00112701

828.7 BYR
BYRON
80/1631

KU-204-775

DISCARD

B.C.H.E. – LIBRARY

00134564

'Between two worlds'

BYRON'S LETTERS AND JOURNALS
VOLUME 7
1820

Between two worlds Life hovers like a star,
  'Twixt Night and Morn, upon the horizon's verge.
How little do we know that which we are!
  How less what we may be! The eternal surge
Of Time and Tide rolls on and bears afar
  Our bubbles; as the old burst, new emerge,
Lashed from the foam of ages; while the graves
Of Empires heave but like some passing waves.

DON JUAN, 15, 99

BYRON AND TERESA GUICCIOLI.   Drawing by Thomas Unwins.

Newstead Abbey Collection. *Reproduced by kind permission of the City Librarian of Nottingham*

'Between two worlds'

BYRON'S LETTERS AND JOURNALS

Edited by
LESLIE A. MARCHAND

*The complete and unexpurgated text of
all the letters available in manuscript and
the full printed version of all others*

VOLUME 7
1820

JOHN MURRAY

———————————————

© Editorial, Leslie A. Marchand 1977
© Byron copyright material, John Murray 1977

All rights reserved. No part of this
publication may be reproduced, stored in
a retrieval system, or transmitted, in any
form or by any means, electronic, mechanical,
photocopying, recording or otherwise,
without the prior permission of
John Murray (Publishers) Ltd.,
50 Albemarle Street, London, w1x 4bd.

Printed in Great Britain by
William Clowes & Sons, Limited
London, Beccles and Colchester
0 7195 3345 7

BATH COLLEGE
OF
HIGHER EDUCATION
NEWTON PARK
LIBRARY

DISCARD

CLASS
No.   828. 7 byR

ACC.
No.   80/1631

CONTENTS

This volume contains the Italian letters of Byron to the Countess Guiccioli which show the intensity of his attachment and the progress of their romance through the year 1820. It began with misunderstandings and jealousies on both sides but became more serene when Byron moved into the Guiccioli Palace in Ravenna. Then came the Guiccioli separation and Byron's loyalty to Teresa and his gradual change of attitude which caused him to treat her as a loved but wayward child. We see also in his letters to Murray, Hobhouse, and Kinnaird his growing absorption in the Italian fight for freedom from the Austrian yoke. And we see him producing, despite distractions of love and revolution, three new cantos of *Don Juan* and the first of his historical dramas, *Marino Faliero*. His letters to his English correspondents, like all his letters from Italy, are full of "pastime and prodigality". Through it all we see his life in Ravenna with the colouring of his own inimitable style.

EDITORIAL NOTE

In order to make the volume as self-contained as possible, the statement concerning editorial principles is repeated at the end of this note. With the same end in view, other editorial information relating to the letters in this volume is supplied in the appendixes. The index of proper names is meant to serve the reader until the general index and subject index appear in the last volume.

ACKNOWLEDGMENTS. (Volume 7). My first and greatest debt is to my publisher, John Murray, whose enthusiasm never flags and whose interest in the project is matched by his untiring attention to details. My work has been immeasurably aided and advanced by a Research Grant from the National Endowment for the Humanities. Donald H. Reiman, editor of *Shelley and his Circle* for the Carl H. Pforzheimer Library, has given me constant assistance and encouragement. Doris Langley Moore continues to be a source of valuable information about Byron and his times upon which I have drawn frequently. I want to thank again the Marchesa Iris Origo for her permission to use her translations of Byron's Italian letters, which first appeared in her *The Last Attachment* (1949). And I am again indebted to Professor Nancy Dersofi of the Italian Department of Bryn Mawr College for translating other Italian letters. John Gibbins of the Murray editorial staff deserves special thanks for his meticulous attention at all stages of publication. To Sir Rupert Hart-Davis I am indebted for skilful tracing of many of Byron's elusive quotations.

For permission to get photocopies of letters in their possession and to use them in this volume I wish to thank the following libraries and individuals: Berg Collection, New York Public Library; Biblioteca Classense, Ravenna; Bodleian Library; British Museum (Department of Manuscripts); Clark Library, University of California at Los Angeles; Fitzwilliam Museum, Cambridge; Houghton Library, Harvard University; Henry E. Huntington Library; Lord Kinnaird; Central Public Libraries, Liverpool; The Earl of Lytton; Mr. John Murray; Pierpont Morgan Library; National Library of Scotland; National Historical Museum, Athens; Carl H. Pforzheimer Library; Stark Library, University of Texas; Walpole Library, King's School, Canterbury.

For assistance of various kinds I am grateful to the following: John G. Bowen; John Buxton; John Clubbe; Gene De Grusen; Mrs. E. E. Duncan-Jones; David V. Erdman; Paul Fussell; Mihai H. Handrea; Peter Janson-Smith; Jerome J. McGann; Virginia Murray; Stewart Perowne; Gordon N. Ray; Dr. Rolf P. Lessenich; Brian Rigby; David H. Stam; Keith Walker; Lindsay Waters; Carl Woodring.

* * * * * *

EDITORIAL PRINCIPLES. With minor exceptions, herein noted, I have tried to reproduce Byron's letters as they were written. The letters are arranged consecutively in chronological order. The name of the addressee is given at the top left in brackets. The source of the text is indicated in the list of letters in the Appendix. If it is a printed text, it is taken from the first printed form of the letter known or presumed to be copied from the original manuscript, or from a more reliable editor, such as Prothero, when he also had access to the manuscript. In this case, as with handwritten or typed copies, or quotations in sale catalogues, the text of this source is given precisely.

When the text is taken from the autograph letter or a photo copy or facsimile of it, the present whereabouts or ownership is given, whether it is in a library or a private collection. When the manuscript is the source, no attempt is made to indicate previous publication, if any. Here I have been faithful to the manuscript with the following exceptions:

1. The place and date of writing is invariably placed at the top right in one line if possible to save space, and to follow Byron's general practice. Fortunately Byron dated most of his letters in this way, but occasionally he put the date at the end. Byron's usual custom of putting no punctuation after the year is followed throughout.

2. Superior letters such as S^r or 30th have been lowered to Sr. and 30th. The & has been retained, but $\&^c$ has been printed &c.

3. Byron's spelling has been followed (and generally his spelling is good, though not always consistent), and *sic* has been avoided except in a few instances when an inadvertent misspelling might change the meaning or be ambiguous, as for instance when he spells *there* t-h-e-i-r.

4. Although, like many of his contemporaries, Byron was inconsistent and eccentric in his capitalization, I have felt it was better to let him have his way, to preserve the flavour of his personality and his times. With him the capital letter sometimes indicates the importance he gives to a word in a particular context; but in the very next line it

2

might not be capitalized. If clarity has seemed to demand a modification, I have used square brackets to indicate any departure from the manuscript.

5. Obvious slips of the pen crossed out by the writer have been silently omitted. But crossed out words of any significance to the meaning or emphasis are enclosed in angled brackets ⟨ ⟩.

6. Letters undated, or dated with the day of the week only, have been dated, when possible, in square brackets. If the date is conjectural, it is given with a question mark in brackets. The same practice is followed for letters from printed sources. The post mark date is given, to indicate an approximate date, only when the letter itself is undated.

7. The salutation is put on the same line as the text, separated from it by a dash. The complimentary closing, often on several lines in the manuscript, is given in one line if possible. The P.S., wherever it may be written in the manuscript, follows the signature.

8. Byron's punctuation follows no rules of his own or others' making. He used dashes and commas freely, but for no apparent reason, other than possibly for natural pause between phrases, or sometimes for emphasis. He is guilty of the "comma splice", and one can seldom be sure where he intended to end a sentence, or whether he recognized the sentence as a unit of expression. He did at certain intervals place a period and a dash, beginning again with a capital letter. These larger divisions sometimes, though not always, represented what in other writers, particularly in writers of today, correspond to paragraphs. He sometimes used semicolons, but often where we would use commas. Byron himself recognized his lack of knowledge of the logic or the rules of punctuation. He wrote to his publisher John Murray on August 26, 1813: "Do you know anybody who can *stop*—I mean point—commas and so forth, for I am I fear a sad hand at your punctuation". It is not without reason then that most editors, including R. E. Prothero, have imposed sentences and paragraphs on him in line with their interpretation of his intended meaning. It is my feeling, however, that this detracts from the impression of Byronic spontaneity and the onrush of ideas in his letters, without a compensating gain in clarity. In fact, it may often arbitrarily impose a meaning or an emphasis not intended by the writer. I feel that there is less danger of distortion if the reader may see exactly how he punctuated and then determine whether a phrase between commas or dashes belongs to one sentence or another. Byron's punctuation seldom if ever makes the reading difficult or the meaning unclear. In rare

3

instances I have inserted a period, a comma, or a semicolon, but have enclosed it in square brackets to indicate it was mine and not his.

9. Words missing but obvious from the context, such as those lacunae caused by holes in the manuscript, are supplied within square brackets. If they are wholly conjectural, they are followed by a question mark. The same is true of doubtful readings in the manuscript.

Undated letters have been placed within the chronological sequence when from internal or external evidence there are reasonable grounds for a conjectural date. This has seemed more useful than putting them together at the end of the volumes. Where a more precise date cannot be established from the context, these letters are placed at the beginning of the month or year in which they seem most likely to have been written.

ANNOTATION. I have tried to make the footnotes as brief and informative as possible, eschewing, sometimes with reluctance, the leisurely expansiveness of R. E. Prothero, who in his admirable edition of the *Letters and Journals* often gave pages of supplementary biographical information and whole letters *to* Byron, which was possible at a time when book publishing was less expensive, and when the extant and available Byron letters numbered scarcely more than a third of those in the present edition. Needless to say, I have found Prothero's notes of inestimable assistance in the identification of persons and quotations in the letters which he edited, though where possible I have double checked them. And I must say that while I have found some errors, they are rare. With this general acknowledgment I have left the reader to assume that where a source of information in the notes is not given, it comes from Prothero's edition, where additional details may be found.

The footnotes are numbered for each letter. Where the numbers are repeated on a page, the sequence of the letters will make the reference clear.

In an appendix in each volume I have given brief biographical sketches of Byron's principal correspondents first appearing in that volume. These are necessarily very short, and the stress is always on Byron's relations with the subject of the sketch. Identification of less frequent correspondents and other persons mentioned in the letters is given in footnotes as they appear, and the location of these, as well as the biographical sketches in the appendix, will be indicated by italic numbers in the index. Similarly italic indications will refer the reader to the principal biographical notes on persons mentioned in the text of the letters.

With respect to the annotation of literary allusions and quotations in the letters, I have tried to identify all quotations in the text, but have not always been successful in locating Byron's sources in obscure dramas whose phrases, serious or ridiculous, haunted his memory. When I have failed to identify either a quotation or a name, I have frankly said so, instead of letting the reader suppose that I merely passed it by as unimportant or overlooked it. No doubt readers with special knowledge in various fields may be able to enlighten me. If so, I shall try to make amends with notes in later volumes.

I have sometimes omitted the identification of familiar quotations. But since this work will be read on both sides of the Atlantic, I have explained some things that would be perfectly clear to a British reader but not to an American. I trust that English readers will make allowance for this. As Johnson said in the Preface to his edition of Shakespeare: "It is impossible for an expositor not to write too little for some, and too much for others . . . how long soever he may deliberate, [he] will at last explain many lines which the learned will think impossible to be mistaken, and omit many for which the ignorant will want his help. These are censures merely relative, and must be quietly endured".

I have occasionally given cross references, but in the main have left it to the reader to consult the index for names which have been identified in earlier notes.

SPECIAL NOTES. The letters to Thomas Moore, first published in his *Letters and Journals of Lord Byron* (1830), were printed with many omissions and the manuscripts have since disappeared. Moore generally indicated omissions by asterisks, here reproduced as in his text.

Byron's letters in Italian to the Countess Guiccioli (and a few other correspondents) I have transcribed from the original autograph manuscripts, most of them now in the Biblioteca Classense, Ravenna. A few are in the Carl H. Pforzheimer Library. I have tried to be faithful to Byron's Italian script so far as possible. His chief slips are to be seen in his carelessness with accents and his tendency to excessive elision with the apostrophe. His spelling is generally good, but he sometimes leaves the English consonant as in *circo(n)stanza*. The Italian text is followed immediately by the English translation as printed by Iris Origo in *The Last Attachment*. The translations of other letters, not translated or not included in that volume, have been made for me by Professor Nancy Dersofi.

Beginning with Volume 7, I have divided some of Byron's longer letters into paragraphs, where a pause or change of subject is indicated. This helps with proof correcting and makes easier the reading of the text, without detracting significantly from the impression of Byron's free-flowing and on-rushing style of composition.

BYRON CHRONOLOGY

1820 Jan.—At Albergo Imperiale, Ravenna.

Jan.—Quarrels with Teresa Guiccioli.

Feb.—Moved into upper floor of Palazzo Guiccioli.

Feb.—Liaison continued in Guiccioli Palace.

Feb.—Twitted Hobhouse on his landing in Newgate.

Feb. 19—Sent Cantos 3 and 4 of *Don Juan* to Murray.

Feb. 21—Completed translation of first canto of Pulci's *Morgante Maggiore*.

March—Became regular Cavalier Servente of Teresa.

March—Finished *Prophecy of Dante*.

March—Wrote ballad on Hobhouse "My Boy Hobbie O".

March 15—Began "Observations" on article in *Blackwood's Magazine*.

April—Engrossed in social life in Ravenna.

April—New interest in Italian politics and rising revolt against Austrians.

May—Crisis with Count Guiccioli, who caught Byron and Teresa "quasi in the fact".

May—Count Gamba, Teresa's father, appealed to Pope for separation of his daughter from Count Guiccioli.

May—Guiccioli in an "interview" proposed that Byron leave.

June—Tension in Palazzo Guiccioli.

July—Finished *Marino Faliero*

July—Sought Italian witnesses for Queen Caroline.

July—Met Count Pietro Gamba, Teresa's brother.

July—Interested in the Neapolitan Revolution.

July 14—Separation decree arrived.

July—Teresa escaped to father's house at Filetto.

Aug.—Through the Gamba family Byron was initiated into the secret revolutionary society of the Carbonari.

Aug.—Found house for Allegra in the country near Filetto.

Aug.—Sent Benjamin Constant's *Adolphe* to Teresa.

Aug. 16—First visit to Teresa at Filetto.

Sept.—Party al fresco at Filetto with Gamba family.

Sept.—Hoppner told Byron story of Shelley's supposed child by Claire Clairmont.

7

Sept. 15—Ferdinando Guiccioli died.

Oct.—Received print of Ada's picture and news of death of Joe Murray, old servant at Newstead.

Oct.—Received from Paris French translation of his works.

Oct. 14—Wrote dedication of *Marino Faliero* to Goethe.

Oct. 16—Began 5th Canto of *Don Juan*.

Nov.—Wrote additions to Memoirs which he sent to Moore.

Nov.—Teresa returned to town house of her father in Ravenna.

Dec. 9—Commandant shot near Byron's door and carried into his apartment.

Dec. 28—Sent Kinnaird 5th Canto of *Don Juan*.

BYRON'S LETTERS AND JOURNALS

[Three short notes]

A. M.+—Forse Luigi sara sbagliato nella risposta ch'io diedi a voce.—Ho detto che sei padrona.—Io sono in libertà.—

sempre [Scrawl]

Vuoi venire?—son solo e nessuno puo venire fin all' Ave Maria—se ti piace più verrò da te—fa ciò che ti pare meglio.—

B. C.+—Tu suoni, è tornato?—Addio

[Scrawl]

[Translation (*a*)]   [*1820?*]

Luigi has probably mistaken the reply I gave him by word of mouth —I said that you are the mistress.—I am at liberty.—

always

Do you want to come?—I am alone and no one can come before the Ave Maria—if you prefer I will come to you—do what seems best to you.—

B. C.+—You are ringing, has he returned? Addio.

[TO COUNTESS TERESA GUICCIOLI (*b*)]   [*1820?*]

Le mie intenzione sono di comprare il quadretto di[Mareschalchi?]— se egli non fa delle domande stravaganti.—Vorrei naturalmente sapere il prezzo prima di decidere.—Io dissi a Lega—che vorrei sapere se gradite che vengo da voi questa sera—non avendo risposta—debbo credere nel' negativo?——

Sono sempre——

[Translation (*b*)]   [*1820?*]

My intentions are to buy the little painting from[Mareschalchi?]— if he does not make unreasonable demands. I would like naturally to know the price before deciding.—I told Lega[1]—that I would like to know if you would be pleased to have me come this evening—not having a reply—must I take it in the negative?—

I am always[2]

---

[1] Lega Zambelli, Byron's secretary servant.
[2] This and the previous notes translated by Professor Nancy Dersofi.

Tu dici che A[lessandro] ha detto che io non "t'amai &c." io non so cosa ⟨quell'uomo⟩ Egli vuol' dire—ma io so di aver' detto in faccia sua—che anche se egli non voleva, io ti voleva—*bene* e *per sempre*.—Si puo dire di più ad un marito? Pel' resto—tu sai se ti *amai*—e come—e quanto—anche nei ultimi dispiaceri più forti—ed *oppresso colla febbre*—sono stato il tuo amante—come sarò sul' letto della morte—fin' almeno che mi resta la medesima forza.—

[On the back of the page]: Questo era il poscritto della ultima lettera—ma non la mandai.

[Translation (*a*)]   [*Jan. 1820?*]

You say that A[lessandro][1] told you that I "did not love you". I do not know what he means, but I know that I said to his face—that even if he did not want you, I was *fond of you* and would be *for ever*. Can one say more to a husband? As to the rest—you know whether I *loved* you—and how—and how much—even in the last and greatest troubles—and *oppressed with fever*—I was your lover—as I shall be on my deathbed, at least while I have the same strength in me.

[On the back of the page]: This was the postscript to my last letter, but I did not send it.

Verrò.——Mi pare che ho fatto giustizia a quelle qualità le quali sono veramente vostre—e pei difetti che vi ho detto (con troppa onestà forse) gli avete in commune con una nazione entiera—e con un' morale di società fatale per un' straniero che ama un' Italiana.—

[Translation (*b*)]   [*Jan. 1820?*]

I will come. I think I have done justice to those qualities which really are yours—and as to the faults I have told you about (perhaps with too much frankness) you have those in common with a whole nation—and with social morals fatal to a foreigner who loves an Italian woman.

---

[1] Teresa's husband, Count Alessandro Guiccioli.

Amor Mio—Mi dispiace che non posso accompagnarti—ma sto poco bene questa sera—e poi il cambiare di casa domanda la mia cura particulare—ciò tu intenderai bene conoscendo il carattere di mia gente.—Penso venire da te in pochi momenti—ma pure non voglio che tu te privi della conversazione della C. C. [Marchesa Clelia Cavalli?] per causa mia.—

                                                            sono
                                                         [scrawl]
Scusate questa Charta *della locanda.*

[Translation (*c*)]   [*Jan. 1820?*]

My Love—I am sorry that I cannot go with you—but I am not feeling well this evening—and then this removal requires my own particular attention—which you will understand well enough, knowing the character of my people. I am thinking of coming to you in a few minutes, but I do not want you to give up the conversation of C[lelia] C[avalli] on my account. I am

Forgive this Inn's paper.[1]

[TO COUNTESS TERESA GUICCIOLI (*d*)]   [*Jan. 1820?*]
[Fragment of a letter]
Sì—e *se no*—pagarò il viaggio qui—e di ritorno a F[irenze] con qualche cosa di più per il disturbo &c. &c.—ma voglio riservare a me stesso il diritto di rifiutare in caso che il *landau* non corrisponde alla descrizione.—A[lessandro] è un' buffone—che non sa cosa volere o dire quando è imbestialito di mal' umore.—ditelo.——

[TRANSLATION (*d*)]   [*Jan. 1820?*]

Yes—and *if not*—I will pay the journey here—and back to F[lorence] with something more for their pains—but I wish to reserve for myself the right to refuse, in case the *landau* does not correspond to the description. A[lessandro] is a buffoon—who does not know what he wants or says when he is in a raging temper. Tell him so.

---

[1] Byron was living in the Albergo Imperiale in Ravenna. Early in February he moved into the Palazzo Guiccioli. Notes and letters passed by hand between him and Teresa both before and after the move.

13

Dearest Augusta—There is but time to write you two words in answer to yr. last. The enclosed is for Lady B.—Address to me as usual;—I wrote to you from Venice enclosing a note of H's about the settled property.——You may open the enclosed if you like—if there is any answer it may come through you—I want none in her writing to me—which would be but a trouble to herself—and assuredly no pleasure to me.——Pray excuse the hurry of this—I wrote to you from Bologna the other day—

ever yrs

B

[TO JOHN MURRAY]   *Jy 2 1820*

Dear Murray—If you want my news—and Moore is not yet arrived —you may open the enclosed letter—and write to me an answer if you like it——

[Scrawl]

[TO AUGUSTA LEIGH]   *January 2d, 1820*

Dearest Augusta,—In your reply about the funds some time ago, you quote Lady B.'s acquiescence, "though she did not partake in the apprehensions," which suggested an investment elsewhere. What does she say *now*? When, if I can believe the papers, the very members of government are transferring property to the *French* funds. Let her remember that I can only judge from what I hear, not being on the spot to observe. She would probably be sorry to be my ruin more than once; since if the funds were to go, you do not suppose that I would sit down quietly under it: no, in that case I will make one amongst them, if we are to come to civil buffeting; and perhaps not the mildest. I would wish to finish my days in quiet; but should the time arrive, when it becomes the necessity of every man to act however reluctantly upon the circumstances of the country, I won't be roused up for nothing, and if I do take a part, it will be such a one as my opinion of mankind, a temper not softened by what it has seen and undergone, a mind grown indifferent to pursuits and results, but capable of effort and of strength under oppression or stimulus, but

14

without ambition, because it looks upon all human attempts as conducting to no rational or practicable advantage, would induce me to adopt. And perhaps such a man, forced to act from necessity, would, with the temper I have described, be about as dangerous an animal as ever joined in ravage.

There is nothing which I should dread more than to trust to my own temper, or to have to act in such scenes as I think must soon ensue in England. It is this made me think of S[ou]th. America, or the Cape, or Turkey, or any where, so that I can but preserve my independence of means to live withal. But, if, in this coming crash, my fortunes are to be swept down with the rest, why then the only barrier which holds me aloof from taking a part in these miserable contests being broken down, I will fight my way too, with what success I know not, but with what moderation I know but too well. If you but knew how I despise and abhor all these men, and all these things, you would easily suppose how reluctantly I contemplate being called upon to act with or against any of the parties. All I desire is to preserve what remains of the fortunes of our house, and then they may do as they please. This makes me anxious to know what has been done. I sent you a letter of D[ougla]s K[innaird] several weeks ago from Venice, proposing an Irish Mortgage to me: I wished you to show this to Lady B[yron].

The other day I wrote to you from hence.

Address to Venice as usual.

Yours ever,

B

[TO DOUGLAS KINNAIRD]   *January 2d. 1820*

Dear Douglas—In the present state of the funds and of the Country —you will hardly wonder at my anxiety to be informed whether you have succeeded in investing the settled property elsewhere—or what has been done towards that object.—I wrote to you twice lately to tell you that I had postponed my intention of return for some time.— Neither the Season nor length of the journey would have suited my daughter's [Allegra's] health after her illness.——You will do me a great favour in letting me know—all about any steps that may have been or are to be taken.—You do not write—nor like to receive long letters—so I will not trail this further.——I read your speeches in Galignani—is H[obhouse] or is he not the author of "a trilling mistake" or is the house mistaken and not H.?[1]—I always said—that I should "have to bail my old friend out of the round-house"[2] & so it seems.—What will be the issue of it all?—he has not written to me these four months——but it is no time to reproach his silence when he is in a scrape.—Don't forget to let me know all about him

yrs. ever truly and faithly.
B

P.S.—You may remit my half-year to the usual address—Venice—in *circulars* as most universal.——

[TO THOMAS MOORE]   *January 2d, 1820*

My Dear Moore,—

> To-day it is my wedding-day;
> And all the folks would stare
> If wife should dine at Edmonton,
> And I should dine at Ware.[1]

Or *thus*:

> Here's a happy new year! but with reason,
> I beg you'll permit me to say—
> Wish me *many* returns of the *season*,
> But as *few* as you please of the *day*.

My [sic] this present writing is to direct you that, *if she chooses*, she may see the MS. Memoir in your possession. I wish her to have fair play, in all cases, even though it will not be published until after my decease. For this purpose, it were but just that Lady B. should know what is there said of her and hers, that she may have full power to

---

[1] Soon after the defeat of Hobhouse for the Westminster Parliamentary seat in the autumn of 1819, Lord Erskine, who had been a defender of the people during the treason trials of 1794, was provoked by the Reformers' denunciation of the Whigs, and published a pamphlet in their defence. Hobhouse countered with an anonymous pamphlet, "A Trifling Mistake in Thomas Lord Erskine's Recent Preface", in which he wrote: "What prevents the people from walking down to the House, and pulling out the members by the ears, locking up their doors, and flinging the key into the Thames?" The only reason, he said, was that the members were protected by the Horse Guards. This alone permits "those who have got the tax-power [to] keep it, and hang those who resist." On December 11, 1819, the pamphlet was voted a breach of privilege and Hobhouse, when he admitted the authorship to spare the printer, was committed to Newgate prison where he remained until the dissolution of Parliament in February, 1820.

[2] Garrick said this of Johnson's association with Beauclerk. (Boswell, *Life of Johnson* [Oxford], I, 165.)

[1] See Cowper's *John Gilpin*.

16

remark on or respond to any part or parts, as may seem fitting to herself. This is fair dealing, I presume, in all events.

To change the subject, are you in England? I send you an epitaph for Castlereagh:

* * * * * * * * * * * * * * *

[Posterity will ne'er survey
A nobler grave than this;
Here lie the bones of Castlereagh:
Stop traveller, * *]²

Another for Pitt:—

With death doom'd to grapple,
Beneath this cold slab, he
Who lied in the Chapel
Now lies in the Abbey.

The gods seem to have made me poetical this day:—

In digging up your bones, Tom Paine,
Will. Cobbett has done well:
You visit him on earth again,
He'll visit you in hell.

Or,

You come to him on earth again,
He'll go with you to hell.

Pray let not these versiculi go forth with *my* name, except among the initiated, because my friend H. has foamed into a reformer, and, I greatly fear, will subside into Newgate; since the Honourable House, according to Galignani's Reports of Parliamentary Debates, are menacing a prosecution to a pamphlet of his. I shall be very sorry to hear of any thing but good for him, particularly in these miserable squabbles; but these are the natural effects of taking a part in them.

For my own part, I had a sad scene since you went. Count Gu[ic-cioli] came for his wife, and *none* of those consequences which Scott prophesied ensued. There was no damages, as in England, and so Scott lost his wager. But there was a great scene, for she would not, at first, go back with him—at least [*sic*] [last?] she *did* go back with him; but he insisted, reasonably enough, that all communication should be broken off between her and me. So, finding Italy very dull, and having a fever tertian, I packed up my valise, and prepared to cross the Alps; but my daughter fell ill, and detained me.

² This "Epitaph" was omitted by Moore. It was published anonymously in *The Republican*, Aug. 23, 1822, and was included in Murray's 1833 edition of Byron's works.

17

After her arrival at Ravenna, the Guiccioli fell ill again too; and, at last, her father (who had, all along, opposed the liaison most violently till now) wrote to me to say that she was in such a state that *he* begged me to come and see her,—and that her husband had acquiesced, in consequence of her relapse, and that *he* (her father) would guarantee all this, and that there would be no further scenes in consequence between them, and that I should not be compromised in any way. I set out soon after, and have been here ever since. I found her a good deal altered, but getting better:—*all* this comes of reading Corinna[3].

The Carnival is about to begin, and I saw about two or three hundred people at the Marquis Cavalli's the other evening, with as much youth, beauty, and diamonds among the women, as ever averaged in the like number. My appearance in waiting on the Guiccioli was considered as a thing of course. The Marquis is her uncle, and naturally considered me as her relation.

The paper is out, and so is the letter. Pray write. Address to Venice, whence the letters will be forwarded.

Yours, etc.,

B

[TO COUNTESS TERESA GUICCIOLI] *Genaio 3. 1820*

Amica—Farai ciò che ti pare meglio.—Io non ho dettato ciò che debbi fare,—ho risposto quando tu mi rimproverasti di aver fatto visita alla Vicari—"che era meno disonorante per me visitare la tua amica più riconosciuta—che per te avere in casa una persona come la Teresa,—mantenuta da tanti anni—allora per *un oggetto*—e adesso— secondo a tutte le apparenze—per un' *altro*—"Se non avevi cominciato rimproverarmi per una cosa la più innocente—ti avrei lasciato senza dire una parola sopra quel' articolo—con tutto ciò—che ora credo come che ho sempre creduto—dagli indicii esterni—da ciò che ho opinato—e da ciò che ho sentito—che quella donna—e il suo antico drudo—vi hanno imbrogliato per loro servizio.——

Le familiarità di quel' uomo possono esser' innocenti—ma *decenti* non sono—anche questa sera—quando tu credevi che io legeva— quell' manoscritto che A. mi metteva nelle mani—io osservava (presso al' fuoco) certe cose che non mi convengono,—e che tu saprai ben intendere—senza che ti dico di più.——

Avresti fatto assai meglio nel'lasciarmi partire prima di venire

---

[3] Madame de Staël's *Corinne*.

18

qui;—dopo la mia venuta—ho provato dei piacere—che tu sola puoi darmi—ma dell' altra parte—ho sofferto moltissimo nel' vederti al' mio parere—o disonorata o debole.—V'è del mistero—delle cose che io non posso intendere;— un' morale senza principii—un' amor senza fede—e un' amicizia senza stima o confidenza—sono pur troppo manifestati ultimamente in un' grado che è stato impossibile per me cavare una parola di verità, della parte di una persona per quale io ho abandonato tutto.— —

Se voi potete reconciliare i vostri principii come una donna ben nata colla vostra difesa della sopradetta persona ora in vostro servizio; se potete reconciliare il amor vostro per me colle libertà che avete permesso a un' altro in mia presenza—la vostra amicizia più sincera— (o *piu finta*) per la Vicari colla maniera in cui avete parlato di lei questa sera—vi riconoscerò per una dama di grandissimo talento—ma non più per mia amica. Il vostro A. questa sera mi accusò di indecisione —*Egli* mi *accusò*—va bene.—*Egli* dopo tutte le scene di Venezia— tutti i suoi progetti—di viaggi a Vienna—a Firenze—a cangiar' paese—di mandar' i suoi figli in Collegio; poi in Inghilterra—di rompere la vostra relazione &c. &c. &c.—veramente questo è bello!— —

Cosa voleva Costui?—che io—straniero—lontano della patria e degli costumi—morale—e maniera di pensare—e di agire di miei connazionale—che io *decidessi* pei *indecisi* di un' altro paese.—Dopo averti conosciuto—ho vissuto per *te*—e con *te*—questa è forse indecisione;—se vedo la mia patria in pericolo di perdersi—gli miei amici— alcuni in arresto—e gli altri nel punto di esser precipitati in una guerra civile—la mia famiglia senza il mio appoggio—molti dei miei beni non troppo ben' assicurati—nelle circonstanze attuali del' governo vacillante—se in un' tal' momento—pare a voi—o ai altri che sono torbato—merita questo il nome di indecisione? poiche debbo pensare che ho lasciato tutto in un' tal' stato—per una donna che non solamente non mi ama—ma non . . . . [a line has been cut out and some words torn out.] amato.—Io non posso negarvi il talento e la bellezza;—scrivete dei biglietti eloquenti—. . . nelle vostre qualità fisiche—siete che non si puo desiderare del' meglio.—

My Friend—You must do as you think best—I have not dictated what you should do—I replied when you reproached me for calling

19

on the Vicari[1],—"that it was less improper for me to visit your most intimate friend than for you to retain in your house a woman like Teresa,[2] kept for so many years, for *one reason*—and now—according to all appearances—for *another.*"

If you had not begun by reproaching me about a most innocent matter, I should have gone away without saying a single word on the subject. Nevertheless I now believe, as I always have believed—from outward signs—from what I have suspected—and heard—that that woman and her former lover have deceived you for their own purposes.

The familiarities of that man may be innocent—but decent they are not—even this evening when you thought I was reading the manuscript that A[lessandro] put into my hands, I observed, by the fire certain things that do not suit me. You will know well enough what I mean, without my saying any more.

You would have done better to let me go away from you before I came here; since my arrival I have enjoyed pleasures that only you can give me—but on the other hand I have suffered very much in seeing you, in my opinion, either degraded or weak. There is a mystery about these things that I cannot understand;—a morality without principle—a love without faith—and a friendship without esteem or trust—these have unfortunately shown themselves lately to such a degree that it has been impossible for me to extract a word of truth from a person for whom I have given up everything.

If you can reconcile your code as a lady with your defence of the aforesaid woman who is now in your service; if you can reconcile your love for me with the liberties you have permitted to another man in my presence;[3] and your most sincere (or most affected) friendship with the Vicari with the way in which you spoke of her to me tonight—I shall admit that you are a lady of great gifts—but no longer my friend.

Your A[lessandro] accused me this evening of indecision. *He* accused *me*—very fine! *He*, after all the scenes in Venice—all his plans to travel to Vienna—to Florence—to change his country—to send his sons to school, then to England—to break off your relationship—

[1] Geltrude Vicari, a friend of Teresa's, with whom Byron had flirted briefly.

[2] Teresa was a maid whom Guiccioli had taken into his service, as Byron believed, to spy on his wife and her lover.

[3] In her note accompanying this letter Teresa Guiccioli tried to make it appear that the reference was to "a family friend (aged 60) Count R." But it seems apparent from later letters that Byron meant that he was annoyed by the familiarities she permitted her husband Count Guiccioli in his presence.

20

really, that is fine! What does he want? That I, a foreigner, far from my own country and from the manners and customs and ways of thought and behaviour of my fellow-country-men—that I should decide things for the people of another land!

Since I have known you I have lived *for you*—and *with you*—is this indecision? If I see my country in danger of destruction—some of my friends arrested—others on the point of being involved in civil war—my family without support—much of my property none too safe—in the conditions prevalent under this insecure government—if in such a moment it seems to you or to others that I am upset—does this deserve the name of indecision?—For I must consider that I have left everything in such a state—for a woman who not only does not love me,—but never . . . [page torn and a line missing] . . . loved.—I cannot deny your gifts and your beauty; you write eloquent notes; in your physical attributes you are all that one can desire . . . [the page is torn and the rest of the letter is missing]

[TO COUNTESS TERESA GUICCIOLI (*a*)]   *G.o.4.o 1820*

In risposta alla vostra di questa mattina non posso dire altro—senonche—non ci intendiamo bene.—Se voi non m'avete rimproverato per esser' stato per un' momento far' una visita la più insignificante—ad una vostra amica—carissima sei mesi fa—e come io credeva—cara anche *adesso*—non mi sarebbe mai venuto il pensiere di dirvi ciò che mi pareva poco per onor' vostro—in una casa—ben ordinata.——

Per il resto io non posso esser' il latore delle vostre communicazioni per il Sr. C. R. nè per bene nè per male—e non voglio in nessuna maniera entrare nei affari di quei due personaggi.—Per il ricevere delle persone in casa—perche *non tutto il mondo?*—allora sarebbe niente.—Intanto—mi importarebbe poco chi veniva o andava—se voi eravate di quella sincerità che disgraziamente non puo esistere nelle vostre circonstanze—secondo lo stato attuale del morale Italiano.—Solamente vorrei dire che quando fate un' accoglienza cosi graziosa—e gentile alla vostra amica—è ben difficile per me indovinare che in quel'momento l'odiate più.——Io non ho più dire sopra questo argomento non troppo aggradevole.——Mi dispiace moltissimo sentire che non state troppo bene questa sera—e spero che domani vi troverate meglio.——

Sono stato con Lega al' quartiere Bacinetti—che non trovo conveniente per il locale—il sito mi piace—ma in quel' apartamento sarebbe impossibile—per mi abitare colla mia famiglia—senza quasi rifabbricando la casa.——

Vi prego di credermi ciò che son sempre stato per voi—e non attribuirmi dei motivi indegni—come sarebbe "il *provarvi*" io dico ciò che sento.——Non sono venuto qui—per oggetti cosi triviali.——Io non metto gran' fede nel' bel' stile—nè nel' eloquenza del' biglietto —che nessuno possiede più di voi—ma nelle azioni oneste—nella sincerità—colle amiche come coi amici—e in una condotta non equivocha nè anche nelle apparenze.——Sono &c. &c. &c.

[scrawl for signature]

[TRANSLATION (*a*)]   *January 4th, 1820*

In reply to your letter of this morning, I can only say that we do not understand each other. If you had not reproached me for paying a brief and most unimportant call on a friend of yours, very dear to you six months ago—and as I believed still dear *now*—I should never have thought of mentioning what seemed to me little to your credit, in a well-ordered household. For the rest I cannot be the bearer of your communications to C.R. either for good or evil, and I will not in any way enter into the affairs of those two creatures. As to receiving people in your house—why not everybody?—then it would have no importance. Meanwhile, it would matter little to me who comes or goes, if you showed the sincerity that unfortunately cannot exist in your circumstances, in the present state of Italian morals. Only I should like to tell you that when you give such a gracious and friendly welcome to your friend, it is difficult for me to guess that in that very moment you are hating her most. I have nothing more to say about this hardly pleasant subject.

I am very sorry to hear that you have not felt well this evening, and I hope that tomorrow you will be better.

I have been with Lega to the Bacinetti apartment, of which I do not think the accommodation convenient—the position I like—but in those quarters it would be impossible for me to live with my family— without almost rebuilding the house.

Pray believe that I feel as I have always felt towards you—and do not attribute unworthy motives to me—such as trying "to test you". I say what I feel; I have not come here for such trivial reasons. I do not put great faith in a fine style, nor in eloquent notes—which no one can do better than you—but in honest deeds, in sincerity—with women as with men friends—and in a conduct which is unequivocal even in appearances. I am etc. etc.

Ti Scrissi la lettera acchiusa—prima di recevere la tua—Lega non essendo tornato dal' porto che in questo momento.—Ciò mostrerà il mio sentimento e la mia risoluzione—che era ed è inalterabile.—Del resto—la T. non perderà molto (fuori della tua Grazia—che sarebbe assai più per mi perdere che per lei) in rapporto delle interesse—io farò tutto che si puo fare finche essa può collocarsi—e l'avrei fatto senza nessuna sforza,—io non cerco nè *vendetta*—nè vedere le persone *soffrire*—ma solamente che quella donna non sia vicina a te, non solamente per causa [tua] e mia—ma per tante altre persone che tu conosci.—Io ho dato ordini a Lega—provve[derà] in tutto——

I wrote you the enclosed letter before receiving yours—Lega having returned only this moment from the port. This will confirm my feelings and my resolution, which was and is unalterable.

Anyway T[eresa] will not lose much (except your good graces, which I would mind losing much more than she would). As to her interests, I will do all that can be done until she finds another place, and will do so very willingly. I am not seeking *vengeance*—or to cause pain—but only that that woman should not be near you, not only for [your] sake and mine, but for all the other people you know. I have given orders to Lega—he will see to everything.

Mio Bene—Ti prego spiegare ciò che A[lessandro] ha detto questa sera—dell' associazione per le feste.—l'Intendo pochissimo—la cosa può essere una Gentilezza Romagnola, o una malagrazia.—Io per sicuro non avrei esibito associarmi se la presenza di A[lessandro] e di Cristino R[asponi] non mi avrebbero guarantito quando lo feci.— In ogni modo mi stimo essere almeno al'pari dei Socii PER NASCITÀ— che non dipende da noi, e per tutto il resto che può dipenderne da noi stessi.—Ti prego istruirmi per norma mia—poiche non voglio

avvilirmi—nè anche per causa tua, ma in tutto ciò tu desideri (creden-
domi sicuro che tu non puoi desiderare ciò che mortificarebbe il tuo
amico) sono e sarò sempre tuo (come tu dici) *"in eterno"*.

[scrawl] +

B

P.S.—Ti giuro che mi piacerebbe assai più il non andare in queste
feste—e che solamente perche tu lo desideri pensava andare.

[TRANSLATION] *January 10th, 1820*

My Love—Pray explain what A[lessandro] said this evening about
the membership for the assemblies—I don't understand very well—
the thing may be a Romagnole politeness or a discourtesy. I most
certainly should not have become a member myself, if the presence of
A[lessandro] and of Cristino R[asponi] had not reassured me as I was
doing it. In any case I consider myself at least the equal of the members
as to *birth*, which is not within our control, and also as to everything
else, which is. Pray instruct me for my guidance—for I do not want
to demean myself—not even for your sake,—but in all that you desire
(feeling certain that you would not desire anything that could mortify
your friend) I am and always shall be yours (as you say) *"eternally"*.

[scrawl] +

B

P.S.—I vow I should vastly prefer not to go to these assemblies—and
only thought of going because you wished it.

[TO RICHARD BELGRAVE HOPPNER] *Ravenna. January 10th. 1820*

My dear Hoppner—I have not decided anything about remaining
at Ravenna—I may stay a day—a week—a year—all my life—but all
this depends upon what I can neither see nor foresee.—I came because
I was called—and will go the moment that I perceive what may render
my departure proper;—my attachment has neither the blindness of
the beginning—nor the microscopic accuracy of the close to such
liaisons—but "time and the hour"[1] must decide upon what I do—I can
as yet say nothing because I hardly know anything beyond what I
have told you.——I wrote to you last post for my moveables—as

---

[1] *Macbeth*, Act I, scene 3.

there is no getting a lodging with a chair or table here ready—and as I have already some things of the sort at Bologna which I had last Summer there for my daughter;—I have directed them to be moved—& wish the like to be done with those of Venice—that I may at least get out of the "Albergo Imperiale" which *is imperial* in all true sense of the Epithet. Buffini may be paid for his Poison.—I forgot to thank you and Mrs. Hoppner for a whole treasure of toys for Allegra before our departure—it was very kind & we are very grateful.——Your account of the Weeding of the Governor's party is very entertaining;—if you do not understand the Consular exceptions—I do—and it is right that a man of honour—and a woman of probity—should find it so—particularly in a place—where there are not "ten righteous"[2].—As to Nobility—in England none are strictly noble but peers—not even peers' Sons—though titled by Courtesy—nor knights of the Garter—unless of the peerage—so that Castlereagh himself would hardly pass through a foreign Herald's ordeal—till the death of his father.——

I don't see why the Spanish Consul's wife should have been excluded—because I have always understood her to be a very respectable woman—that is for Italy—She is a Padouan—had money—and has not I believe very much annoyed her husband hitherto.—As for Madame Cicognara—it seems a mystery—not her present exclusion—but her former presentations at the Courts specified—at least if her tale be true, as told by her Co-harlots.——I should imagine that the new rules must have caused a strong *Con-catin*-ation of Venetian Gentildonne—upon the occasion of their enactment.—

The Snow is a foot deep here.——There is a theatre—and Opera—the Barber of Seville.—Balls begin on Monday next.——Pay the Porter—for never looking after the gate—and ship my chattels—and let me know or let Castelli let me know how my lawsuits go on—but fee him only in proportion to his success.——Perhaps we may meet in the Spring yet—if you are for England.—I see Hobhouse has got into a Scrape—which does not please me—he should not have gone so deep among those men—without calculating the consequences.—I used to think myself the most imprudent of all among my friends and acquaintances but almost begin to doubt it.

yrs [scrawl]

---

[2] A reference to the destruction of Sodom (*Genesis VIII*, 32). Byron compared Venice to Sodom in *Marino Faliero* Act V, scene 3: "Gehenna of the waters! thou Sea-Sodom".

Mio Bene—Elisei mi confirmò ciò che tu dicesti sulla *"prima donna"* per conto mio—ma era già persuaso che non era vero—ed io l'ho pregato di bel nuovo caldamente di contradire quella ciarla dappertutto;—ed Egli m'ha promesso anche con premura. Non ho veduto Giulio Rasponi—quando lo vedo—dirò la medesima cosa anche a lui. Non sono venuto da te—perche tu sei andata far visita, e poi A[lessandro] non ritrovò la chiave del' palcho—dunque come fare?—Vuoi che vengo alle 6. or no?—e come debbo regolarmi in riguardo tuo all festa? A[lessandro] mi pareva di mal umore;—Credi che io sono in *fatto* ciò che tu sei in *detto*—il tuo *"amante in eterno"* +

[TRANSLATION]   *January 17th, 1820*

My Love—Elisei has confirmed what you said about the *"prima donna"*[1] in connection with me, but was already convinced that it was not true—and I asked him once more, warmly, to contradict that bit of gossip everywhere—and he promised to, very gladly.

I have not seen Giulio Rasponi—when I do I shall say the same thing to him too. I did not come to see you, because you had gone out calling, and then A[lessandro] did not find the key of the box—so what was to be done? Do you want me to come at 6 or not—and how shall I behave with regard to the assembly? A[lessandro] seemed to me in a bad humour. Believe that I am in *deeds* what you are in *words*—Your *"lover for ever"*[2] +

[TO COUNTESS TERESA GUICCIOLI]   *Ravenna G.o 29. 1820*

Ben Mio—Tu hai sbagliato—io non mi ricordo niente—e ti prego non fare delle cose simili senza ragione.—Tu non hai debiti con me se non del' *Amor* per cui "resto in credito ['] a tutto il presente giorno R.i 1000000000.

                                                                B

Ti rimando i tuoi quattrini.—Cosa so io—sei pazza?

[1] The "prima donna", Mme. Pasta, was much admired by Byron who offered to contribute £200 to engage her for the Ravenna Theatre. It seems apparent also that Teresa was jealous of Byron's interest in her. This was also the subject of a dispute with Count Guiccioli, who was head of the Ravenna Theatre Committee.

[2] Teresa frequently ended her letters with the initials *a. a. in e.* (amante ed amico in eterno) which Byron adopted for the closing of many of his later letters to her.

Ravenna January 29, 1820

My Love—You are mistaken—I remember nothing of it—and I beg you not to do anything similar without reason.—You have no debts with me if not of *Love* for which there "remains in credit" for the whole of the present day R.i 1000,000,000.

B

I return you your money.—This much I know—are you mad?[1]

[TO RICHARD BELGRAVE HOPPNER] *Ravenna. January 31st. 1820*

My dear Hoppner—You would hardly have been troubled with the removal of my furniture, but there is none to be had nearer than Bologna—and I have been fain to have that of the rooms which I fitted up for my daughter there in the Summer removed here.— The expence will be at least as great of the land Carriage—so that you see it was necessity and not choice—*here*—they get every thing from Bologna—except some lighter articles from Forli or Faenza.——

I am fully sensible of Mr. Dorville's past and present cares and attentions—and wish I knew how to requite them—as I considered him as your *Vice*—I could not from delicacy—offer him any recompence —otherwise I assure you it would be a great relief to me—if by any present in any shape—I could evince my sense of his troubles.—Perhaps—without saying anything to *him*—you could show me the line to take—and I assure you I shall be the most obliged of the two.—

If Scott[1] is returned—pray remember me to him—and plead laziness—the whole and sole cause of my not replying; dreadful is the exertion of letter writing.——What you say of Mrs. Prescott[2]— and her Sclavonian marriage does not surprize me—it is a match of *your* making—I was sure that such or some such result would be the consequence of any remonstrance——it is the very essence of human nature to act thus;—but I think I see *your face* upon the occasion—which would interest me a great deal more than anything of the Venetian Carnival.—The Carnival here is less boisterous—but we have balls and a theatre—I carried Bankes[3] to both—and he carried away I

---
[1] Editor's translation.
[1] Alexander Scott, a close friend of Byron at Venice.
[2] Unidentified.
[3] William Bankes, Byron's Cambridge friend, had just returned from extensive travels in the East.

believe a much more favourable impression of the Society here—than of that of Venice—recollect that I speak of the *native* Society only.——

I am drilling very hard to learn how to double a Shawl, and should succeed to admiration—if I did not always double it the wrong side out—and then I sometimes confuse and bring away two—so as to put all the Serventi out—besides keeping their *Servite* in the cold—till everybody can get back their property.—But it is a dreadfully moral place—for you must not look at anybody's wife except your Neighbour's, if you [go] to the next door but one—you are scolded—and presumed to be perfidious.——And then a relazione or an amicizia seems to be a regular affair of from five to fifteen years—at which period if there occur a widowhood—it finishes by a sposalizio;—and in the mean time it has so many rules of it's own that it is not much better.——A man actually becomes a piece of female property; they won't let their Serventi marry until there is a vacancy for themselves.—I know two instances of this in one family here.——

To-night there is a [Tom]bola or lottery after the Opera—it is an [odd?] ceremony.——Bankes and I took tickets [for?] it—and buffooned together very merrily.——He is gone to Firenze.—— Mrs. Zambelli should have sent you my postscript—there was no occasion to have bored you in person.—I never interfere in anybody's squabbles—she may scratch your face herself.——The weather here has been dreadful—Snow several feet——*fiume* broke down a bridge— and flooded Heaven knows how many Campi,—then rain came—and it is still thawing—so that my saddle horses have a sinecure till the roads become more practicable.——

Why did Lega give away the goat? a blockhead—I must have him again.——Will you pay Missiaglia—and the Buffo Buffini—of the Gran Bretagna.—I heard from Moore who is at Paris—I had previously written to him [in] London —but he has not yet got my letter apparently.——Have you Clawed Edgecombe? if you see him— tell him that if he and I foregather again—I shall have to say that which he will remember for some time.——Castelli should proceed with the law suits—and if there is any other I shall have no objection. With my benediction on Mrs. Hoppner—who has made Mrs. Prescott's marriage—believe me

yrs. ever very truly
BYRON

Voi avete sentito il vostro Genitore parlare di quella donna—e se non volete sentire nè lui nè il vostro amico—basta sentire il paese.— Essa ha portato dei dispiaceri in tutte le famiglie dove è stata.—Io pregava Ferdinando dirvi *in orecchio*;—forse egli m'avra mal inteso.— L'altra sera—vi diedi la mia parola d'*onor* di non intrare più in casa dove stava quella donna—e in mia patria—questa diviene più d'un giuramento.—Per il resto—ognano è padrone di Casa sua—e nessuno più di *A*[*lessandro*]—egli farà ciò che lo piace—e farà bene—io ho parlato con voi—ed anche in presenza del Conte Ruggiero—credete che c'è una differenza d'opinione sopra la vostra protezione di questa donna?—domandate.—

Io non cerco l'avvilimento di nessuno—ma nè il vostro onore— nè il mio mi permetterà tacere quando vedo delle cose alle quali non voglio dare loro *vero* nome per non dirvi delle parole che potrebbero offendervi.—L'imprudenza di Ferdinando è stata Colpa mia in parte, ma io non aveva altra maniera in quel'momento communicare con voi— e credeva ch' egli vi direbbe in un'momento più opportuno—ciò che era solamente la replica della mia risoluzione già presa, e spiegata da molto tempo.——

La mia intenzione non era di offendere nè A[lessandro]—nè nessuno—ma non sono pentito di avere ad ogni rischio—fatto il possibile per impedire il progresso di un' imprudenza che andava per finire in un' disonore.—Bisogna fare ciò che se debbe—e non quello che può piacere solamente—cosi ho fatto io.—— Sono e sarò il vostro umil. Serv. ed ami[c]o

B

You have heard your father talk about that woman—and if you will not listen to him or to your friend, it is enough to listen to the town. She has caused trouble in every household where she has been.

I asked Ferdinando to whisper in *your ear*—perhaps he misunderstood.

The other evening I gave you my *word of honour* not to go into any house where that woman is—and in my country this counts for more than an oath. As to the rest—everyone is master in his own house, and no one more than A[lessandro]. He will do what he likes and will be right. I have told *you*—even in the presence of Count Ruggero.[1]

[1] Count Ruggero Gamba, Teresa's father.

Do you think there is any difference of opinion between us about your defence of this woman? Ask him.

I am not trying to humiliate anyone—but neither your honour nor mine will allow me to be silent when I see things to which I will not give their *real* name, so as not to use words which might offend you. The imprudence of Ferdinando was my fault,—in part—but I had no other way at the time of communicating with you—and I thought he would tell you at a more suitable moment what was only repeating a resolution already taken and explained a long time ago.

My intention was not to offend either A[lessandro] or anyone, but I do not regret having done everything possible at any cost—to prevent the continuance of an imprudence which would have ended dishonourably.

One must do what one must—and not only what is agreeable—and this I have done. I am and shall be your most humble servant and friend.

[TO COUNTESS TERESA GUICCIOLI (*b*)]   7 *ore* [*Jan. 31, 1820?*]

Amor mio—È difficile prevedere come questo affare abbia a terminare.—In ogni caso tu poui essere sempre certo del' amor il più sincero, il più sviscerato.—Tu sei in caso di sapere più di me l'idee di A[lessandro]—io ho mandato Lega a dirlo che nè Papa—nè la Rasponi m'aveva parlato—nè fatto parlare—di questa cosa—come è il fatto.— Della donna—ritengo la mia opinione e la mia risoluzione—adesso le ragioni si radoppiano ad ogni momento perche io non potrei intrare nessuna casa dove abita questa bella Elena della nuova guerra di Troja—tu sai che il nome di *Paride* nel' Greco è *Alessandro*—come tu avrai veduto nella traduzione di'Omero da Monti.—Cosa sarà di te—io non so—cosa sarà di me—ora e sempre—dipende quasi tutto di te—e del' grado e costanza del' bene che tu mi vuoi.—Io non sono venuto a R[avenna] per abbandonarti—ma le circonstanze—la fortuna e la morte—sono i Sovrani dei uomini;—vedremmo col tempo, lo sviluppo di nostro destino.—Ti bacio 100000 volte— Carissima.—

[TRANSLATION (*b*)]   7 o'clock [*Jan. 31, 1820?*]

My Love—It is difficult to foresee how this affair may end. In any case you can always be certain of my most sincere, my most passionate love. You are in a position to know better than I what A[lessandro]'s ideas are. I have sent Lega to tell him that neither Papa nor the

Rasponi had spoken to me or sent me a message about the matter—
as is the case.

Of the woman I retain my opinion and my resolution—since the
reasons are constantly increasing against my entering any house
inhabited by this fine Helen of the new Trojan war. You know that
the name of Paris in Greek is *Alexander*—as you saw in Monti's
translation of Homer.

What will happen to you—I don't know—what will happen to me,
now and always—depends almost completely on you, and on the degree
and constancy of your love for me. I did not come to R[avenna] to
give you up—but circumstances—chance—and *death* are the rulers of
men; we shall see, in time, the unfolding of our destiny. I kiss you
100,000 times—my dearest.

[TO COUNTESS TERESA GUICCIOLI]   [*Feb. 1820?*]

P + O + [1]—Hai ragione—io ho sempre pensato di *quello*, e mi
spaventa più di tutte le Gazzette dell' Europa. Se perdessi li denti per
cagione dell'aria di Ravenna—tu non mi baciaresti più con buona
volontà—& se quell' aria grossa mi fece divenire troppo grosso—la
[several words erased] delle cose più necessarie ancora per te & per il
tuo

                                                            B

P.S.—Dunque l'affare è anche tuo, *la volpe* è morta—dunque—
tutti quanti di quella cera dovrebbero guardarsi—in questa stagione.—
Amami + + ⟨sempre tuo⟩ ti abraccio mille + + + + +

                                                        [Scrawl]

[TRANSLATION]   [*Feb., 1820?*]

P + O + [1]—You are right—I have always thought of *that*, and it
frightens me more than all the Newspapers in Europe. If you were
to lose your teeth because of the air of Ravenna—you would no longer
kiss me gladly—and if that thick air made me become too thick—
the [words erased] of the things still most necessary for you and for
your

                                                            B

1 Pessimo O. Iris Origo translates this: "Very naughty O." The "O" was some
private epithet never written out.

31

P.S.—Then the matter is yours also, the fox is dead—well then—
everyone of that complexion—should take care—in this season.—
Love me + + ⟨always yours⟩ I embrace you a thousand + + + + +[1]

Attendo con impazienza—mio Bene—la tua lettera—che debbe
decidere molto—forse tutto per me.—Io sono così persuaso di aver
ragione nella risoluzione mia—che anche se mi costasse la mia felicità
—mi ritengo fermo.—La nuova predilezione di A[lessandro] in
favor—di quella persona di cui si tratta—io non posso ben capire;—
a Venezia—egli aveva un'opinione tutta opposta—e se tu ti ricordi—
la diceva anche in parole molto grosse.—Le mie ragione ho già
spiegato—ho delle altre—ma non torno a ripeterle.—Io non ho
diritto di dire nè a lui nè a te più di ciò che ho detto—ma sono anche io
padrone di mi stesso di venire o non venire in una casa dove habita
una persona che io conosco per essere cativa in ogni rapporto;—
particolarmente quando si tratta—(come recentemente si trattò) del'
mio occupare una parte della casa.——

Ti prego dirmi una volta la decisione;—se dopo tutto quello che ho
passato debbo essere sacrificato, mi dispiace che non sia per una
miglior ragione—e per un soggetto un poco più degno che questa
mantenuta, ma ciò che sarà sarà.—Ricordati—che sono venuto due
volte a Ravenna—per compiacerti—*che ti amai con tutto il mio cuore*—e
che partirò non per capriccio mio—nè per stanchezza—nè per mancanza
della minima parte di quel' amor che t'ho sempre portato—e *che
sempre ti portarò*—ma perche vedo che il restar in un' paese dove non ti
vedrò, più che di ben' rado, sarebbe peggiore della lontananza—per
tutti due.—Fammi sapere ti prego; e subito—se puio—poiche—ho
delle ordini di dare a Lega—e ti raccomando spiegare a Papa—e al tuo
fratello che la nostra relazione finiva per nessuna leggerezza della
parte mia.—

I am awaiting with impatience—my Love—your letter, which must
decide a great deal—perhaps everything—for me. I am so convinced
of being right in my resolution—that even should it cost me my
happiness—I hold firm. The recent predilection of A[lessandro] in

---

[1] Translated by Professor Nancy Dersofi.

favour of the person in question I cannot well understand. In Venice he had quite the opposite opinion—and if you remember, expressed it in very plain language. My reasons I have already explained—I have no others—but I shall not repeat them here again. I have no right to say more than I have already said either to you or to him—but I am also my own master to go or not to go into a house where some-one lives whom I deem to be evil in every way; especially when it is a case (as recently it has been) of my occupying part of the same house.[1]

Pray tell me your decision once for all;—if, after all that I have endured, I am to be sacrificed, I am sorry that it is not to be for a better reason—and for a subject more deserving than this kept woman; but what will be, will be. Remember that I have come twice to Ravenna to please you—that *I loved you with all my heart*—and that I shall go away not owing to a whim of my own, nor from fatigue, nor from a failure of the slightest part of the love I have always felt and *always shall feel* for you—but because I realize that to remain in a town where I should only see you very seldom would be worse than separation—for both of us.

Pray answer me and at once—if you can—for I have orders to give to Lega, and do not fail to explain to Papa and to your brother that our relation is not ending through any instability on my part.

[TO COUNTESS TERESA GUICCIOLI]   *6 ore* [*Feb. 2, 1820?*]

Ben Mio—Jersera ho detto *"forse"* e con tutto ciò che per più ragioni fuori anche dell' amor che sento per te—vorrei vederti in casa tua—non posso risolvere in'un' momento prendere un' passo che mi sembra una viltà—e di cui sono sicuro che dopo i primi momenti che *fanno dimenticare tutto* io non perdonarei a mi stesso di aver' fatto—riflettendo sopra tutte le circonstanze che sono le cause e compagni di questa discordia—Io lascio all' bella Elena tutto il vantaggio di suo degno trionfo.—ho promesso ed in ogni modo tenerò parola—di non cercare più farla sortire direttamente nè indirettamente—e questo è in fatto—il solo partito—perche A[lessandro] ha il vero diritto di licenziarla.—Io ho pensato tutta la notte—ma con tutto l'amor che ti porto—non posso in' un' momento reconciliarmi a tornare dove

---

[1] Byron was being urged by Teresa to rent an apartment in the Guiccioli Palace, but he refused unless Guiccioli dismissed the maid "Teresa the second", whom he did not trust. Guiccioli was adamant and Byron finally succumbed to Teresa's wish and moved into the Palazzo Guiccioli.

questa abita—forse—col' tempo sarà possibile—ma in questo punto—
sarebbe comprare troppo caramente anche il piacere di rivenire nelle
tue braccia.—Ci vedremo alla festa spero—io vado alle 7 precisamente.
—A[lessandro] voleva che io facessi una risposta a lui questa mat[t]ina
—ma sono troppo combattuto per darla finora,—potrei darla facil-
mente—il mio Cuor la dittarebbe pur troppo—ma *dopo?*—Intanto ci
vedremo alle feste—credimi sempre e tutto tuo.

[scrawl]

[TRANSLATION]   *6 o'clock [Feb. 2, 1820?]*

My Love—Last night I said "perhaps"—and although for many
reasons besides the love I feel for you, I should like to see you in
your own house—I cannot suddenly resolve to take a step that seems
to me cowardly, and which I am sure, after the first moments, which
cause *everything to be forgotten*, I should never forgive myself for
having taken in view of all the circumstances that have been the cause
and the accompaniment of this disagreement. I leave the fair Helen all
the advantages of her worthy triumph. I have promised, and I shall
certainly keep my word, not to try any more to get rid of her either
directly or indirectly—and this conduct is the only possible course—
since only A[lessandro] has a true right to dismiss her. I have thought
about it all night—but in spite of all my love for you—I cannot
suddenly reconcile myself to going back to a house where she is living.
—Perhaps in time it will be possible—but now—it would be buying
too dearly the pleasure of returning to your arms.

We shall see each other at the assembly, I hope—I shall go punctu-
ally at 7. A[lessandro] wanted me to give him an answer this morning
—but I am still too tormented to do it. I could do it easily—my
Heart would only too gladly dictate it—but *afterwards?*

Meanwhile we shall see each other at the assembly. Believe me ever
and always yours

[TO JOHN MURRAY]   *Ravenna. February 7th 1820*

Dear Murray—I have had no letter from you these two months—
but since I came here in Decr. 1819—I sent you a letter for Moore—
who is—God knows *where*—in Paris or London I presume. I have
copied and cut the third Canto of Don Juan *into two*—because it was
too long—and I tell you this before hand—because in case of any
reckoning between you & me—these two are only to go for *one*—as

this was the original form—and in fact the two together are not longer than one of the first.—So remember that I have not made this division to *double* upon *you*—but merely to suppress some tediousness in the aspect of the thing.—I should have served you a pretty trick if I had sent you for example cantos of 50 stanzas each—like that Oriental Country Gentleman Mr. Galley Knight with his Eastern Sketches[1] blessings on his pretty poesy.——I am translating the first Canto of Pulci's Morgante Maggiore—& have half done it but these last days & nights of the Carnival confuse and interrupt every thing.——

I have not yet sent off the Cantos—and have some doubt whether they ought to be published—for they have not the Spirit of the first— the outcry has not frightened but it has *hurt* me—and I have not written "con amore" this time.—It is very decent however—and as dull "as the last new Comedy".—I think my translation of Pulci will make you stare—it must be put by the original stanza for stanza and verse for verse[2]—and you will see what was permitted in a Catholic country and a bigotted age to a Churchman on the score of religion;— and so tell those buffoons who accuse me of attacking the liturgy.—— I will give you due notice—if I send off the two Cantos—or the trans- lation of the Morgante.——I write in the greatest haste—it being the hour of the Corso—and I must go and buffoon with the rest—my daughter Allegra is just gone with the Countess G. in Count G.'s coach and six to join the Cavalcade—and I must follow with all the rest of the Ravenna world—our old Cardinal is dead—and the new one not appointed yet—but the Masquing goes on the same—the Vice- Legate being a good Governor.——We have had hideous frost and snow—but all is mild again—

yrs. ever truly

B

[TO COUNTESS TERESA GUICCIOLI]   *7 Feb[brai]o 1820*

Amor Mio—La rivoluzione Guiccioli è la conseguenza della rivoluzione in Spagna ed il buon'umore di Alassandro dopo aver letto il supplemento alla Gazetta di Lugano.—Gran cosa ch'è la Politica in questo mondo!—Basta—che le buone nuove non siano contradette

---

[1] *Phrosyne, a Grecian Tale* and *Alashtar, an Arabian Tale,* both by Henry Gally Knight, were published in 1817.

[2] Byron's translation of the first canto of the *Morgante Maggiore* was thus published with the Italian original in the 4th and last number of *The Liberal* in 1823.

la domenica ventura—allora avrei paura che il despotismo di Ferdinando il settimo—e di Teresa la seconda si rinascerebbe ensieme—per altro—la Cameriera ha più talento di sua Maesta Catholica—ed è altrotanto piu pericolosa.——Siccome tu lo desideri—la Signorina Biron sarà alle tue ordini—ma—ma—non importa.——Io vengo da te quando tu vuoi;—andare alla festa senza te non sarebbe nè convenienza nè piacere almeno per me—io non penso di farti veruno dispiacere ma se tu lo temi è assai facile restare ensieme in casa—la festa stessa è la cosa più indifferente ed anche noiosa—io sono stato alle passate perche tu volevi—e non per altra ragione.——Vieni—se tu vuoi—per la bambina—è gia vestita.——Credimi—con tutta l'anima sempre e tutto tuo

amante in e[tern]o
B

[TRANSLATION]   *February 7th, 1820*

My Love—The Guiccioli revolution is the consequence of the revolution in Spain, and the good humour of A[lessandro] is caused by his having read the supplement to the *Lugano Gazette*. What a good thing Politics are in this world! Enough—so long as the good news is not contradicted next Sunday—for then I am afraid that the despotism of Ferdinand VII and of Teresa II would come to life again—indeed the Maid has more talent than his Catholic Majesty—and is so much the more dangerous.

As you wish—Miss Biron will be at your orders—but—but—never mind.

I will come to you whenever you wish. To go to the assembly without you would be neither suitable nor pleasureable—at least for me. I do not want to disappoint you, but if that is what you fear, it would be quite easy to stay at home together; the assembly itself is the most indifferent and tedious affair. I went to the others because you wished me to, and for no other reason.

Come—if you will—for the child; she is already dressed. Believe me with all my soul always and entirely. Your lover forever

B

[TO COUNTESS TERESA GUICCIOLI (*a*)]   [*After Feb. 7, 1820?*]

Pessimo O.—Bramerei sapere cosa era quella charta che tu legesti al' ritorno della Conversazione in questo momento—e che poi non

hai voluto mostrarmi.—Aveva tutta l'aria d'un' contrabando.——
Pensate subito di un' ripiego e mandatemi la bugia più probabile che
potete inventare.—

[scrawl]

[TRANSLATION (a)]   [After Feb. 7, 1820?]

Very Naughty O.—I should like to know what that paper was,
which you were reading just now, after getting back from the Conversazione—and which you would not show me. It looked very much
like contraband. Think of a good excuse at once and send me the most
probable lie you can invent.

[TO COUNTESS TERESA GUICCIOLI (b)]   [After Feb. 7, 1820?]

Adesso la tua testina è riscaldata con quell' maladetto romanzo di
quale l'autore è sempre in ogni paese—ed in ogni tempo—stato il mio
Genio maligno.—Del resto. vi giuro che non so cosa vi ho fatto—non
v'era la Tuda—della Zinnantina tu non puoi dubitare—la Zinnani tu
conosci—dunque cosa è?— Io non vado a Cavallo oggi—dunque
quando tu puoi—o vuoi—sono qui e sempre

e tutto tuo
B

[TRANSLATION (b)]   [After February 7, 1820?]

Your little head is heated now by that damned novel—the author of
which has been—in every country and at all times—my evil Genius.[1]

As for the rest, I vow I don't know what I have done to you.
Zinnantina's Tuda was not there—and you know the Zinanni—so
what is it?

I am not riding today—so when you can—or wish—I am here and
ever and entirely yours.

B

[TO COUNTESS TERESA GUICCIOLI (c)]   [After Feb. 7, 1820?]

Il biglietto è copiato da qualche libro Francese.—Le Sentenze sono
attacate come cavalli di diverso colore—e fanno una muta piuttosto

---

[1] The book was Caroline Lamb's novel *Glenarvon*, which Byron had lent to
Teresa.

37

singolare.—"*Besoin*" non ha bisogno di un' *e* per terminarlo.—Dieu *sait* e non "*sais*" (come tu scrivi) che tu sei una pessima piccinina—e un' pessimo O.——La vostra fedeltà è come il vostro progresso nella nuova lingua,—⟨difficile⟩ [two lines crossed out]

Bon Soir.—

Bon repos.

Bonne nuit non è F[rancese]

[TRANSLATION (*c*)]   [*After Feb. 7, 1820?*]

The note is copied from some French book. The sentences are coupled together like horses of different colours—and form a rather singular team.—"*Besoin*" does not need an *e* at the end. Dieu *sait* not "*sais*" (as you write) that you are a very bad child and a very naughty O.——Your fidelity is like your progress in this new language, ⟨vacillating⟩ [two lines crossed out].

Bon soir—bon repos—*bonne nuit* is not F[rench].

[TO COUNTESS TERESA GUICCIOLI (*d*)]   [*After Feb. 7, 1820?*]

A. M. in E.—Ci vedremo. Io non ho le lettere di Maintenon—la quale era una p——[puttana] divota—e non allegra come la Clemilda —dunque non posso nemmeno capire cosa la detta Clemilda puo volere col'tal libro—se l'avessi—per certo ti avrei mandato.—Ho letto le vostre "due righe di biglietto" con tutta la dovuta attenzione—sono scritte colla solita eloquenza che non ti manca mai—finche non ti manca—non *Cuore* ma *Corinna*.——

                                             B

[TRANSLATION (*d*)]   [*After February 7, 1820?*]

My Love for Ever: We shall be meeting. I have not got the Letters of the Maintenon—who was a devout wh[ore]—and not a merry one like Clemilda—so I can't even understand what the aforesaid Clemilda can want with such a book. If I had it—I would certainly send it you.

I have read the "few lines" of your note with all due attention— they are written with your usual eloquence, which you will never lose, until you lose—not a Heart, but *Corinne*.

38

I have room for you in the house here, as I had in Venice, if you think fit to make use of it; but do not expect to find the same gorgeous suite of tapestried halls. Neither dangers nor tropical heats have ever prevented your penetrating wherever you had a mind to it, and why should the snow now?—Italian snow—fie on it!—so pray come. Tita's[1] heart yearns for you, and mayhap for your silver broad pieces; and your playfellow, the monkey, is alone and inconsolable.

I forget whether you admire or tolerate red hair, so that I rather dread showing you all that I have about me and around me in this city. Come, nevertheless,—you can pay Dante a morning visit, and I will undertake that Theodore and Honoria will be most happy to see you in the forest hard by. We Goths, also, of Ravenna hope you will not despise our arch Goth, Theodoric. I must leave it to these worthies to entertain you all the fore part of the day, seeing that I have none at all myself—the lark, that rouses me from my slumbers, being an afternoon bird. But, then, all your evenings, and as much as you can give me of your nights, will be mine. Ay! and you will find me eating flesh, too, like yourself or any other cannibal, except it be upon Fridays. Then, there are more cantos (and be d—d to them) of what courteous reader, Mr. S[aunders],[2] calls Grub Street, in my drawer, which I have a little scheme to commit to your charge for England; only I must first cut up (or cut down) two aforesaid cantos into three, because I am grown base and mercenary, and it is an ill precedent to let my Mecaenas [Maecenas], Murray, get too much for his money. I am busy, also, with Pulci—translating—servilely translating, stanza for stanza, and line for line, two octaves every night,—the same allowance as at Venice.

[1] Giovanni Battista Falcieri (1798–1874), who went by the name of Tita, came of a family of Venetian gondoliers, his father and brothers being employed by the Mocenigo family. Byron took him into his service soon after he moved into the Mocenigo Palace. He accompanied Byron to Ravenna and became one of his most trusted servants. His great black beard made him seem more ferocious than he was. Although he was brave enough, he had a most gentle nature and had a thoroughly loyal devotion to his master. He remained with Byron through the rest of the poet's life. It was Tita who gave him most comfort and care during his last illness. He was later a servant of Isaac D'Israeli, and Benjamin Disraeli got him various government posts. He lived to the age of 76, enjoying the fame of having been a favourite and faithful servant of the poet.

[2] According to Moore, Bankes had told Byron that a Mr. Saunders, whom he met in Venice, had said that "Don Juan was all Grub-street". Bankes told Moore that Byron was so affected by this disparagement that he could not bring himself to write another line of the poem for some time.

Would you call at your banker's at Bologna, and ask him for some letters lying there for me, and burn them?—or I will—so do not burn them, but bring them,—and believe me,

Ever and very affectionately yours,

BYRON

P.S.—I have a particular wish to hear from yourself something about Cyprus, so pray recollect all that you can.—Good night.

[TO LADY BYRON] *Ravenna. February 20th. 1820*

D[ea]r. Lady Byron—At the request of Mr. Kinnaird—I address you upon business.—Perhaps it will be best explained by copying a part of his letter.—"You should at the same time write to Lady Byron sending her a copy of the letter you have written to me and Mr. Blande [sic][1]—& requesting that She will write a similar one—or such a one as may be deemed right by Mr. Blande as her proper consent and another to him—and a similar one to myself as She is to be guaranteed for all the interest she can have in it. I presume no difficulties &c. &c.["]—the long and short of all this is—that Hanson is throwing difficulties in the way because Lord *Portsmouth* wants a mortgage— and D. Kinnaird is not pleased—and I am at my wit's end—for as to my writing and copying all these letters I really don't think I could— and I hope that it won't be necessary for me to try.—I request you to consent—and above all not to let me have to copy any letters to anybody.—The Mortgage as represented to me is most eligible—and has my full consent and concurrence—but yours is as necessary as mine—so do let us concur for once—if we never agreed before—for the singularity of the thing—as well as the importance of the object.——

And above all—expedite that eternal dawdle Hanson—who has sent me in such a *bill!*—but I suppose you know all that Story long ago—from D. Kinnaird, or others.—Your consent will save me the horrors of a journey to England which I assure you I contemplate with the most repugnant feelings.—Since I was twenty one I have passed six years out of the eleven in other countries—so that I am as much expatriated in habits as in climate, and should feel hardly less strange in London than in Pekin.—I perceive that the King is dead—

---

[1] Thomas Davidson Bland, a friend of Lady Byron's family, was one of the trustees of the Byron marriage settlement.

but I shall not trouble you with my company at the Coronation—
unless compelled by business to return,—or by any disgust which
might ⟨make⟩ induce me to strike my tents.——I recommend this
affair to your earnest consideration—and am &c. &c.

yrs.
BYRON

P.S.—I shall be very glad of Ada's picture whenever it can be
forward[ed]. I wrote to you on that—and other m[atters] in December
last.——On second thoughts, to put all imagination of my story out
of the question—I enclose you at once Douglas's letter—judge for
yourself.—You perhaps did right though not delicately in making a
clause for yourself in case of *my death*;—which I confess has hurt me a
little—for I assure you—I never contemplate the idea of yours without a heavy heart—and would rather precede than follow you—notwithstanding all that has happened, and notwithstanding all that may
happen.——Recollect one thing only—that in all acts of Settlement I
gave you *every advantage*—that you will be a great gainer by my
decease—and that by yours I stand where I am only—in short that
I acted fairly and liberally in such transactions previous to our marriage
—recollect all this—when the time comes—and then do not forget my
Sister Augusta—and her children—were I but sure of this—I should be
relieved from a weight—that was upon my heart like lead—when I was
ill three months ago—it was my last request on leaving England—
and it would be my last on leaving this world.——
[On cover]: To be forwarded immediately.—

[TO JOHN MURRAY]   *Ravenna. February 21st. 1820*

Dear Murray—The Bulldogs will be very agreeable—I have only
those of this country who though good—& ready to fly at any thing
yet have not the tenacity of tooth and Stoicism in endurance of my
canine fellow citizens, then pray send them—by the readiest convey-
ance, perhaps best by Sea.——Mr. Kinnaird will disburse for them &
deduct from the amount on your application or on that of Captain
Fyler.—I see the good old King is gone to his place—one can't help
being sorry—though blindness—and age and insanity are supposed to
be drawbacks—on human felicity—but I am not at all sure that the
latter at least—might not render him happier than any of his subjects.——I have no thoughts of coming to the Coronation—though I
should like to see it and though I have a right to be a puppet in it—

but my division with Lady Byron which has drawn an equinoctial line between me and mine in all other things—will operate in this also to prevent my being in the same procession.

——By Saturday's post—I sent you four packets containing Cantos third and fourth of D[on] J[uan]—recollect that these two cantos reckon only as *one* with you and me—being in fact the third Canto cut into two—because I found it too long.—Remember this—and don't imagine that there could be any other motive.—-The whole is about 225 Stanzas more or less—and a lyric of 96 lines—so that they are no longer than the first *single* cantos—but the truth is—that I made the first too long—and should have cut those down also had I thought better.——Instead of saying in future for so many cantos— say so many *Stanzas* or pages—it was Jacob Tonson's way—and certainly the best—it prevents mistakes—I might have sent you a dozen cantos of 40 Stanzas each—those of "the Minstrel" (Beatties's) are no longer—and ruined you at once—if you don't suffer as it is;— but recollect you are not *pinned down* to anything you say in a letter and that calculating even these two cantos as *one* only (which they were and are to be reckoned) you are not bound by your offer,— act as may seem fair to all parties.——I have finished my translation of the first Canto of the "Morgante Maggiore" of Pulci—which I will transcribe and send—it is the parent not only of Whistlecraft—but of all jocose Italian poetry.——You must print it side by side with the original Italian because I wish the reader to judge of the fidelity—it is stanza for stanza—and often line for line if not word for word.——

You ask me for a volume of manners &c.—on Italy; perhaps I am in the case to know more of them than most Englishmen—because I have lived among the natives—and in parts of the country—where Englishmen never resided before—(I speak of Romagna and this place particularly) but there are many reasons why I do not choose to touch in print on such a subject—I have lived in their houses and in the heart of their families—sometimes merely as "amico di casa" and sometimes as "Amico di cuore" of the Dama—and in neither case do I feel myself authorized in making a book of them.——Their moral is not your moral—their life is not your life—you would not understand it—it is not English nor French—nor German—which you would all understand—the Conventual education—the Cavalier Servitude—the habits of thought and living are so entirely different—and the difference becomes so much more striking the more you live intimately with them—that I know not how to make you comprehend a people— who are at once temperate and profligate—serious in their character

42

and buffoons in their amusements—capable of impressions and passions which are at once *sudden* and *durable* (what you find in no other nation) and who *actually* have *no society* (what we would call so) as you may see by their Comedies—they have no real comedy not even in Goldoni—and that is because they have no society to draw it from.——

Their Conversazioni are not Society at *all*.—They go to the theatre to talk—and into company to hold their tongues—The *women* sit in a circle and the men gather into groupes [sic]—or they play at dreary Faro—or "Lotto reale"—for small sums.—Their Academie are Concerts like our own—with better music—and more form.—Their best things are the Carnival balls—and masquerades—when every body runs mad for six weeks.——After their dinners and suppers they make extempore verses—and buffoon one another—but it is in a humour which you would not enter into—ye of the North.——

In their houses it is better—I should know something of the matter—having had a pretty general experience among their women—[from] the fisherman's wife—up to the Nobil' Donna whom I serve.—— Their system has it's rules—and it's fitnesses—and decorums—so as to be reduced to a kind of discipline—or game at hearts—which admits few deviations unless you wish to lose it.——They are extremely tenacious—and jealous as furies—not permitting their Lovers even to marry if they can help it—and keeping them always close to them in public as in private whenever they can.——In short they transfer marriage to adultery—and strike the *not* out of that commandment.—The reason is that they marry for their parents and love for themselves.—They exact fidelity from a lover as a debt of honour—while they pay the husband as a tradesman—that is not at all.——You hear a person's character—male or female—canvassed—not as depending on their conduct to their husbands or wives—but to their mistress or lover.——And—and—that's all.—If I wrote a quarto—I don't know that I could do more than amplify what I have here noted.——

It is to be observed that while they do all this—the greatest outward respect is to be paid to the husbands—and not only by the ladies but by their Serventi—particularly if the husband serves no one himself —(which is not often the case however) so that you would often suppose them relations—the Servente making the figure of one adopted into the family.—Sometimes the ladies run a little restive—and elope—or divide—or make a scene—but this is at starting generally— when they know no better—or when they fall in love with a foreigner—

or some such anomaly—and is always reckoned unnecessary and extravagant.———

You enquire after "Dante's prophecy"—I have not done more than six hundred lines but will vaticinate at leisure.———Of the Bust I know nothing—no Cameos or Seals are to be cut here or elsewhere that I know of in any good style.—Hobhouse should write himself to Thorwalsen—the bust was made and paid for three years ago.———Pray tell Mrs. Leigh to request Lady Byron—to urge forward the transfer from the funds—which Hanson is opposing because he has views of investment for some Client of his own—which I can't consent to—I wrote to Lady B. on business this post addressed to the care of Mr. D. Kinnaird.—Somebody has sent me some American abuse of "Mazeppa"—and "the Ode";—in future I will compliment nothing but Canada—and desert to the English.———

By the king's death[1]—Mr. H[obhouse] I hear will stand for Westminster—I shall be glad to hear of his standing any where except in the pillory—which from the company he must have lately kept—(I always except Burdett—and Douglas K. and the genteel part of the reformers) was perhaps to be apprehended. I was really glad to hear it was for libel instead of larceny—for though impossible in his own person he might have been taken up by mistake for another at a meeting.———All reflections on his present case and place are so ⟨very⟩ *Nugatory*—that it would be useless to pursue the subject further.———

I am out of all patience to see my friends sacrifice themselves for a pack of blackguards—who disgust one with their Cause—although I have always been a friend to and a Voter for reform.———If Hunt had addressed the language to me—which he did to Mr. H[obhouse] last election—I would not have descended to call out such a miscreant who won't fight—but have passed my sword-stick through his body—like a dog's and then thrown myself on my Peers—who would I hope—have weighed the provocation;—at any rate—it would have been as public a Service as Walworth's chastisement of Wat. Tyler.—If we must have a tyrant—let him at least be a gentleman who has been bred to the business, and let us fall by the axe and not by the butcher's cleaver.———No one can be more sick of—or indifferent to politics than I am—if they let me alone—but if the time comes when a part must be taken one way or the other—I shall pause before I lend myself to the views of such ruffians—although I cannot but approve of a Constitutional amelioration of long abuses.———Lord

[1] On the death of the King a new Parliament had to be elected.

George Gordon[2]—and Wilkes—and Burdett—and Horne Tooke—
were all men of education—and courteous deportment—so is
Hobhouse—but as for these others—I am convinced—that Robespierre was a Child—and Marat a quaker in comparison of what they
would be could they throttle their way to power.———

[scrawl]

[TO WILLIAM BANKES] *Ravenna, February 26th, 1820*

Pulci and I are waiting for you with impatience; but I suppose we
must give way to the attraction of the Bolognese galleries for a time. I
know nothing of pictures myself, and care almost as little: but to me
there are none like the Venetian—above all, Giorgione. I remember
well his Judgment of Solomon in the Mariscalchi in Bologna. The real
mother is beautiful, exquisitely beautiful. Buy her, by all means, if
you can, and take her home with you: put her in safety: for be assured
there are troublous times brewing for Italy; and as I never could keep
out of a row in my life, it will be my fate, I dare say, to be over
head and ears in it; but no matter, these are the stronger reasons for
coming to see me soon.

I have more of Scott's novels (for surely they are Scott's) since we
met, and am more and more delighted. I think that I even prefer them
to his poetry, which (by the way) I redde for the first time in my life
in your rooms in Trinity College.

There are some curious commentaries on Dante preserved here,
which you should see.

Believe me ever, faithfully and most affectionately,

Yours, etc.

[TO JOHN MURRAY] *Ravenna. February 28th. 1820*

ARGUMENT.

While Charlemagne, the Emperor is living
 all his Paladins in feast and glee
With
 the Paladins in festival and glee,
Orlando, 'gainst the traitor Gano giving
 Way to his wrath, departs for Paganie,

---

[2] Lord George Gordon, born 1751, youngest son of the 3rd Duke of Gordon,
instigated anti-Roman Catholic riots in 1774. He died in Newgate in 1793.

And saves an Abbey, in a wild arriving,
  All from the beastly rage of Giants three.
Slays two of them, and with Morgante ends
  In goodly fellowship by making friends.

Dear Murray—When you publish the enclosed—it must be with the *Italian text*—as I wish it to be proved with the original—for good or no—Surely you will find a *Pulci* in London.—

yrs. truly
B

P.S.—Write—an answer suddenly. I sent you last week the two Cantos of D.J. Respond—Show this translation to Frere and *Rose*—and Hobhouse.——

[TO LEGA ZAMBELLI] [*March, 1820?*]

Signore Lega Zambelli—Non può essere bisogno di tante parole—io mi sono già spiegato.——Io sono pronto a pagare il [incremento?] in questo punto *ma sempre colla condizione di avere una ricevuta*, il primo dovere del' uomo onesto che riceve.—Il signor Cavaliere dovrebbe averlo dato sul' incremento—la sua scusa è che il pagamento non è per la somma totale—è la metà pero—e io desiderava *una ricevuta solamente* per ciò che io ⟨abbia⟩ pagava—e non per il resto.— Per terminare l'affare—io sono prontissimo a pagare ⟨il⟩ l'altri due cento scudi—sul' incremento—basta che ho la mia ricevuta, e che non ho più a fare con uno che si [?] nelle liti [fino?] delle miserie.—— Voi sapete che il sistema di mia famiglia è di avere delle ricevute anche ⟨delle⟩ per le più piccole cose—così so cosa che pago—e cosa debbo pagare.—In ogni modo non [stata?]—

BYRON

[TRANSLATION] [*March, 1820?*]

Signor Lega Zambelli—Many words cannot be needed—I have already explained myself. I am ready to pay the [increment?] at this point, but always on condition of having a receipt, the first duty of an honest man who receives. The Signor Cavaliere should have given it on the increment—his excuse is that the payment was not for the entire amount—it is, however, half—and I wished a receipt only for that which I paid—and not for the rest.[1] To put an end to the matter—I

---

[1] See March 3, 1820, to Teresa, note 1.

46

am very ready to pay the other two hundred scudi—on the increment—
so long as I have my receipt, and have nothing more to do with someone who [thrusts?] himself into quarrels to the point of blackguardly
tricks [?]——

You know that the system in my family is to have receipts even for
the smallest things—thus I know what I pay, and what I must pay.—
In any case [?]

BYRON[2]

Ravenna. March 1st. 1820

Dear Murray—I sent you by last post the translation of the first
Canto of the Morgante Maggiore—and the week before the 3d. & 4th.
Cantos of D[on] J[uan]—In the translation I wish you to ask Rose
about the word *Sbergo*—i.e. *Usbergo* which I have translated Cuirass—
I suspect that it means *helmet* also—now if so—which of the senses is
best accordant with the text?—I have adopted Cuirass—but will be
amenable to reasons.—Of The Natives some say one and some
t'other, but they are no great Tuscans, in Romagna—however I will
ask Sgricci (the famous Improvisatore) tomorrow—who is a native
of Arezzo—The Countess Guiccioli—who is reckoned a very cultivated young lady—and the dictionary—say Cuirass—I have written
Cuirass—but *helmet* runs in my head nevertheless—and will run in
verse very well whilk is the principal point.—I will ask the "Sposa
Spina Spinelli" too, the Florentine bride of Count Gabriel Rasponi[1]—
just imported from Florence—and get the sense out of Somebody.——

I have just been visiting the new Cardinal[2] who arrived the day
before yesterday in his legation—he seems a good old gentleman pious
& simple—and not like his predecessor who was a bon vivant in the
worldly sense of the words.[3]——Enclosed is a letter which I received
some time ago from Dallas.—It will explain itself—I have not answered it.——This comes of doing people good.—At one time or

[2] Translated by Professor Nancy Dersofi.
[1] One of several noble friends of the Gambas in Ravenna.
[2] Cardinal Antonio Rusconi was Cardinal Legate in Ravenna from 1819 to
1824.
[3] Cardinal Alessandro Malvasia had come to Ravenna in 1816 as the first
Cardinal Legate on the reestablishment of the Papal States after the Napoleonic
occupation. He died in 1819 and was succeeded by Cardinal Rusconi. See July 5,
1819, to Lord Kinnaird (Vol. 6, p. 176). Besides being a lover of parties and a
"bon vivant", he was a celebrated scholar and founder of the literary academy called
after him the "Malvasiana".

another—(including copy-rights)—this person has had about fourteen hundred pounds of my money—and he writes what he calls a posthumous work about me—and a scrubby letter accusing me of treating him ill—when I never did any such thing.—It is true—that I left off letter writing as I have done with almost every body else—but I can't see how that was misusing him.——I look upon his epistle as the consequence of my not sending him another hundred pounds—which he wrote to me for about two years ago—and which I thought proper to withhold he having had his share methought of what I could dispone upon others.—

In your last you ask me after my articles of domestic wants—I believe they are as usual—the bulldogs—Magnesia—Soda powders—tooth-powder—brushes—and everything of the kind which are here unattainable.——You still ask me to return to England—Alas to what purpose?—you do not know what you are requiring—return I must probably some day or other—(if I live)—sooner or later—but it will not be for pleasure—nor can it end in good.——You enquire after my health—and *Spirits* in large letters—my health can't be very bad—for I cured myself of a sharp Tertian Ague—in three weeks—with cold water—which had held my stoutest Gondolier for months—notwithstanding all the Bark of the Apothecary;—a circumstance which surprized Dr. Aglietti—who said it was a proof of great Stamina—particularly in so epidemic a Season.—I did it out of dislike to the taste of Bark (which I can't bear)—and succeeded—contrary to the prophecies of every body—by simply taking nothing at all.—— As to *Spirits* they are unequal—now high now low—like other people's I suppose—and depending upon circumstances.——

Pray send me W. Scott's new novels—what are their names and characters?[4] I read some of his former ones at least once a day for an hour or so.—The last are too hurried—he forgets Ravenswood's name—and calls him *Edgar*—and then *Norman*—and Girder—the Cooper—is—styled now *Gilbert* and now *John*—and he don't make enough of Montrose—but Dalgetty is excellent—and so is Lucy Ashton—and the bitch her mother.[5]——What is *Ivanhoe?*—and what do you call his other—are there *two?*—Pray make him write at least two a year.—I like no reading so well.——Don't forget to answer forthwith—for I wish to hear of the arrival of the packets—

[4] Scott's new novels were *Ivanhoe* (1819) and *The Monastery* (1820).

[5] Edgar, Master of Ravenswood, is the hero of Scott's *The Bride of Lammermoor.* His union with Lucy Ashton was prevented by her proud and ambitious mother. Dalgetty, a soldier of fortune, enrolled as a Major under the Marquis of Montrose, leader of the Royalist forces in the Highlands in *A Legend of Montrose.*

viz.—the two Cantos of Donny Johnny—and the translation from Morgante Maggiore—or Major Morgan.——Have you sent the letter to Moore?—Why do you abuse the Edin[burgh] Magazine and Wilson?—last year you were loud & long in praise of both—and now damnify them.—You are somewhat *capricious*—as we say here in Romagna—when a woman has more than the usual Staff establishment of Aides de *Cons*.——

The Editor of the Bologna Telegraph has sent me a paper with extracts from Mr. Mulock's (his name always reminds me of Muley Moloch of Morocco) "Atheism Answered"[6]—in which there is a long eulogium of my poesy—and a great "compatimento" for my misery.——I never could understand what they mean by accusing me of irreligion—however they may have it their own way.——This Gentleman seems to be my great admirer—so I take what he says in good part—as he evidently intends kindness—to which I can't accuse myself of being insensible.—

yrs.
[scrawl]

[TO JOHN CAM HOBHOUSE]   *Ravenna. March 3d. 1820*

My dear Hobhouse—I have paused thus long in replying to your letter not knowing well in what terms to write—because though I approve of the object—yet with the exception of Burdett and Doug. K. and one or two others—I dislike the companions of your labours as much as the place to which they have brought you.——I perceive by the papers that "ould Apias Korkus"[1] has not extricated you from the "puddle" into which your wit hath brought you.—However if this be but a prologue to a seat for Westminster—I shall less regret your previous ordeal, but I am glad that I did not come to England—for it would not have pleased me to find on my return from transportation my best friends in Newgate.[2] "Did I ever—no I never"—but I will say no more—all reflections being quite *Nugatory* on the occasion;—still I admire your Gallantry and think you could not do otherwise *having* written the pamphlet[3]—but *"why bitch Mr. Wild!"*[4]—why

---

[6] Thomas Mulock's *Answer Given by the Gospel to the Atheism of all Ages* was published in 1819. The passages referring to Byron are given in *LJ*, IV, 496–97.

[1] Habeus Corpus.

[2] Hobhouse was released from Newgate on February 28, 1820.

[3] See Jan. 2, 1820, to Kinnaird, note 1.

[4] Fielding's *Life of Mr. Jonathan Wild*, Book III, chapter 8.

write it?—why lend yourself to Hunt and Cobbett—and the bones of Tom Paine? "Death and fiends"—You used to be thought a prudent man—at least by me whom you favoured with so much good counsel—but methinks you are waxed somewhat rash at least in politics.——

However the King is dead—so get out of Mr. Burns's apartments—and get into the House of Commons—and then abuse it as much as you please, and I'll come over and hear you. Seriously—I did not "laugh" as you supposed I would—no more did Fletcher—but we looked both as grave as if we had got to have been your Bail—particularly that learned person who pounced upon the event in the course of spelling the Lugano Gazette.——So—Scrope is gone[5]—down—*diddled*—as Doug. K. writes it—the said Doug. being like the Man who when he lost a friend went to the St. James's Coffee House and took a new one—but to you and me—the loss of Scrope is irreparable—we could have "better spared" not only "a better man"[6] but the "best of Men".—Gone to Bruges—where he will get tipsy with Dutch beer and shoot himself the first foggy morning.——Brummell—at *Calais*—Scrope at Bruges—Buonaparte at St. Helena—you in—your new apartments—and I at Ravenna—only think so many great men!—there has been nothing like it since Themistocles at Magnesia—and Marius at Carthage.——But—Times change—and they are luckiest who get over their worst rounds at the beginning of the battle.—The other day—February 25th. we plucked violets by the way side *here* at Ravenna—and now March 3d. it is snowing for all the world as it may do in Cateaton Street.——

We have nothing new here but the Cardinal from Imola—and the news of the Berricide in France by a Saddler[7];—I suppose the Duke had not paid his bill.——I shall let *"dearest Duck"* [Lady Byron] waddle alone at the Coronation—a ceremony which I should like to see and have a right to act Punch in—but the Crown itself would not bribe me to return to England—unless business or actual urgency required it.——I was very near coming—but that was because I had been very much "agitato" with some circumstances of a domestic description—here in Italy—and not from any love of the tight little Island.—Tell Doug. K. that I answered his last letter long ago—and enclosed in the letter an order peremptory to Spooney—to make me

[5] Scrope Davies, like Beau Brummell, was ruined by gambling and escaped to the Continent. He spent his last days in Paris.

[6] *Henry IV*, Part 1, Act V, scene 4.

[7] Pierre-Louis Louvel, a saddler, assassinated the Duc de Berri, grandson of Louis XVIII, February 13, 1820.

an Irish Absentee according to Doug's own directions.———I like the security in Dublin Houses "an empty house on Ormond Quay"— but pray are they insured in case of Conflagration?—Deliver me that— and let us be guaranteed—otherwise what becomes of my fee?—My Clytemnestra stipulated for the security of her jointure—it was delicately done—considering that the poor woman will only have ten thousand a year more or less for life on the death of her mother.——

I sent Murray two more Cantos of Donny Johnny—but they are only to reckon as *one* in arithmetic—because they are but one long one cut into *two*—whilk [which] was expedient on account of tedium.— So don't let him be charged for these two but as one.———I sent him also a translation close and rugged—of the first Canto of the Morgante Maggiore to the published with the original text side by side— "cheek by jowl by Gome!" on account of the superlative merits of both.———All these are to be corrected by you—by way of solace during your probation.——

William Bankes came to see me twice—once at Venice—and he since came a second time from Bologna to Ravenna on purpose—so I took him to a Ball here and presented him to all the Ostrogothic Nobility—and to the Dama whom I serve;—I have settled into regular Serventismo—and find it the happiest state of all—always excepting Scarmentado's.[8] —I double a shawl with considerable alacrity—but have not yet arrived at the perfection of putting it on the right way—and I hand in and out and know my post in a Conversazione—and theatre—and play at cards as well as [a] man can do who of all the Italian pack can only distinguish "Asso" and "Re" the rest for me are hieroglyphics.—Luckily the play is limited to "Papetti" that is pieces of four Pauls—somewhere in or about two shillings. I am in favour & respect with the Cardinal and the Vice-legato—and in decent intercourse with the Gonfalonicre—and all the Nobiltà of the middle ages.—Nobody has been stabbed this winter—and few new liaisons formed—there is a Sposa Fiorentina—a pretty Girl yet in abeyance— but no one can decide yet who is to be her Servente—most of the men being already adulterated—and she showing no preferences to any who are not.—There is a certain Marchese who I think would run a good chance—if he did not take matters rather too philosophically.— Sgricci is here improvising away with great success—he is also a celebrated Sodomite a character by no means so much respected in Italy as it should be; but they laugh instead of burning—and the Women talk of it as a pity in a man of talent—but with greater

8 See [July, 1814] to Moore, note 1 (Vol. 4, p. 139).

tolerance than could be expected—and only express their hopes that
he may yet be converted to Adultery.——He is not known to have
b——d anybody here as yet but he has paid his addresses "fatto la
corte" to two or three.——

[scrawl]

[TO COUNTESS TERESA GUICCIOLI] *Marzo 3.o 1820*

"Egli creditore a me?" come? e si fosse vero, avendo pagato due
cento scudi—non v'e una ragione di più per darmi una ricevuta?—
Egli non dovrebbe aver' sottoscritto veruna obbligazione—ma queste
sono inezie.——Veniamo al' fatto.——La Somma che io dovrei
pagare al' Commune—o ai Signori deputati—è di 400 Scudi—*l'ho
esibito*—e lo *faccio ben volontieri* e con tutto il *piacere* possibile.—Di
questo è già pagata la Somma di due Cento Scudi—pei quali Egli mi
rifiuta *una ricevuta*—per delle ragioni—ch'io non m'intendo, e non
voglio intendere.——Io sono prontissimo pagare la somma totale
dimane—e fra le altre ragioni—per non aver' il Signor C[onte]
G[uiccioli] esposto alle obbligazioni pel'conto mio—ma pagandolo,—
torno a domandare una ricevuta—il primo dovere di lui *chi riceve* se
fosse di un'suo Contadino.——

[TRANSLATION] *March 3rd, 1820*

"He is my creditor." How? And if it were so, since he has been paid
200 scudi—is that not a reason the more for giving me a receipt?[1] He
should not have signed any obligation—but these are trifles. Let us
come to the facts. The sum that I have to pay to the Com[m]une—or to
the Deputies—is 400 scudi. I have acknowledged it, and I do so very
gladly, with all possible pleasure. Of this, the sum of 200 scudi has
already been paid—for which He refuses me a receipt—for reasons
which I do not understand and do not want to understand. I am quite
ready to pay the whole sum tomorrow—and among other reasons for
this—not to let Count Guiccioli be placed under an obligation on my
behalf—but if I pay, I shall once again ask for a receipt—the first
duty of anyone who *receives* anything, even from one of his own
peasants.

[1] Byron had advanced 200 Scudi of 400 promised for the engagement of the
prima donna, Mme. Pasta, and Count Guiccioli, head of the Ravenna Theatre
Committee, had refused to give him a receipt for the sum. See Jan. 17, 1820, to
Teresa.

La tua Immagionazione è troppo forte.—Il mandarti un libro che
tu da qualche tempo desiderasti vedere non ha niente nè sorprendente—
nè di riflesso.—"Tu non mi vedrai più"—Perche?—Cosa t'ho fatto?—
E vero che non sono stato al' tuo fianco per giocare alle Charte questa
sera in Casa C[avalli]—perche tu sei messa in un' cantone dove non si
trovava luogo per il tuo amico—per delle ragioni forse più conosciute
da te—che da me.——Ma questa non mi pare una ragione sufficiente
per disfare un'amicizia di qualche tempo e di molto prove.—Se sono
reo di torti contro te—tu puoi informarti.—In un piccolo paese—si
puo trovare la verità quando si vuole o dir' male, o sentirlo. Se tu
sei *seria* nella tua risoluzione—Io non sono l'uomo per importunarti—
ma voglio *in sangue freddo*—*tu ripeti in iscritto* questa risoluzione—
ed allora io prenderò il mio partito.——Ricordati solamente che *tu*
vuoi cosi, ed io no.—
[The page is torn and some words are missing.]

Your imagination is too active—To have sent you a book which you
have wanted to see for some time, is not surprising and is no reflection
on you.

"You will not see me again." Why—What have I done to you? It is
true that I did not stay by your side during cards this evening at the
C[avalli]'s, because you put yourself in a corner where there was not
room for your friend—for reasons which perhaps you know better
than I. But this does not seem to me a sufficient reason to end a friendship of some duration and many trials.[1]

If I have been guilty towards you—you can find it out. In a small
town one can find out the truth, when one wishes either to speak evil
or to hear it.

If you are serious in your resolution—I am not a man who will be
importunate—but I require you *to repeat* this resolution in *cold blood*
in writing—then I shall draw my own conclusions. Remember only
that *you* want this, and not I.

---

[1] Teresa had deliberately tried to make Byron jealous to keep him, Iris Origo
suggests, from becoming bored with their relationship. Several letters at this
period refer to their lovers' quarrels.

[TO JOHN MURRAY] *Ravenna. March 5th. 1820*

Dear Murray—In case in your country you should not readily lay hands on the Morgante Maggiore—I send you the original text of the 1st. Canto to correspond with the translation which I sent you a few days ago.—It is from the Naples Edition in Quarto of 1732—*dated Florence* however by a trick of *the trade*—which you as one of the Allied Sovereigns of the profession will perfectly understand without any further Spiegazione.——It is strange that here nobody understands the real precise meaning of *"Sbergo"* or *"Usbergo"*—an old Tuscan word which I have rendered *Cuirass* (but am not sure it is not *Helmet*) I have asked at least twenty people—learned and ignorant—male and female—including poets and officers civil and military.—The Dictionary says *Cuirass*[1]—but gives no authority—and a female friend of mine says *positively Cuirass*—which makes me doubt the fact still more than before.—Ginguené[2] says "bonnet de Fer" with the usual superficial decision of a Frenchman—so that I can't believe him—and what between The Dictionary—the Italian woman—and the Frenchman—there is no trusting to a word they say—The Context too which should decide admits of either meaning equally as you will perceive—Ask Rose—Hobhouse—Merivale—and Foscolo—and vote with the Majority—is Frere a good Tuscan? if he be bother him too— I have tried you see to be as accurate as I well could—this is my third or fourth letter or packet within the last twenty days

[scrawl]

[TO COUNTESS TERESA GUICCIOLI] *Marzo 5. 1820*

Vi ho mandato due volte per la risposta vostra alla *mia* di jersera.— Almeno qualunque che sia la vostra decisione—mi pare che per la mia giustificazione dovreste indicarmi più precisamente per norma mia— la vostra risoluzione—e la ragione.—Io ho un' dovere col' vostro padre—con cui prima di prendere le misure che (in caso che tu sei veramente decisa in questa stranissima risoluzione) bisognerà che prendo—voglio parlare per un momento.———Ricordati sempre che *tu* sei quella che vuole terminare la relazione—e non io—e che io non vi ho mai fatto torto in detto in fatto nè in pensiere.———[In] caso che sei attualmente risoluta—[word torn out] perche—non vi impor-

---

[1] Modern Italian dictionaries agree that the word meant cuirass or coat of mail.
[2] P. L. Ginguené, *Histoire Littéraire d'Italie*, tom. IV, p. 219 (1811–1819).

tunerò più—é partirò sul momento. Sono nonostante sempre il vostro amico ed amante.

[scrawl]

[TRANSLATION] *March 5th, 1820*

I have sent twice for a reply to my last night's letter. At least, whatever your decision may be, I think that in justice to me you should tell me, for my guidance, your definite decision and the reasons for it. I have a duty towards your father, with whom—before taking the steps which I must take if you are really determined to hold me to this very strange decision—I must speak for a moment.

Remember always that you are the one who wants to break off our relationship—and not I—and that I have never wronged you in word, or deed or thought.

[Paper torn]. . . . . . [In] case you really are resolved . . . because—I shall not importune you any more and shall leave at a moment's notice.

I am nevertheless always your friend and lover.

[TO COUNTESS TERESA GUICCIOLI (*a*)] *[After March 5, 1820?]*

Sarebbe meglio dirmelo questa sera—tutto è meglio del' incertezza. ——Io sono partito perche la serata minacciava divenire ben lunga—e vedeva Papa—che non ebbe l'aria di partire presto.——Vi prego dirmi adesso ciò ch'avete a dire in vece di dimane—perche io ho anche le mie ragioni per voler' sapere, e ho delle cose a decidere prima di Sabbato.

[Scrawl]

P.S.—Luigi è tornato dicendo che siete andata a letto. Direte ciò che vi commoda—ma vi prego dirlo presto—perche io non voglio essere più esposto ai capricci nè di mariti—nè di amiche che sono compiaciute nel fare tutte le malagrazie possibili.——

[TRANSLATION (*a*)] *[After March 5, 1820?]*

It would be better to tell me tonight—anything is better than this uncertainty.—I left because the evening showed signs of becoming very long—and I saw Papa—who did not look as if he would be leaving soon. Pray tell me what you have to say now instead of tomorrow because—I too have my own reasons for wanting to know, and have some things to decide before Saturday.

[Scrawl]

P.S.—Luigi has come back saying that you have gone to bed. You will say what suits you,—but pray say it soon—for I will not be exposed any longer to the caprices either of husbands or of "amiche" who take a pleasure in being as ungracious as possible.

[TO COUNTESS TERESA GUICCIOLI (*b*)]   [*After March 5, 1820?*]

Amor mio—[page torn—some words missing] Voi contate sopra il potere che finora avete avuto sopra me e le mie azioni—i miei pensieri—il mio cuore—per farmi creder' ciò—e tutto ciò che volete— e che vi commoda più per ora e per sempre.—Non dirò che ora non riuscirete perche avete già riuscita troppo spesso—ma vi prevengo che un'momento verrà quando vostre [arti] saranno in vano.

[Scrawl]

[TRANSLATION (*b*)]   [*After March 5, 1820?*]

My Love—You count on the power that you have had over me until now and over my actions—my thoughts—my heart—to make me believe this—and everything else you want—and that is most convenient to you: now and for ever. I do not say that you will not succeed now, because you have already succeeded only too often—but I warn you that a moment will come when your [arts] will be in vain.

[TO COUNTESS TERESA GUICCIOLI (*c*)]   [*After March 5, 1820?*]

E' meglio che non ci vediamo più questa sera—dimane parleremo forse con più tranquillità.—Io sono disposto creder ciò che tu dici— ma anche io ho dei miei sospetti qualche volta e tu che sei almeno egualmente sospettosa dovresti piuttosto compatire che condannarmi. —Ti prego di non venire da me adesso—perche il vederci in questo momento non puo fare altro se nonche accrescere il mio dolore— dimane ti vedrò e parleremo.

[Scrawl]

It is better that we should not see each other again tonight—
tomorrow perhaps we can talk more quietly.—I am inclined to believe
what you say—but I also have my suspicions sometimes, and you,
who are at least equally suspicious, ought rather to pity than blame
me.—I beg you not to come to me now—because to see each other at
this moment could do nothing but increase my grief. Tomorrow I shall
see you and we will talk.

[TO JOHN MURRAY]   *Ravenna. March 14th. 1820*

Dear Murray—Enclosed is Dante's Prophecy—Vision—or what
not[1]—where I have left more than *one* reading—(which I have done
often) you may adopt that which Gifford & Frere—Rose—and Hobhouse (is he still in Newgate?) and others of your Utican *Senate* think
the best—or least bad—the preface will explain all that is explicable.—
These are but the four first cantos—if approved I will go on like
Isaiah.——Pray mind in printing—and let some good Italian
Scholar correct the Italian quotations.——

Four days ago I was overturned in an open carriage between the
river and a steep bank—wheels dashed to pieces slight bruises—
narrow escape—and all that—but no harm done—though Coachman—
footman—horses—and vehicle were all mixed together like Maccaroni.
——It was [owing] to bad driving—as I say—but the Coachman
swears to a start on the part of the horses—we went against a post—
on the verge of a steep bank—and capsized.——I usually go out of the
town in a carriage—and meet the saddle horses at the bridge—it was
in going there—that we boggled—but I got my ride as usual—after
the accident.——They say here it was all owing to St. Antonio of
Padua (serious I assure you) who does thirteen miracles a day—that
worse did not come of it;—I have no objection to this being his fourteenth in the four and twenty hours—he presides over overturns—
and all escapes therefrom it seems; and they dedicate pictures &c. to
him as the Sailors once did to Neptune after "the high Roman
Fashion".[2]——

Yours in haste
[scrawl]

P.S.—Write directly.—I have sent you Don Juan—Translation of
Morgante Maggiore—and now Dante's &c. Acknowledge all.—

1 *The Prophecy of Dante* was published with *Marino Faliero* on April 21, 1821.
2 *Antony and Cleopatra*, Act IV, scene 3.

D[ea]r Murray—Last post—I sent you the "Vision of Dante["]—4 first Cantos.———Enclosed you will find *line for line* in *third rhyme* (*terza rima*) of which your British Blackguard reader as yet understands nothing—Fanny of Rimini—you know that She was born here—and married and slain from Cary, Boyd, and such people already.—I have done it into *cramp* English line for line & rhyme for rhyme to try the possibility.———You had best append it to the poems already sent by last three posts.———I shall not allow you to play the tricks you did last year with the prose you *post*scribed to Mazeppa—which I sent to you *not* to be published if not in a periodical paper, & there you tacked it without a word of explanation and be damned to you.——— If this is published—publish it *with the original*—and *together* with the *Pulci* translation—or the *Dante Imitation*[1]—I suppose you have both by now—& the *Juan* long before—

[scrawl]

[note in margin of manuscript of "Francesca of Rimini"]: In some of the editions it is *"diro"* in others *"faro"* an essential difference between *"saying"* and *"doing"* which I know not how to decide.—Ask Foscolo, the damned editors drive me mad.—

[TO JOHN MURRAY (*a*)] *March 23d. 1820*
Varied readings of the translation from Dante.—

———

The Land where I was born sits by the Seas
Upon that shore to which the Po descends
With all his followers in search of Peace.
Love, which the gentle heart soon apprehends,
Seized him for the fair person, which in its
Bloom was taen from me, yet the mode offends.

——— or ———

Seized him for the fair form, of which in it's
Bloom I was reft, and yet the mode offends.
Love which to none beloved to love remits
with mutual wish to please

---

[1] Byron's translation of the episode of *Francesca of Rimini* from Dante's *Inferno*, canto V, was first published by Moore in 1830 (Moore, II, 309–311).

Seized me with wish of pleasing him, so strong,
                     with the desire to please
That, as thou seest, not yet that passion quits.
Love &c. &c.

———————

D[ea]r. M[urra]y—You will find these readings vary from the
M.S. I sent you—they are closer but rougher—take which is liked
best, or if you like—print them as variations—they are all close to the
text.————

[Scrawl]

I sent the translation by last post—on ⟨Saturday⟩ Tuesday—Today
is Thursday.————

[TO JOHN MURRAY (*b*)]   *Ravenna. March 23d. 1820*

Dear Murray—I have received yr. letter of the 7th.—Besides the 4
packets you have already received I have sent the Pulci—a few days
after—and since (a few days ago) the 4 first Cantos of Dante's prophecy (the best thing I ever wrote if it be not *unintelligible*) and by last
post a *literal* translation word for word (versed like the original) of
the episode of Francesca of Rimini.——I want to hear what you think
of the new Juans, and the translations—and the Vision—they are all
things that are or ought to be very different from one another.——If
you choose to make a print from the Venetian you may—but she don't
correspond at all to the character you mean her to represent—on the
contrary the Contessa G[uiccioli] does (except that She is remarkably
fair) and is much prettier than the Fornarina—but I have no picture
of her—except a miniature which is very ill done—and besides it
would [not] be proper on any account whatever to make such a
[use] of it—even if you had a copy.———Pray give *Hobhouse* the enclosed song[1]—and tell him I know he will never forgive me—but I
could not help it—I am so provoked with him and his ragamuffins for
putting him in *quod*, he will understand that word—being now resident
in the flash capital.——I am now foaming an answer (in prose) to the
Blackwood Article of last August—you shall have it when done—it will
set the kiln in a low.———Recollect that the *two* new Cantos only count
with us—for *one*.—You may put the Pulci and Dante Together—

———

[1] This was Byron's satire on Hobhouse's association with the "Mobby O"
among the reformers which caused him to be sent to Newgate. It had the refrain
"My boy Hobby O" and was quite offensive to Hobhouse who felt that Byron
did not understand the principles on which he stood.

59

perhaps that were best—so you have put *your* name to Juan—after all your panic and the row—you are a rare fellow.——I must now put myself in a passion to continue my prose.

yrs.

[scrawl]

Saturday March 25th. 1820

I have caused write to Thorwalsen [sic].—Pray be careful in sending my daughter's picture—I mean that it be not hurt in the carriage—for it is a journey rather long and jolting.—

[TO JOHN MURRAY]   *Ravenna. March 28th. 1820*

D[ea]r M[urra]y—Inclosed is "a Screed of Doctrine for you" of which I will trouble you to acknowledge the receipt by next post.— Mr. Hobhouse must have the correction of it—for the press, you may show it first to whom you please.——I wish to know what became of my two epistles from St. Paul (translated from the Armenian three years ago and more) and of the letter to Roberts of last autumn, which you never [have even] alluded to.——There are two packets [with] this—

[scrawl]

P.S.—I have some thoughts of publishing the "hints from Horace" written ten years ago[1]—if Hobhouse can rummage them out of my papers left at his father's—with some omissions and alterations previously to be made—when I see the proofs.——

[TO JOHN MURRAY]   *Ravenna. March 29th. 1820*

Dear Murray,—I sent you yesterday eight sheets of answer to Jack Wilson and the Edin[burgh] Mag[azine] of last August.[1]—Herewith you will receive a note (enclosed) on Pope, which you will find tally

---

[1] The *Hints from Horace*, intended as a kind of sequel to *English Bards and Scotch Reviewers*, was written in Athens in the spring of 1811. It was not published as a whole until 1831. Moore published extracts in his life of Byron in 1830.

[1] *Blackwood's Edinburgh Magazine* for August, 1819, had a review of *Don Juan* in which the writer (not John Wilson as Byron supposed) referred to the "filthy and impious poem, with an elaborate satire on the character and manners of his wife . . . from whom, even by his own confession, he has been separated only in consequence of his own cruel and heartless misconduct. . . ." Byron's reply, "Some Observations upon an Article in Blackwood's Magazine" was not published during his lifetime. It finally appeared in Vol. 6 of Murray's collected edition (1832).

with a part of the text of last Post.[2] I have at last lost all patience with the atrocious cant and nonsense about Pope, with which our present blackguards are overflowing, and am determined to make such head against it, as an Individual can by prose or verse—and I will at least do it with good will.——There is no bearing it any longer, and if it goes on, it will destroy what little good writing or taste remains amongst us.——I hope there are still a few men of taste to second me, but if not, I'll battle it alone—convinced that it is in the best cause of English literature.——I have sent you so many packets verse and prose lately, that you will be tired of the postage if not of the perusal.——

I want to answer some parts of your last letter—but I have not time, for I must "boot and saddle" as my Captain Craigengelt[3] (an officer of the old Napoleon Italian army) is in waiting, and my Groom and cattle to boot.—You have given me a screed of Metaphor and what not about *Pulci*—& manners, "and going *without clothes* like our Saxon ancestors" now the *Saxons did not go* without cloathes [sic] and in the next place they are *not* my ancestors, nor yours either, for mine were Normans, and yours I take it by your name were *Gael*.——And in the next I differ from you about the "refinement" which has banished the comedies of Congreve—are not the Comedies of *Sheridan* acted to the thinnest houses?—I *know* (*as ex-Committed*) that the "School for Scandal" was the *worst Stock piece* upon record.—I also know that Congreve gave up writing because Mrs. Centlivre's balderdash[4] drove his comedies off—so it is not *decency* but Stupidity that does all this—for Sheridan is as *decent* a writer as need be—and Congreve no worse than Mrs. Centlivre—of whom Wilkes (the Actor) said—"not only her play would be damned but She too"—he alluded to a "Bold Stroke for a Wife"[5].——

But last and most to the purpose—Pulci is *not* an *indecent* writer—at least in his first Canto as you will have perceived by this time.——You talk of *refinement*, are you all *more* moral? are you *so* moral?—No such thing,—*I* know what the World is in England by my own proper experience—of the best of it—at least—of the loftiest.—And I have described it every where as it is to be found in all places.—But to return—I should like to see the *proofs* of mine Answer—because there

---

[2] This was probably an early form of Byron's reply to Bowles on the Pope controversy.

[3] Bucklaw's associate in *The Bride of Lammermoor*.

[4] Susanna Centlivre (1680?–1723) wrote 19 plays, the most popular of which were *The Busy Body* (1709) and *The Wonder* (1714)

[5] From the life of Mrs. Centlivre in *Biographica Dramatica*, pp. 97–100.

will be something to omit or to alter—but pray let it be carefully printed——When convenient let me have an answer——

yrs.
[scrawl]

[TO JOHN CAM HOBHOUSE]   *Ravenna. March 29th. 1820*

My dear Hobhouse—I congratulate you on your change of residence, which I perceive by the papers, took place on the dissolution of King and parliament.—The other day I sent (through Murray) a song for you—you dog—to pay you off for them there verses which you compounded in April 1816.—

————"No more shall Mr. Murray
Pace Piccadilly in a hurry—
Nor Holmes with not a few grimaces
Beg a few pounds for a few faces
Nor Douglas—"

but I won't go on—though you deserve it but you see I forget nothing—but good.—I suppose I shall soon see your speeches again and your determination "not to be saddled with wooden shoes as the Gazetteer says"—but do pray get in to Parliament—and out of the company of all these fellows except Burdett and Douglas Kinnaird—and don't be so very violent—I doubt that Thistlewood[1] will be a great help to the Ministers in all the elections—but especially in the Westminster.—What a set of desperate fools these Utican Conspirators seem to have been.[2]—As if in London after the disarming acts, or indeed at any time a secret could have been kept among thirty or forty.—And if they had killed poor Harrowby—in whose house I have been five hundred times—at dinners and parties—his wife is one of "the Exquisites"—and t'other fellows—what end would it have answered?—"They understand these things better in France" as Yorick says—but really if these sort of awkward butchers are to get the upper hand—*I* for one will declare *off*, I have always been (*before you* were—as you well know) a well-wisher to and voter for reform

---

[1] Arthur Thistlewood, leader of the so-called Cato Street conspirators, had planned to murder the Ministers at a dinner at Lord Harrowby's on February 20, 1820. They were apprehended and Thistlewood was captured the following day. Thistlewood was hanged in May.
[2] Byron meant to draw a parallel between the Cato Street conspirators and the Cato who rebelled against Caesar and shut himself up in Utica (near Carthage) and killed himself rather than surrender.

in Parliament—but "such fellows as these who will never go to the Gallows with any credit"———such infamous Scoundrels as Hunt and Cobbett[3]—in short the whole gang (always excepting you B. & D.) disgust and make one doubt of the virtue of any principle or politics which can be embraced by similar ragamuffins.——I know that revolutions are not to be made with rose-water,[4] but though some blood may & must be shed on such occasions, there is no reason it should be *clotted*—in short the Radicals seem to be no better than Jack Cade, or Wat Tyler—and to be dealt with accordingly.——I perceive you talk *Tacitus* to them sometimes—what do they make of it?— It is a great comfort, however to see you termed *"young Mr. Hobhouse"* at least to me who am a year and a half younger—and had given up for these two years all further idea of being

"Gentle and juvenile, curly and gay".—
"In the manner of Ackermann's dresses for May["]

And now—my Man—my Parliament Man I hope—what is become of Scrope?—is he at Bruges?—or have you gone to "the St. James's Coffee house to take another?"[5]——You will have been sadly plagued by this time with some new packets of my poesy and prose for the press but Murray was so pressing & in such a hurry for something for the Season—that I e'en sent him a cargo—otherwise I had got sulky about Juan, and did not mean to print any more—at least *"before term ends"*. You will see that I have taken up the *Pope* question (in prose) with a high hand, and *you* (when you can spare yourself from *Party* to Mankind)[6] must help me:—You know how often under the Mira elms, and by the Adriatic on the Lido—we have discussed that question and lamented the villainous Cant which at present would decry him.——It is my intention to give battle to the blackguards— and try if the "little Nightingale" can't be heard again.——But at present you are on the hustings—or in the Chair.—Success go with you.——

yrs. [scrawl]

[3] Henry ("Orator") Hunt, a radical orator, who ran for parliamentary seats at Bristol and at Westminster, had helped to organize the protest meeting that led to the "Manchester Massacre" (Peterloo). William Cobbett was a leading radical journalist who edited *Cobbett's Weekly Political Register*.
[4] Marmontel, *Mémoires d'un Père*, Livre XIV: "Voulez-vous qu'on fasse des révolutions à l'eau rose?"
[5] See March 3, 1820, to Hobhouse.
[6] Goldsmith's "Retaliation": "and to party gave up what was meant for mankind," in reference to Burke.

63

P.S.—Items of *"Poeshie* of the King your master".—Sent last Moon Cantos of Don Juan—two—to reckon as one only however with Murray on account of their brevity.—First Canto of Morgante Maggiore translated.—Prophecy of Dante—*four short* Cantos.— Prose observations on an article in B[lackwoo]d's Edin[burgh] Magazine.—Poeshie—Episode of Francesca of Rimini translated.— For all these matters you will request the honourable Dougal to arrange the elements with Mr. Murray.——Tell the Dougal I answered him peremptory in favour of the Irish Mortgage long ago— and *against* Spooney [John Hanson]—and hope that he hath done the Needful—but yr. damned parliaments cut up all useful friendship.—— Ask Dougal to get Spooney's bill and try to bring Rochdale to the hammer. I want to buy an Annuity like.

[TO HARRIETTE WILSON]   *Ravenna, March 30th.* [*1820*]

I have just received your letter, dated 15th instant, and will send you fifty pounds, if you will inform me how I can remit that sum; for I have no correspondence with Paris of any kind; my letters of credit being for Italy; but perhaps you can get someone to cash you a bill for fifty pounds on me, which I would honour, or you can give me a safe direction for the remission of a bill to that amount. Address to me at Ravenna, not Venice.

With regard to my refusal, some years ago, to comply with a very different request of yours, you mistook, or chose to mistake the motive: it was not that "I held you much too cheap" as you say, but that my compliance with your request to visit you, would just then have been a great wrong to another person: and, whatever you may have heard, or may believe, I have ever acted with good faith in things even where it is rarely observed, as long as good faith is kept with me. I told you afterwards that I had no wish to hurt your self-love,[1] and I tell you so again, when you will be more disposed to believe me.

In answer to your wish that I shall tell you if I was "happy", perhaps it would be a folly in any human being to say so of themselves, particularly a man who has had to pass through the sort of things which I have encountered; but I can at least say that I am not miserable, and am perhaps more tranquil than ever I was in England.

You can answer as soon as you please: and believe me

Yours, etc.,
BYRON

[1] See [April? 1814] to Harriette Wilson, note 1 (Vol. 4, p. 88).

P.S.—Send me a banker's or merchant's address, or any person's in your confidence, and I will get Langle, my banker at Bologna, to remit you the sum I have mentioned.

It is not a very magnificent one; but it is all I can spare just now.

Dear Hoppner—Laziness has kept me from answering your letter.— It is an inveterate vice—which grows stronger, and I feel it in my pen at this moment.———With regard to Mr. Gnoatto, I doubt that the Chevalier is too honest a man to make a good lawyer.—Castelli is a bustling, sly, sharp Avocato—& will be more likely to make the rascal wince. But I mean to do thus,—that is to say—with your approbation.— You will inform Madame Mocenigo—that till Mr. Gnoatto's money is paid—*I shall deduct that sum* from her rent—in June—till she compels her Servant to pay it. She may make a cause of it, if she likes—*so will I* & carry it through all the tribunals—so as to give her as many years work of it—as she pleases.—At the same time I will prosecute *him* also.—I am not even sure that I will pay her *at all*—till she compels her Scoundrelly dependent to do me justice—which a word from *her* would do.—All this you had better let *her* know as soon as can be.——— By the way—I should like to have my *Gondola* sold—for what it will bring—and do you carry money to the account of expences.—If Mother Mocenigo does as she ought to do—I may perhaps give up her house—and pay her rent into the bargain.—If not—I'll pay nothing and we'll go to law—I *loves* a "*lité*".——

What you tell me of Mrs. Strephon is very amusing—but all private matters must be superseded at present by the public plots—and so forth —I wonder what it will all end in.—I should probably have gone to England for the Coronation—but for my wife—I don't wish to walk in such company, under present circumstances.——Ravenna continues much the same as I described it—Conversazioni all Lent, and much better ones than any at Venice—there are small games at hazard— that is Faro—where nobody can point more than a shilling or two— other Card tables—and as much talk and Coffee as you please— Everybody does and says what they please—and I do not recollect any disagreeable events—except being three times falsely accused of flirtation—and once being robbed of six sixpences by a nobleman of the city—a count Bozzi. I did not suspect the illustrious delinquent— but the Countess Vitelloni and the Marquess Loratelli told me of it

directly—and also that it was a way he had—of filching money—
when he saw it before him—but I did not ax him for the cash—but
contented himself [myself] with telling him that if he did it again—I
should anticipate the law.——There is to be a theatre in April—and
a fair—and an Opera—and another Opera in June—besides the fine
weather of Nature's giving—and the rides in the Forest of Pine.——
Augustine overturned the carriage—a fortnight ago—and smashed
it—and himself and me—and Tita—and the horses—into a temporary
hodge-podge.—He pleaded against the horses—but it was his own bad
driving—Nobody was hurt—a few slight bruises—the escape was
tolerable—being between a river on one side—and a steep bank on the
other.—I was luckily alone—Allegra being with Madame Guiccioli.
——With my best respects to Mrs. Hoppner believe me

ever & very truly yrs.

BYRON

P.S.—Could you give me an Item of what books remain at Venice—
I *don't* want them—but wish to know whether the few that are not
here are there—and were not lost by the way.——I hope and trust you
have got all your wine safe—and that [it] is drinkable.——Allegra is
prettier I think—but as obstinate as a Mule—and as ravenous as a
Vulture.—Health good to judge [from] the Complexion—temper
tolerable—but for vanity and pertinacity—She thinks herself handsome—and will do as she pleases.

[TO COUNTESS TERESA GUICCIOLI (*a*)]   [*April, 1820?*]

A.M. +—"*La Contro-chiave*" ecco perche voleva le mie *lettere* in
mani mie *per ora*—e nonostante tu mi dicesti tutte le ingiurie—per
quella richiesta.——Ti prego guardare bene tutte quelle lettere che
sono chiuse in tua Scrivame (colla musica che era alla Mira) poiche si
potrebbe trovare se non del' *mio*—almeno qualche cosa che non ti
piacerebbe.—La mia opinione è sempre l'istessa—ma se non v'è
rimedio—io per certo farò il mio dovere.—Del' amor mio—tu non
puoi dubitare—e forse la prova più grande è stata—che io preferiva
sagrificare mi stesso—piuttosto—di te.—Credemi sempre e tutto

B

P.S.—La malatia tua non mi pare che *cutanea*—quando ci vedremo—
dimane?—Ricorda—non *sottoscrivere* niente per quel' *Scelerato per
eccellenza.*

My Love—The skeleton key—that is why I wanted my letters in my own hands *for the present*—and nevertheless you violently insulted me, because of my request. Pray look after the letters that are shut up in your writing-desk (with the music that was at La Mira) for something might be found there, if not of *mine*—yet something that you would not like.

My opinion is still the same—but if there is no remedy—I assuredly shall do my duty. Of my love you cannot doubt, and perhaps the greatest proof has been—that I prefer to sacrifice myself, rather than you.

Believe me ever and entirely

B

P.S.—Your illness seems to me only *skin-deep*—when shall we see each other—tomorrow?

Remember—do not sign anything for that arch-scoundrel.[1]

[TO COUNTESS TERESA GUICCIOLI (*b*)]   [*April, 1820?*]

A.M.—Io non lo stimo e non lo temo—Egli farà ciò che vuole. Per me, io ho del'amor e dei doveri, con te—ma non voglio influire in nessun modo sopra la tua decisione.—Dopo aver' fatto ciò ch'Egli ha fatto—nessuna viltà nessuna nefandità dalla parte sua sorprenderebbe nè a me—ne a nessuno.—Parla coi tuoi amici e parenti e come tu decidi—deciderà anche il tuo.

[Scrawl]

[TRANSLATION (*b*)]   [*April 1820?*]

My Love—I do not esteem him and I do not fear him—he will do as he pleases. For my part I feel love and a duty towards you—but I do not wish to influence your decision in any way. After having done what he has done—no vileness—no wickedness—on his part would surprise me—or anyone else.[1]

Talk to your friends and relations and as you decide—so also will decide your

1 This is the first of thirteen letters and notes which Teresa had put in a folder marked "Avant" or "Après l'abbocamento", that is, before or after the interview between Byron and Count Guiccioli. At that interview the Count expressed his displeasure and wanted Byron to leave his house. This led to the separation of Guiccioli and his wife.
1 A reference probably to Count Guiccioli breaking into his wife's writing-desk.

Ravenna. April 3d. 1820

I received yesterday your answer dated March 10th.[1] My offer was an honest one, and surely could be only construed as such even by the most malignant Casuistry.—I *could* answer you—but it is too late, and it is not worth while.——To the mysterious menace of the last sentence—whatever it's import may be—and I really cannot pretend to unriddle it,—I could hardly be very sensible even if I understood it—before it could take place—I shall be where "nothing can touch him further".[2]——I advise you however to anticipate the period of your intention—for be assured no power of yours can avail beyond the present,—and if it could I would answer with the Florentine—

"Et io, che posto son con loro in croce
. . . . .e certo
La *fiera Moglie*, piu ch'altro, mi nuoce."[3]

BYRON

[TO LADY BYRON] *Ravenna. April 6th. 1820*

In February last at the suggestion of Mr. Douglas Kinnaird—I wrote to you on the proposition of the Dublin Investment—and to put you more in possession of his opinions—I enclosed his letter.——I now enclose you a statement of Mr. Hanson's—and to say the truth—I am at a loss what to think or decide upon between such very opposite views of the [same] question.——Perhaps you will lay it before your trustees—I for my own part—am so ignorant of business and [am] so little able to judge—that I should be disposed to think with them—whatever their ideas may be upon the Subject.—One thing is certain—I cannot consent to sell out of the funds at such a loss—and the Dublin House should be insured.——Excuse all this trouble—but as it is your affair—as well as mine—you will pardon it—I have an innate distrust and detestation of the public funds and their precarious tenure—but still the sacrifice of the removal (at least at present) may

---

[1] In her reply to Byron's offer to let her read his "Memoirs" Lady Byron wrote: "I decline to inspect it. I consider the publication or circulation of such a composition at any time as prejudicial to Ada's future happiness. For my own sake, I have no reason to shrink from publication; but, notwithstanding the injuries which I have suffered, I should lament some of the *consequences*."

[2] *Macbeth*, Act III, scene 2.

[3] Dante, *Inferno*, Canto XVI, lines 43–45. Jacopo Rusticucci owed his place in Hell to the savage temper of his wife.

be too great.——I do not know what to think nor does any body else[.]

P.S.—I received yrs of March 10th. & enclosed [an answer] (to Mr. Thomas Moore) to be forwarded [to you.]

[TO JOHN HANSON]   *Ravenna. April 6th. 1820*

Dear Sir—I have just received yours dated March 22d.—Your *January packet* only arrived last Sunday—so that I shall put off *replying to it* for the present (as there is a *witness* wanting for the Scotch deed—&c.) and answer your March epistle—which as you yourself say—is of much more importance.——But how shall I answer?

> Between the devil and deep Sea,
> Between the Lawyer and Trustee?[1]—

it is difficult to decide.—Mr. Kinnaird writes that the Mortgage is *the most advantageous thing possible*—you write that [it] *is quite the contrary*—you are both my old acquaintances—both men of business—and both give good reasons for both your opinions—and the result is that I finish by having no opinion at all.——I cannot see that it could any way be the interest of either to persuade me either one way or the other unless you thought it for my advantage—in short *do settle* it among you if you can—for I am at my wits' end betwixt your contrary opinions.—One thing is positive—*I will not agree to sell out of the funds at a loss*—and the *Dublin House property must be insured*—but *you* should not have waited till the Funds get low again—as you have done—so as to render the affair impracticable.—I retain however my bad opinion of the funds—and must insist on the money being one day placed on better *security somewhere*; of Irish Security—and Irish Law—I know nothing—and cannot take upon me to dispute your Statement—but I prefer higher Interest for my Money (like everybody else I believe) and shall be glad to make as much as I can at the least risk possible.——It is a pity that I am not upon the Spot but I cannot make it at all convenient to come to England for the present.——

I am truly pleased to hear that there is a prospect of terminating the Rochdale Business—in one way or the other—pray see *it out*—it has been hitherto a dead loss of time and expences—but may I suppose pay in the long run—and if *you could for once* be a *little quicker*

---

[1] Cuddie Headrigg in *Old Mortality* (Chapter 33) found himself "atween the deil and the deep sea" in appealing to Claverhouse to save Morton.

about that or anything else it would be a great gain to me and no loss to you—as our final Settlement naturally will depend in some measure upon the result.—If the claim could be adjusted—and the whole brought to the hammer—I could clear every thing—and know what I really possess—Pray write to me (direct to Ravenna) I do not feel justified in the present state of the funds—and on your statement—of urging the fulfilment of the Blessington Mortgage—and yet I feel sorry that it does not seem feasible. At any rate see Mr. Kinnaird upon it & come to some decision.—Let me hear about Rochdale.—

yrs. ever truly

BYRON

P.S.—*Advance old Joe Murray whatever may be necessary & proper*— and it will be deducted from my Bankers acct.

[TO JOHN CAM HOBHOUSE]   *Ravenna. April 6th. 1820*

My dear Hobhouse,—Perceiving that you are likely to get in for Westminster[1]—I shall condescend to patronize you again—conceiving that it will be more creditable and I want besides to make you useful to my private affairs—which is the reason of this present writing— that is to say if your new honours have not made you "proud" like "B—g—g Dick" of traditional memory.——Douglas has all along said that the Irish Mortgage was the best possible thing for my *matters* (notwithstanding that those damned Ribbon men—might be worse for them than the *blue ribbons* for those of Jew King) and I believed him firmly and consented accordingly to insert sixty Thousand pounds on "empty houses on Ormond Quay".[2]——But Spooney writes (I enclose his letter to me to the honourable Doug. by this very post) that it will be the worst of all possible investments for reasons therein stated—for it seems that I should lose eight thousand pounds (English) by selling out just now—and that six means five in Irish—when people talk of interest.——Now I believe Spooney too—and Douglas too—Like Garschattachin[3]—who wished to serve

[1] After his release from Newgate (February 28, 1820) Hobhouse won a seat in the House of Commons for Westminster along with Sir Francis Burdett.

[2] Douglas Kinnaird had recommended that Byron invest in an Irish Mortgage on the property of Lord Blessington, who owned Ormond Quays.

[3] In Scott's novel Duncan Galbraith of Garschattachin, Major of the Lennox militiamen, captured Rob Roy after Rob had been deceived by Rashleigh Osbaldistone's treacherous message.

King George and King James both at once—so how shall I decide?———
Now I wish you to decide for me—weighing both the opinions for I
cannot make up my own mind further than this—*that I won't sell out at
a loss*—and that the Dublin tenements should be *ensured* before we
ventures.———And pray write and let me know—I sent you two letters
and a song some time ago—and am

yrs ever
BYRON

P.S.—I suppose you are in by this time—but I can't come home to
congratulate you, yet awhile.—I have sent a cargo of Poeshie for
Murray—for which Dougal may contract—there is a chance of
Rochdale being settled amicably (so Spooney's letter says) which
would be a felicity—as I should like to convert it into Cash—and
then I'll come to England and get drunk with you.——I sent a
counter-part of Hanson's statement to Lady Byron by this post—as I
did of Douglas's some time ago—I should think She will be as much
puzzled by their antithetical statements as I have been.—There is a
bond of Mr. W. Webster's dated 1813—with a judgment—principle
1000—interest 500—total 1500—will you get it sold—that is desire
Hanson to do so;—I will take any *discount*—but it must be in monies—
and *not* on Mr. *Hanson's account.*—Messrs. Dawson—Capron—
and [Barley?]—of Saville Row—Attorneos are not unlikely to treat
for it—as they are already in W[ebster]'s affairs.—I really can not
afford to lose the whole—and prefer this method to awaken him—
which otherwise I must have done—whenever he returns to England—
I know that Dawson and Capron &c. have lent him money—and are
therefore—of opinion that he is *payable*—and would be likely to buy
his bond—though [for?] but a trifle.—Put Hanson on the Scent—he
likes it.—

[TO DOUGLAS KINNAIRD]   *Ravenna. April 6th. 1820*

My dear Douglas—I have received the enclosed letter from Mr.
Hanson—which I confess *"doth give me pause"*[1]—

Between the *devil* and deep Sea
Between the Lawyer and Trustee,

[1] *Hamlet*, Act III, scene 1.

I am sadly bested.—What *can I decide?*

"Or this way, or that way, or which way I will—
Whate'er I decide, t'other bride will take ill.—[ ]²

and so I decide nothing at all——I love 6 per cent—if *6* it be—(but it seems *six* means *five* in Ireland) but I can't sell out at such a bloody thundering loss—in the funds at present—and then the *housen* maun' be insured—otherwise the Security would be like George Faulkner's burglary—"Last night an empty house on Ormond quay"³—In short—I can't consent, and can't dissent—what the devil is to be done?—Do pray decide anything—and I'll agree—if you will but set the example.——You will be glad to see a distant glimpse of the Settlement of *Rochdale*—pursue it, and don't be wroth with me for my indecision—since I send you the reasons.—Oh—that I had six per cent without risk—that Ireland was England and Dublin—proof against fire and ribbonry—that the funds were high—lawyers tractable, and trustees agreeable—but my feelings overpower me.—

yrs. ever & most truly
BYRON

P.S.—*Mem.* various M.S.S. sent to *Mr. Murray*—the which you will arrange—as usual;—the interruption of the Mortgage—rendering me somewhat more avaricious than usual—in such matters.—I can't come to England till after the coronation—because of family matters—my spouse and I could not march together at it—and I have no great inclination.—

[TO DOUGLAS KINNAIRD]   *Ravenna. April 8th. 1820*

My dear Douglas,—A letter which accompanies this under another cover—will more fully explain all that is explicable at this distance.—Pray—when you transmit the enclosed to Mr. Hanson—*see him*—and combine together if you can an arrangement.—I *do not revoke my Consent, if I can sell out of the funds without loss—but eight thousand pounds is such a* sacrifice that—to do so—would be insanity. I think the H[ouses] also should be insured. Address direct to me at *Ravenna*——

----

² Gay's *Beggar's Opera* (Act III, scene 11):
    "This way and that way, and which way I will,
        What would comfort the one, t'other wife would take ill."
³ Unidentified.

Pray—what was it that Farebrother said was the bona fide bidding for Rochdale? at one of the Auctions?—keep it in sight. I have written to you at some length[.]

yrs ever & truly
BYRON

P.S.—There are various things sent to Mr. Murray.——

[TO JOHN MURRAY]   *Ravenna. —April 9th. 1820*

D[ea]r. S[i]r.—In the name of all the devils in—the printing office— why don't you write to acknowledge the receipt of the second—third— and fourth packets, viz. the Pulci—translation & original—the Danticles—the Observations on &c.—you forget that you keep me in hot water till I know whether they are arrived—or, if I must have the bore of recopying.——I send you "a Song of Triumph" by W. Botherby Esqre. price sixpence—on the Election of J. C. H. Esqre. for Westminster—(*not* for publication).——

> Would you go to the House by the true gate—
> Much faster than ever Whig Charley went.
> Let the Parliament send you to Newgate,
> And Newgate will send you to Parliament.

Have you gotten the cream of translations—Francesca of Rimini— from the Inferno?—why I have sent you a warehouse of trash within the last month—and you have no sort of feeling about you—a pastry-cook would have had twice the gratitude—and thanked me at least for the quantity.——

To make the letter heavier I enclose you the Cardinal Legate's— (our Campeius)[1] circular for his Conversazione this evening—it is the anniversary of the Pope's tiara-tion, and all polite Christians— even of the Lutheran creed—must go and be civil.———And there will be a Circle—and a Faro table—(for shillings that is—they don't allow high play) and all the beauty—nobility, and Sanctity of Ravenna present; the Cardinal himself is a very good natured little fellow— Bishop of Imola—and Legate here—a devout believer in all the doctrines of the Church—he has kept his housekeeper these forty years— for his carnal recreation—but is reckoned a pious man—and a moral

---

[1] Shakespeare, *Henry VIII*, Act II, scene 2, line 96: "This just and learned priest, Cardinal Campeius". In Shakespeare's play Cardinal Campeius was an intriguer against Katherine of Aragon, Henry's Queen.

73

liver.———I am not quite sure that I won't be among you this autumn—for—I find that business don't go on—what with trustees and Lawyers as it should do with all deliberate speed.—They differ about investments in Ireland—

> Between the devil and deep Sea
> Between the Lawyer and Trustee—

I am puzzled—and so much time is lost by my not being upon the spot—what with answers—demurs, rejoinders—that it may be I must come and look to it.—For one says do—and t'other don't—so that I know not which way to turn.——But perhaps they can manage without me.——

yrs. ever
[Scrawl]

P.S.—I have begun a tragedy on the subject of Marino Faliero, The Doge of Venice, but you shan't see it these six years if you don't acknowledge my packets with more quickness and precision.—*Always write if but a line* by return of post—when anything arrives which is not a mere letter. Address direct to Ravenna—it saves a week's time—& much postage.

[TO JOHN MURRAY]   *Ravenna. April 11th. 1820*

Dear Murray—Pray forward the enclosed letter to a fiddler.——In Italy they are called "Professors of the Violin"—you should establish one at each of the universities.

yrs.
[scrawl]

P.S.—Pray forward it carefully with *a frank*—it is from a poor fellow to his musical Uncle—of whom nothing has been heard these three years (though what he can have been doing at Belfast Belfast best knows) so that they are afraid of some mischief having befallen him or his fiddle.——

[TO DOUGLAS KINNAIRD]   *Ravenna. April 14th. 1820*

My dear Douglas—The hopes of the termination of this interminable mortgage—and the breaking of my carriage—(not the traveling one) by an overturn (I was upset a month ago) have induced me to solace myself with a new one—ordered at Florence (a Landau) and to which I have appended a pair of bran new horses—harness—and the like.—All this besides cutting a formidable figure in francs and in Scudi—will look not less repugnant in pounds sterling, so that you will make a fearful face—as becomes a banker-trustee—and particularly as a friend who is privileged to look as disagreeable as possible.—But then as a set-off—I have despatched sundry packets of poeshie to Master Moray of that ilk, cantos of Donny Johnny,—and Translations from Pulci—and Visions of Dante—and a brief translation from the Same &c.—the which added to my *fee* from the funds viz half my year's income in July—will—or ought to bring us right again—to say nothing of a handsome sum in Ransom epistles and Circulars yet itching in my breeches pockets.—

I have sent you Hanson's objections to the Irish Mortgage—but I will do as seems best—only *don't* let me sell out at a loss—and *do* let me hear from you—*and pray follow up the prospect of the Rochdale accommodation (and Sale let us hope)* which you will perceive dawning in the latter end of Spooney's letter.———Tell Murray that he has not written to acknowledge any packets but the two cantos—and that I am extremely angry at his negligence, it is very unbusinesslike—he ought to know this—& put me out of suspense about the *post* at once.——It rejoices me to see that Hobhouse is at last an M.P.—his former fate reminded me of the lines on Guy Faux—

"Guy Faux turpis erat voluitque cremare Senatum
Ast hoc invento, *Ille* (the Constable understood) *recepit eum*
(took him up)."

But now as Garshattachin [sic][1] says "I'm glad you're a Baillie" though he passed through a queer sort of a turnpike to his preferment.——

Would you go to the House by the true gate
Much faster than ever Whig Charley went
Let Parliament send you to Newgate,
And Newgate will send you to Parliament.

Pray are you in Parliament this time? or only as far as Newgate in your way there?—the return or close of the Poll for Bishop's Castle is not given in the Pas de Calais—nor in Galignani—so that I am in ignorance of your proper success.——

[1] In *Rob Roy*.

We are in expectation of a *row* here—in a short time—the Spanish business has set all Italy a constitutioning—and they won't get it without some *fechting* as we Scottish say.———Now this being likely—I shall stay to see what turns up—and perhaps to take a turn amongst them—instead of coming to hear so much—and to see so little done—as seems to be your Anglo-fashion at present.——Here you may believe there will be cutting of thrapples and something *like* a civil buffetting—if they once begin, and there are all the dispositions.—You can have no idea of the ferment in men's minds from the Alps to Otranto.——As I have been inoculated among the people rather within these last four years—if matters wax serious—I should not like to sit twirling my thumbs—but perhaps "take service" like Dugald Dalgetty and his horse on the savage side of the question,[2]—but I must say no more just at present—except desiring you to write now and then as long as the communications are open.——I desire to be remembered to that Hobhouse whom I perceive characterized in the Courier as a cold-blooded conspirator—full of mischiefs—Guy Faux again—"callidus a hothead fellow—frigidus a cold, determined villain" and to all the respectable part of your people, in whose principles however I do *not* fully concur.—

believe me yrs. ever &c.

[scrawl]

P.S.—I enclose to *you*—some rhymes of last year which I have just copied out—I wrote them on passing the Po in June 1819—the subject of them being that at Cavanelli sul' Po—nearer the Sea—and I much higher up.—I send them to you instead of to Moray—as a sign of my high displeasure—and so tell him—in future I shall enclose everything to you—since he neglects to answer by return of post—when I send him nonsense by packets.——As a reward for his rudeness—*bleed* him in the *jugular*—when you treat for the M.S.S. I have a drama too upon the anvil—*not* for the stage.——

[TO JOHN MURRAY]   *Ravenna. April 16th. 1820*

Dear Murray—Post after post arrives without bringing any acknowledgement from you of the different packets (excepting the first) which I have sent within the last two months—all of which

---

[2] The soldier of fortune in Scott's *A Legend of Montrose.*

76

ought to be arrived long ere now—& as they were announced in other letters—you ought at least to say whether they are come or not. —You are not expected to write frequent or long letters—as your time is much occupied—but when parcels that have cost some pains in the composition, & great trouble in the copying are sent to you I should at least be put out of Suspense by the immediate acknowledgement per return of post addressed *directly* to *Ravenna*.—I am naturally —knowing what continental *posts* are—anxious to hear that they are arrived especially as I loathe the task of copying so much—that if there was a human being that could copy my blotted M.S.S.—he should have all they can ever bring for his trouble.——All I desire is two lines to say—such a day I received such a packet—there are now at least *six* unacknowledged.——This is neither kind nor courteous.——

I have besides another reason for desiring *you* to be speedy—which is—that there is *that* brewing in Italy—which will speedily cut off all security of communication and set all your Anglo-travellers flying in every direction with their usual fortitude in foreign tumults.——The Spanish & French affairs have set the Italians in a ferment—and no wonder—they have been too long trampled on.—This will make a sad scene for your exquisite traveller—but not for the resident— who naturally wishes a people to redress itself.—I shall if permitted by the natives remain to see what will come of it—and perhaps to take a turn with them—like Dugald Dalgetty and his horse—in case of business—for I shall think it by far the most interesting spectacle and moment in existence—to see the Italians send the Barbarians of all nations back to their own dens.——I have lived long enough among them—to feel more for them as a nation than for any other people in existence—but they want Union—and they want principle—and I doubt their success—however they will try probably—and if they do— it will be a good cause—no Italian can hate an Austrian more than I do—unless it be the English—the Austrians seem to me the most obnoxious race under the Sky.——But I doubt—if anything be done— it won't be so quietly as in Spain;—to be sure Revolutions are not to be made with Rose-water—where there are foreigners as Masters. —Write while you can—for it is but the toss up of a Paul—that there will not be a row that will somewhat retard the Mail, by and bye.

yrs.
[scrawl]

Address right to *Ravenna*.

Dear Hoppner—I have caused [someone to] write Siri and Willhalm to send with Vincenzo in a boat—the Camp-beds and swords left in their care when I quitted Venice.—There are also several pounds of *Manton's best powder* in a Japan case—but unless I felt sure of getting it away from V[enice] without seizure—I won't have it ventured—I *can* get it *in* here—by means an acquaintance in the Customs who has offered to get it ashore for me—but should like to be certiorated of its safety in leaving Venice. I would not lose it for its weight in gold—there is none such in Italy, as I take it to be.——I *wrote* to you a week or so ago—and hope you are in good plight and Spirits.—Sir Humphry Davy is here, and was last night at the Cardinal's.—As I had been there last Sunday, and yesterday was warm I did not go which I should have done if I had thought of meeting the Man of Chemistry.—He called this morning and I shall go in search of him at Corso time; I believe today being Monday there is no great Conversazione, and only the family are at Marchese Cavalli's where I go as a *relation* sometimes so that unless he stays a day or two we should hardly meet in public.—The theatre is to open in May for the fair—if there is not a Row in all Italy by that time—the Spanish business has set them all a Constitutionizing, and what will be the end no one knows—it is also necessary thereunto to have a beginning.—You see the blackguards have brought in Hobhouse for Westminster.—Rochefoucauld says that "there is something in the misfortunes of our best friends not unpleasing to us" and it is to this that I attribute my not being so sorry for his election as I ought to be seeing that it will eventually be a millstone round his neck, for what can he do? he can't take place? he can't take power in any case—if he succeeds in reforming—he will be stoned for his pains—and if he fails—there he is stationary as Lecturer for Westminster.——

> Would you go to the House by the true gate
> Much faster than ever Whig Charley went
> Let Parliament send you to Newgate
> And Newgate will send you to Parliament.

But Hobhouse is a man of real talent however and will make the best of his situation as he has done hitherto.

yrs. ever & truly
BYRON

P.S.—My benediction to Mrs. Hoppner.—How is the little boy? Allegra is growing, and has increased in good looks and obstinacy.——

[TO RICHARD BELGRAVE HOPPNER]   *Ravenna. April 22d. 1820*

My dear Hoppner—With regard to Gnoatto—I cannot relent in favour of Madame Mocenigo who protects a rascal and retains him in her service.—Suppose the case of your Servant or mine—you having the same claim upon F[letche]r or I upon your Tim—would either of us retain them an instant unless they paid the debt?—As "there is no force in the decrees of Venice"[1] no Justice to be obtained from the tribunals—because even conviction does not compel payment—nor enforce punishment—you must excuse me when I repeat *that not one farthing of the rent shall be paid* till either Gnoatto pays me his debt— or quits Madame Mocenigo's service;—I will abide by the consequences—but I could wish that no time was lost in apprizing her of the affair;—you must not mind her relation Seranzo's statement—he may be a very good man—but he is but a Venetian—which I take to be in the present age—the ne plus ultra of human abasement in all moral qualities whatsoever.—I dislike differing from you in opinion—but I have no other course to take—and either Gnoatto pays me—or quits her Service—or I will resist to the uttermost the liquidation of her rent.—I have nothing against her—nor for her—I owe her neither ill will nor kindness;—but if she protects a Scoundrel—and there is no other redress I will *make* some.—It has been & always will be the case where there is *no law*, Individuals must then right themselves.— They have set the example "and it shall go hard but I will better the Instruction".[2]—Two words from her would suffice to make the villain do his duty—if they are not said—or if they have no effect—let him be dismissed—if not—as I have said—so will I do.———I wrote last week to Siri to desire *Vincenzo* to be sent to take charge of the beds and Swords to this place by Sea.———I am in no hurry for the books—none whatever—and don't want them.—Pray has not Mingaldo the Biography of living people?[3]—it is not here—nor in your list.—I am not at all sure that *he* has it either—but it may be possible.—Let Castelli go on to the last—I am determined to see Merryweather[4] *out* in this business just to discover what is or is not to be done in their tribunals—and if ever I cross him—as I have tried the law in vain—(since it has but convicted him and then done nothing in consequence)—I will try a shorter process with that personage.

[1] *Merchant of Venice*, Act IV, scene 1.
[2] *Merchant of Venice*, Act III, scene 1.
[3] Probably Colburn's *Biographical Dictionary of the Living Authors of Great Britain and Ireland* (1816).
[4] See Aug. 2, 1819, to Alexander Scott, note 1 (Vol. 6, p. 213).

About Allegra—I can only say to Claire—that I so totally disapprove of the mode of Children's treatment in their family—that I should look upon the Child as going into a hospital.—Is it not so? Have they *reared* one?—Her health here has hitherto been excellent—and her temper not bad—she is sometimes vain and obstinate—but always clean and cheerful—and as in a year or two I shall either send her to England—or put her in a Convent for education—these defects will be remedied as far as they can in human nature.——But the Child shall not quit me again—to perish of Starvation, and green fruit—or be taught to believe that there is no Deity.——Whenever there is convenience of vicinity and access—her Mother can always have her with her—otherwise no.—It was so stipulated from the beginning.—The Girl is not so well off as with *you*—but far better than with them;—the fact is she is spoilt—being a great favourite with every body on account of the fairness of her Skin—which shines among their dusky children like the milky way, but there is no comparison of her situation now—and that under Elise—or with them.—— She has grown considerably—is very clean—and lively.——She has plenty of air and exercise at home—and she goes out daily with M[adam]e Guiccioli in her carriage to the Corso.—The paper is finished & so must the letter be—

yrs.

[scrawl]

My best respects to Mrs. H. and the little boy—and Dorville.——

[TO JOHN CAM HOBHOUSE] *Ravenna. April 22d. 1820*

Dear Hobhouse—By yesterday's post I had yrs. of the 31st. Ulto. ——The papers told me that you had got *out*, and got *in*, I am truly glad of both events—though I could have wished the one had had no connection with the other.——I beg your pardon for confounding you with Hunt and Cobbett—but I thought that the Manchester business had effected a reconciliation—at least you all (bating Cobbett) attended one meeting, soon after it—but I am glad to hear you have nothing to do with those scoundrels—I can understand and enter into the feelings of Mirabeau and La Fayette—but I have no sympathy with Robespierre—and Marat—whom I look upon as in no respect worse than those two English ruffians—if they once had the power.——You will hardly suppose that I should deny to you— what I said to another—I *did* use such an expression on the subject of

Bristol Hunt—and I repeat it—I do not think the man who would overthrow all laws—should have the benefit of any, he who plays the Tyler or Cade might find the Walworth or Iden—he who enacts the Clodius—the Milo[1]—and what is there in Bristol Hunt and Cobbett— *so* honest as the former—or *more* patriotic than the latter?—"Arcades Ambo" blackguards both.[2]——Why our classical education alone— should teach us to trample on such unredeemed dirt as the *dis*honest bluntness—the ignorant brutality, the unblushing baseness of these two miscreants;—and all who believe in them.——I think I have neither been an illiberal man nor an unsteady man upon politics—but I think also that if the Manchester Yeomanry had cut down *Hunt only*— they would have done their duty—as it was—they committed *murder* both in what they did—and what they did *not* do,—in butchering the weak instead of *piercing* the wicked, in assailing the seduced instead of the seducer—in punishing the poor starving populace, instead of that pampered and dinnered blackguard who is only less contemptible than his predecessor *Orator Henley* because he is more mischievous. ——What I say thus—I say as publicly as you please—if to praise such fellows be the price of popularity—I spit upon it, as I would in their faces.——

Upon reform you have long known my opinion—but *radical* is a new word since my time—it was not in the political vocabulary in 1816—when I left England—and I don't know what it means—is it uprooting?—As to yourself it is not in the power of political events to change my sentiments—I am rejoiced to see you in parliament because I am sure you will make a splendid figure in it, and have fought hard to arrive there—and I esteem and admire Burdett as you know—but with these and half a dozen more exceptions—I protest, not against *reform*—but my most thorough contempt and abhorrence— of all that I have seen, heard, or heard of the persons calling themselves *reformers*, *radicals*, and such other names,—I should look upon being free with such men, as much the same as being in bonds with felons.—— I am no enemy to liberty however, and you will be glad to hear that there is some chance of it in Italy—the Spanish business has set the

[1] Sir William Walworth, Lord Mayor of London, killed Wat Tyler, leader of the Peasants' Revolt in 1381. Jack Cade led the Kentish rebellion in 1450 and came to a like end at the hands of Alexander Iden, the Sheriff of Kent. Publius Clodius, (92–52 B.C.), gained power in Rome with the aid of the mob. He exiled Cicero and burned his house but, in a factional struggle with Titus Annius Milo, Clodius was killed.
[2] *Don Juan*, canto 4, stanza 93. "Arcades Ambo" comes from Virgil, *Eclogue VII*.

Italians agog, and if there turns up anything as is not unlikely, I may perhaps "wink and hold out mine iron"[3] with the rest, or at any rate be a well wishing spectator of a push against those rascally Austrians who have desolated Lombardy, and threaten the rest of the bel paese.——I should not like to leave this country in case of a row, but if nothing occurs, and you could come out during the recess in autumn—I might revert with you—though only four years of the usual term of transportation are expired.——I wrote to you last week about my affairs which are puzzling, Dougal says the Irish thing is excellent, Hanson says it is ruinous, decide between them.——I have sent lots of poeshie to Murray who has not condescended to acknowledge but two of half a dozen packets—*"bleed him in the Jugular"* as they did our char a banc driver in the Simmenthal in 1816.
——believe me,

yrs ever & truly

B

P.S.—I have written in great haste, and it is bed time—my monkey too has been playing such tricks about the room as Mr. Hunt at his meetings—so that I have hardly had time to be common-sensible but never mind.——

[TO JOHN MURRAY]   *Ravenna. April 23d. 1820*

Dear Murray—The proofs don't contain the *last* stanzas of Canto second—but end shortly after the 105th. Stanza.——I told you long ago—that the new Cantos were *not* good—and I also *told you ⟨the⟩ a reason*—recollect I do not oblige you to publish them, you may suppress them if you like—but I can alter nothing—I have erased the six stanzas about those two impostors Southey and Wordsworth—(which I suppose will give you great pleasure) but I can do no more—I can neither recast—nor replace—but I give you leave to put it all in the fire if you like—or *not* to publish—and I think that's sufficient;—I told you that I wrote on with no good will—that I had been *not* frightened but *hurt*—by the outcry—and besides that, when I wrote last November—I was ill in body and in very great distress of mind about some private things of my own—but *you would* have it—so I sent it to you—& to make it lighter *cut* it in two—but I can't piece it together again. I can't cobble; I must "either make a spoon or spoil a

---

[3] *Henry V*, Act IV, scene 1.

horn"[1] and there is an end—for there is no remeid [sic]; but I leave you free will to suppress the *whole* if you like it.—

About the *Morgante* Maggiore—I *wont have a line omitted*—it may circulate or it may not—but all the Criticism on earth shan't touch a line—unless it be because it is *badly* translated—now you say—and I say—and others say—that the translation is a good one—and so it shall go to press as it is.———Pulci must answer for his own irreligion— I answer for the translation only.——I am glad you have got the *Dante*—and there should be by this time a translation of his Francesca of Rimini arrived—to append to it.——I sent you a quantity of *prose* observations in answer to Wilson—but I shall not publish them *at present*—keep them by you—as *documents*.———Pray let Mr. Hobhouse look to the *Italian* next time in the *proofs;—this time* while I am scribbling to you—they are corrected by one who passes for the prettiest woman in Romagna and even the Marches as far as Ancona—be the other who she may.——I am glad you like my answer to your enquiries about Italian Society—it is fit you should *like something* and be damned to you.——

My love to Scott—I shall think higher of knighthood[2] ever after for his being dubbed—by the way—he is the first poet titled for his talent —in Britain—it has happened abroad before now—but on the continent titles are universal & worthless.——Why don't you send me Ivanhoe & the Monastery?—— I have never written to Sir Walter— for I know he has a thousand things & I a thousand nothings to do— but I hope to see him at Abbotsford before very long, and I will sweat his Claret for him—though Italian abstemiousness has made my brain but a skilpit[3] concern for a Scotch sitting "inter pocula".—I love Scott and Moore—and all the better brethren—but I hate & abhor that puddle of water-worms—whom you have taken into your troop in the *history* line I see.———I am obliged to end abruptly.

yrs
[Scrawl]

P.S.—You say that *one half* is very good,[4] you are *wrong*—for if it were it would be the finest poem in existence—*where* is the poetry of which *one half* is good—is it the *Æneid?* is it *Milton's*, is it *Dryden's*— is it anyone's except *Pope's* and Goldsmith's; of which *all* is good—& yet these two last are the poets—your pond poets would explode.—

[1] See *Rob Roy*, chap. 22.
[2] Scott was not knighted but was gazetted baronet on March 20, 1820.
[3] See *Waverley*, chap. 11
[4] Of *Don Juan*.

But if *one half* of the two new Cantos be good in your opinion—what the devil would you have more?—no—no—no poetry is *generally* good—only by fits & starts—& you are lucky to get a sparkle here & there—you might as well want a Midnight *all stars*—as rhyme all perfect.——

We are on the verge of a *row* here—last night they have overwritten all the city walls—with "up with the Republic['] & ['] death to the Pope &c. &c." this would be nothing in London where the walls are privileged—& where when Somebody went to Chancellor Thurlow to tell him as an alarming sign that he had seen "Death to the king" on ⟨Hyde⟩ the park wall——old Thurlow asked him if he had ever seen "C—t" chalked on the same place, to which the alarmist responding in the affirmative—Thurlow resumed "& so have I for these last 30 years and yet it never made my p——k stand."—— But here it is a different thing[;] they are not used to such fierce political inscriptions—and the police is all on the alert, and the Cardinal glares pale through all his purple.——

April 24th. 1820 8 o'clock **P.M**

The police have been all Noon and after searching for the Inscribers— but have caught none as yet—they must have been all night about it— for the "Live republics—death to popes & priests" are innumerable— and plastered over all the palaces—ours has plenty.——There is "down with the Nobility" too—they are down enough already for that matter.——A very heavy rain & wind having come on—I did not get on horseback to go out & "skirr the country"5 but I shall mount tomorrow & take a canter among the peasantry—who are a savage resolute race—always riding with guns in their hands.——I wonder they don't suspect the Serenaders—for they play on the guitar all night here as in Spain—to their Mistresses.——Talking of politics— as Caleb Quotem6 says—pray look at the *Conclusion* of my Ode on *Waterloo*,7 written in the year 1815—& comparing it with the Duke de Berri's catastrophe in 1820—tell me if I have not as good a right to the character of *"Vates"* in both senses of the word as Fitzgerald & Coleridge.—

"Crimson tears will follow yet."8

and have not they?——I can't pretend to foresee what will happen

---

5 *Macbeth*, Act V, scene 3.

6 In *The Review, or the Wags of Windsor*, by George Colman the Younger.

7 Byron's "Ode from the French", published anonymously in the *Morning Chronicle*, March 15, 1816.

8 The last line of Byron's "Ode from the French".

among you Englishers at this distance—but I vaticinate a *row* in Italy—& in which case I don't know that I won't have a finger in it.— I dislike the Austrians and think the Italians infamously oppressed, & if they begin—why I will recommend "the erection of a Sconce upon Drumsnab"⁹ like Dugald Dalgetty.

My dear Douglas—I wrote to you not very long ago—enclosing Hanson's letter of objections to the Irish Investment, upon which you must decide—I have already given you *my consent* provided I am not to be a heavy loser by selling out of the funds—a loss H[anson] estimates at 8000 pounds—which if truly stated—forms an insurmountable objection. If that can be done away with—and the houses are insured—I see no further obstacle on our part.——As he holds out the prospect also of either a speedy legal termination of the *Rochdale Suit*—or in the meantime some accommodatory proposition on the part of the defendants—I wish you would turn a sharp eye that way too—a moderate accommodation is preferable to the uncertainty & delay of law—but you will have read H[anson]'s letter & can judge for yourself.—Pray what did *Farebrother* say was bid for R[ochdale] *bona fide*—at the last auction?—Recollect that in settling for it—we shall have no hampering with trustees—it not being in the Settlement.——

I have to congratulate Hobhouse on his election—but I do not know whether I have yet to pay you the same compliment.——I must now trouble you with a small bit of booksale—& back-shop business. Jno. Murray was very impatient for some more of Juan—so I sent him *two* Cantos—that is *one long canto* cut into two—but *expressly stated & stipulated by me* to *reckon* (in money matters) *only* as *one*, in fairness to him—as well as from this having been the original form—in fact the two are not so long—as *one* of those already published—which are both very tedious.——It seems that *one* half of these cantos do not please the said John—& his Synod—& they are *right*;—I *know*—& said to him always—that they were *not* good—but he was very eager, so I sent them.—Now I am by no means anxious for the publication— & have written to say so—I have also sent him over various other things—verse and prose—(the *prose* I *don't* mean in any case to publish *just now*) so that you may let him off if he likes.—I don't

---

⁹ *A Legend of Montrose*, chap. 10.

care about the money—only do *you* let me know in time that I may not calculate upon any extra sum beyond the income funds in July next.——I had made no bargain with him—leaving all that to you—and he has behaved very fairly—& I wish to do as much by him—as I would whether he had or no. If he chooses to decline—let him—and let the thing rest in abeyance—I don't want any other publisher nor publication.—If he wishes to publish he may—and you may settle as seems fair to both.—I enclose you his letter to me—for you to go upon, you will, I think, agree with him that the trash is not very brilliant this time; but I can't alter—I can't cobble—I have struck out a few stanzas—& that is all I can do—except suppressing the whole new Cantos, to which I have no objection.——

News I have none to send—except that we expect a rising in Italy—for a constitution. I sometimes think of going to England after the Coronation, and sometimes not,—I have no thoughts at least no wish—of coming before—& not much after, but I am very undecided & uncertain, & have quite lost all *local* feeling for England without having acquired any *local* attachment for any other spot, except in the occasional admiration of fine landscapes—& goodly cities.——It is now turned of four years since I left it—& out of the last Eleven I have passed upwards of six years a Gipsy-ing.—You tell me nothing of the "whereabouts" of Scrope, our old Crony—nor does Hobhouse—you worldly gentlemen make excellent friends—however you lent him money—and *I* dare say it was that more than yr. memory that he liked,—but he was a fine fellow and as he never had any of *my* cash—to authorise me to forget him—I should be glad to know what hath become of him.—

yrs. ever very truly
Byron

P.S.—I want to ax Hobhouse a question, in his last letter—he denies that any reconciliation—has taken place between him and *Hunt*, & yet I see Hunt at *the Dinner* and an eulogium from Burdett on the blackguard who called Hobhouse an Ape—or a Monkey—at the last election—I wish to know why he sate down to table with him?—I don't mean that such a fellow could merit a gentlemanly resentment or give either satisfaction or apology, but why *eat* in his company

[TO COUNTESS TERESA GUICCIOLI (*a*)]   [*May, 1820?*]

A. M. + "Donne! Donne!—che v'arriva &c." Cosa vuoi che ne faccia? tu non sai—egli mai fa niente senza un' perche—e questo è

solamente il principio.—Io torno a dirti che non c'è e non sarà mai
altro rimedio ch'il mio partire.—*Del' amor mio sei certa*—ma io non
capisco come può essere un' amor *vero* il quale sagrifica l'amato
oggetto—con *me* sareste infelice—e sagrificata nei occhi del' mondo—
con' lo marito sareste se non felice almeno sempre rispettabile e
rispettata.—Come che non vedo alternativo senon una disunione che
tosto o tardi dovrebbe accadere—io voglio salvarti—anche al' prezzo
del' odio tuo—ingiusto—ma che col' tempo darà luogo a un sentimento
di riconoscenza.—Di cosa puoi accusarmi?—son' venuto, son' partito—
son' tornato, sono stato—v'è più d'un anno che non ho fatto altro
ch'ubbidirti in tutto—finche poteva conciliare il tuo ben essere
⟨colla nostra rispettabilità⟩ coll'tuo desiderio ed ora chi vedo che
questo non si può fare di più, prenderò il solo partito che può essere o
ragionevole o nobile.——Verrò da te questa sera—e parlaremo.——
Credemi sempre & tutto il tuo vero am.o ed am.te!

[Scrawl]

[TRANSLATION (*a*)]   [*May? 1820*]

My love + "Women! Women! Who can guess . . . etc."[1]—What
do you want me to do about it? You do not realize—he never does
anything without a reason—and this is only the beginning.—I repeat
to you that there is not and cannot be any remedy but my departure.

Of my love be assured—but I cannot understand how a love can be
true that sacrifices the beloved object.——with me you would be unhappy—and compromised in the eyes of the world—with your husband
you would be, if not happy, at least respectable and respected.—So I
see no alternative except a separation, which sooner or later would in
any case have to come. I want to save you—even at the price of your—
unjust—hatred—which however, in time, would give place to a feeling of gratitude.

Of what can you accuse me? I have come, I have gone—I have come
back, I have remained. It is more than a year that I have done nothing
but obey you in every respect—so long as it was possible to reconcile
your welfare with your wishes,—and now that I see that this is no
longer possible,—I shall take the only course that can be either
reasonable or honourable.

I shall come to you this evening—and we will talk. Believe me ever
and wholly your true friend and lover.

[1] Rossini, *Barber of Seville*, Act 1, scene 7.

87

[TO COUNTESS TERESA GUICCIOLI (*b*)]   [*May, 1820?*]

A. M. +—Verrò, ma quando e come?—Se non temi per te stessa—si debbe pensare di tua famiglia—perche è in fatto contra di loro—che queste cose sono dirette.—Contra me stesso (finche di ciò che sento per te) non possono far niente—ma non sarebbe gran' Eroisma in me compromettervi tutti quanti senza participare nel' pericolo.—Dunque voglio prima essere istruito—come debbo condurmi—e per quel' oggetto vorrei parlare con'Papa.—

+ [Scrawl]

[TRANSLATION (*b*)]   [*May, 1820?*]

My love—I will come—but when and how?—If you do not fear for yourself, we must think of your family—for it is really against them that these things are directed—Against myself (apart from what I feel for you) they cannot do anything—but it would not be very heroic of me to compromise you all without sharing in the danger. So I would like to be instructed beforehand—how to behave—and for this purpose I should like to speak to Papa.

[TO COUNTESS TERESA GUICCIOLI (*c*)]   [*May, 1820?*]
[Two fragments cut from a longer letter]
    . . . In fatto è meglio per te in ogni modo essere con A[lessandro]—In sei mesi tu anche penserai così—e sarai persuasa che io sono stato il tuo amico *vero*—e sacrificato.— — Tu m'accusi—io non lo merito—e tu lo sai.—Il tempo di decidere è stata prima di partire da V[enezia] in quale infelice paese tu ricorderai quanto e come ti pregava non sforzarmi ritornare.—Ecco le conseguenze.

[TRANSLATION (*c*)]   [*May, 1820?*]

Indeed it is better for you in every way to be with A[lessandro], in six months you will think so too—and will be assured that I have been your *true* and sacrificed friend.— —
    You accuse me—I do not deserve it—and you know it. The time for deciding was before leaving V[enice], in [to?] which unhappy place you will remember how, and how much, I implored you not to force me to return. Behold the consequences!

A. M.—Cosa vuoi che ne rispondo?—Egli ha saputo—e debbe aver' saputo tutte queste cose per molti mesi—v'è del' mistero che non capisco e che non mi preme capire.—E' solamente *adesso* che Egli sa della tua *infedeltà?* [Teresa tried to change the sentence to read: sospetta la tua *fedeltà*] cosa avra creduto—che siamo di stucco?— o che io sono *più* o *meno* d'un'uomo? Io non conosco che un' sol rimedio—ciò che ho già suggerito, *il mio partire*—sarebbe un *sagrifizio grande*—ma piuttosto che incontrare ogni giorno di cose simili deviene necessario—quasi un' dovere in me—il non rimanere più in queste parti.——Egli dici ch'è impossibile per lui più soffrire questa ralazione—io rispondo che non *dovrebbe* averlo mai sofferto—e che per certo non è lo stato più felice ne anche per me esser' esposto alle sue 'stravaganze ormai troppo tarde.—Ma farò ciò che un' galant' uomo dovrebbe fare ciò'è non portare dei disturbi nelle famiglie.— tutto questo sarebbe stato già finito—se quel uomo—m'avesse permesso di partire in 10bre del' anno scorso.—Egli non solamente *voleva* che venissi—ma—mi diceva colla sua propria bocca che non *dovrei* partire "essendo un' rimedio troppo lontano". In queste circonstanze non ci vedremmo questa sera—Sempre e *tutto tuo!*

B

My love—What do you want me to reply? He has known—or ought to have known, all these things for many months—there is a mystery here that I do not understand, and prefer not to understand. Is it only now that he knows of your infidelity?[1] What can he have thought—that we are made of stone—or that I am *more* or *less* than a man? I know of one remedy only—what I have already suggested, *my departure. It would be a great sacrifice*, but rather than run into things like this every day it becomes necessary—almost a duty—for me not to remain any longer in these parts.

He says that it is impossible for him to tolerate this relationship any longer—I answer that he *never* should have tolerated it. Assuredly it is not the happiest condition, even for me, to be exposed to his scenes, which come too late, now. But I shall do what a gentleman should do, that is, not cause disturbance in a family. All this would already be over—if that man had allowed me to leave in December of

---

[1] Teresa tried to change this to "is suspicious of your fidelity".

last year.—He not only *wished* me to *come*, but he said to me with his own lips that I ought not to go away—"This being too far-fetched a remedy".

In these circumstances we shall not see each other tonight. Always and *all yours*!

A. M.+—Nelle circonstanze attuali è meglio *non* venire—in questo momento—per prudenza.—Se Egli è serio—farà il possibile (secondo sua indole—& per vendetta) di non lasciarti pretendere nessun' mantenemento—in ciò bisogna *non cedere*—non tanto per la cosa in se stessa—ma per la tua reputazione.——Qualche fine egli ha per certo—è un' uomo—in cui non si può fidare un momento.——Me pare che la sua intenzione era sempre di ⟨far la cosa⟩ finire *così*—e che mi fece venire la *seconda volta* apposto.——Parla con papa—e poi (o prima) ci parleremo.—Vuoi che ti conduco al' teatro o no!—Fammi sapere.——Se l'affare va'finire nel' disunirti da lui—(ciòch'io non desidero—ma che per l'altra parte non mi sorprenderebbe) noi prenderemmo il nostro partito—ed io farò tutto che si debbe fare in tali circonstanze.——Mi dispiace solamente per te—ed appunto perche *ti amo*; mi dispiace anche per la tua famiglia—per me—non può importare—se posso contribuire a renderti meno infelice.—— Adesso sento doppiamente il peso di non essere in libertà per renderti più giustizia nei occhi del' mondo—e per assicurarti dell'independenza dopo il mio mancare—in caso che (come spero) tu mi sopravivi.—— Ma farò in qualche maniera—per superare quella difficoltà.——Verrò da te dopo il vestirmi al mio ritorno dalla Pigneta.—Credimi sempre & tutto tuo am.o ed am.e.

[Scrawl]

My love—As things are now it is better *not* to come—just now— out of prudence. If He is in earnest—he will do everything possible (according to his nature—and for revenge) not to let you obtain any *allowance*. In this you must not *give way*—not so much for the thing in itself, but on account of your reputation.

He assuredly has some end in view—he is a man who cannot be trusted for a moment.

I fancy that it has always been his intention to make the matter end like this, and that he made me come the *second time* on purpose.

Speak to Papa—and then (or before) we will talk. Do you want me to take you to the theatre or not? Tell me.

If the matter ends with your separation from him—(which I do not wish—though, on the other hand, it would not surprise me) we shall make our decision,—and I shall do all that should be done in the circumstances.—

I am only sorry for you—and just because *I love you*; I am sorry too for your family,—For me—it doesn't matter—if I can help in any way to make you less unhappy.—

Now I feel doubly the burden of not being free to render you greater justice in the eyes of the world[1]—and also to assure your independence after my death—in case (as I hope) you should survive me. But I shall manage somehow to overcome this difficulty.

I will come to you after changing when I come back from the Pineta. Believe me always and wholly your friend and lover.

[TO COUNTESS TERESA GUICCIOLI (*f*)]   [*May, 1820?*]

A. M.+—Io non vado in nessun luogo di divertimento—sinche questo affare non viene terminato in una maniera o l'altra.——Anderò a cavallo perche quello è un esercizio—in un sito solitario—e non per farsi vedere.——Se A[lessandro] vuole parlare con me—è padrone— ma per certo io avrò ben poco a risponderlo.—Se dopo l'insulto di esser divisa da letto—per la pazzia di un maniaco—tu torni a cedere alle sue falsissime lusinghe e tenerezze di vecchio rimbambito—il torto si rigetterà sopra di te, e il tuo carattere per debolezza sarà più che mai confirmato.—Farai ciò pero che ti commoda—basta che io lo so per norma mia, Sono

[Scrawl]

[TRANSLATION (*f*)]   [*May, 1820?*]

My love +—I shall not go to any place of amusement—until this affair is finished one way or the other. I shall ride, because that is

---

[1] That Byron was willing to marry Teresa if they were both free is evident in this letter and was expressed more explicitly later. In July, 1819, he wrote to Augusta: "if you see my Spouse—do pray tell her I wish to marry again—and as probably she may wish the same—is there no way in *Scotland?* without compromising *her* immaculacy—cannot it be done there by the *husband* solely?" (See Vol. 6, p. 171.)

exercise—in a solitary place—and not in order to be seen. If A[les-sandro] wants to speak to me, let him—but assuredly I shall have very little to say in reply. If, after suffering the insult of his requiring separate rooms—owing to his mad folly—you go back to yielding to his false blandishments and dotardly caresses, it is you who will be to blame, and your weakness of character will be more confirmed than ever. However do what suits you—so long as I know it for my own guidance. I am

[TO COUNTESS TERESA GUICCIOLI (*g*)]   [*May, 1820?*]

E' appunto perche ti amo tanto—che non posso avere pazienza quando s'entra del' *interesso*—particolarmente con *lui*.——Farei qualunque sagrifizio per te—ma in tal' caso ti voglio *a me*—entiere-mente adesso—tutte quelle cose m'avviliscono nella mia opinione.——A lui non posso cedere—Egli mi tratta con tutta l'insolenza d'un suo dipendente, e nol soffrirò più delle cose simili.——Mi assoggetterò alla decisione di qualunque Signore, che in questo affare, Egli ha mancato equalmente in gentilezza ed in buona fede.——Ma basta.—Addio ti bacio

[Scrawl]

[TRANSLATION (*g*)]   [*May, 1820?*]

It is just because I love you so much—that I cannot be patient where money matters are involved[1]—especially with *him*. I would make any sacrifice for you—but in that case I want you *to myself*—entirely and now—all these things belittle me in my own opinion.

To him I cannot give way. He treats me with the insolence that he would show to one of his servants, and I will not bear such things any longer. I will submit to the opinion of any gentleman, that in this affair he has been equally lacking in courtesy and good faith—but enough! Farewell, I kiss you.

[TO COUNTESS TERESA GUICCIOLI (*h*)]   [*May, 1820?*]

Amor Mio +—Si voleva anche questo per compire la nostra infelicità.—Non mi sorprende pero. E in queste circonstanze non sarà

[1] Count Guiccioli had borrowed some money from Byron in Bologna the previous year, and had hoped to avoid repayment by allowing Byron to occupy the upper floor of his Ravenna palace rent free. According to a contemporary chronicle he had also asked Teresa to ask Byron for another 4000 scudi. See Origo, pp. 179–180.

accordato che vengo trovarti.—Ma più di tutto mi affligono le ultime parole di tuo biglietto,—sono ingiusto sempre e più che mai adesso.— Io t'ebbi consigliato sempre per il tuo bene—e vedendo ch'era inutile, finalmente cedeva al' tuo desiderio—e per ciò tu mi rimproveri.— Malgrado questo sono e sarò eternamente il tuo più sincero ed amantissimo amico

Bn

[TRANSLATION (h)]   [*May, 1820?*]

My Love +—Only this was lacking to complete our unhappiness![1] I am, however, not surprised. And in these circumstances I shall not be allowed to visit you.

But most of all I am distressed by the last words of your note. They would be unjust at any time, and now more than ever. I always advised you for your good—and on seeing that it was useless, finally gave way to your wishes—and for this you now reproach me. In spite of this, I am constantly, and shall ever be your ever most sincere and loving friend

Bn

[TO COUNTESS TERESA GUICCIOLI (*i*)]   [*May, 1820?*]

A. M. + + + —Le solite cose inconcludenti—ed *inconcludibile*— se sia una tale parola.—Egli propone o che io *parto* (dicendo que questa è l'opinione e il *desiderio publico*—e che il suo amico Marini se meraviglia che io ne resto per portare dei dispiaceri nelle famiglie) o che mi servo della mia ascendenza sopra di te—per persuaderti di distaccarti da *me* ed *amare lui*—ed anche per *attaccarmi* il più presto che posso ad *un'altra.*——Per la separazione dice che egli non la vuole— non essendo disposto "perdere la donna["]—disgustare i suoi parenti—e sopra tutto *pagare* un assegnamento.—Non vuole fare la figura di "b[ecco] contento" (dice) e m'incarica di persuaderti che il vero amore e quello dei *conjugi*.—Mi servo delle sue proprie parole.— Dice che l'amor mio non essendo una prima passione—come la tua— io dovrei agire cosi &c. &c. &c. *non vuole*—*non vuole*—e non sa cosa vuole—ma intanto non vuole che ci vogliamo bene—ciò pero che io farò sempre

[Scrawl]

---

1 Teresa was suffering from an attack of erysipelas.

My Love + + + —The usual inconclusive business—and incon-
cludable, if there be such a word.

He proposed that I should *go away* (saying that this is the *general
desire* and opinion—and that his friend Marini is surprised that I
should stay to cause trouble in the life of a family) or else that I
should use my influence over you to persuade you to detach yourself
from *me* and to love *him*—and also that I should attach myself, as
soon as possible, to *another*.

As to separation—he says that he does not want it—not being disposed to "lose the woman"—to disgust his relations—and, above all,
to *pay* an allowance. He does not want to cut the figure, he says, of a
"complacent cuckold"—and he charges me to persuade you that true love
is *conjugal* love. I am using his own words.—He says that, my love
not being a first passion—like yours—I should not behave like this,
etc. etc. etc. He does not want this—he does not want that—and does
not know what he does want—but meanwhile he does not want us to
love each other—which however I always shall.

[TO DOUGLAS KINNAIRD]   *Ravenna. May 3d. 1820*

My dear Douglas—I have written to you twice lately—once
enclosing a letter of Hanson's & secondly a letter of Murray's—I shall
therefore not trouble you now at great length on the subject of yours of
the 18th. Ulto. It holds out no great inducements to visit England—
which you say you yourself would like to quit.——I see the funds
are improving—if they get high enough to enable us to sell out without
loss—do so—& place the money any where or how rather than have
it in the three per cents.—I have already given my consent to complete the Mortgage for Ireland—if it can be done without a heavy
loss, & so that the house property is ensured—I once more recommend *Rochdale* to your notice—the more so—that you will perceive
that Hanson particularly alludes to it—& to the proposal of accommodation made by the other party.——I have had no letter from Murray
since the one I sent you—with my opinions thereupon—& shall therefore not intrude upon the man of books for the present with my
correspondence.—I will just repeat that my *prose* (an Answer to the
Edin[burgh] Magazine) is *not* for present publication—but I wish

¹ This letter and those following were labelled by Teresa: "Après l'abboc-
camento", "After the Interview".

you to read it—because as how I think you will find it very smart in the invective line.———

I sometimes think of making one among you (*not* among the radicals by the way) in the coming autumn—*after the Coronation* for I won't waddle with "dearest duck" but really the encouragement you hold out is not very great, and I don't know how my finances may stand for an English visit—unless a better interest of the settled property or a sale of Rochdale take place.—I have been obliged to be at expences in changing my sea-residence for a land house much as a Triton would on coming ashore.—I have had to buy me a landau in lieu of a Conch or Gondola—to get me horses—to alter my tarpaulin liveries into terra firma fashions, and to leave nothing of the Sea about us but the crest on my carriage—a Mermaid, as you may remember.——I have bought me furniture & new Saddles and all that from Milan—& chairs & tables from various parts of the Globe—at some cost & great trouble.—However I am still in respectable cash—having no occasion to spend money except upon *myself* & *family* which only consists of my daughter & Servant. Sir Humphrey Davy was here the other day & much pleased with the *primitive Italian* character of the people—who like Strangers because they see so few of them, he will tell you himself all about it being on his way to England.——I am glad to hear any good of any body—& particularly of our Hobhouse—pray get in for Bishop's Castle—& let me hear from you—how you are & all that—& what you may have settled or *not* settled with Spooney and Moray "the *dear*"

yrs. ever & truly
BYRON

[TO HENRY BROUGHAM]   *May 6th. 1820*

Sir—The Circumstances which will form the subject of this application were unknown to me till some time after their occurrence, when you were in one country and I in another & consequently I could not then reach you. In the month of ⟨March &⟩ April 1816—you expressed yourself to Mr. Perry a day or two after my leaving England in harsh & ungentlemanly terms with regard to the rent of a house occupied by me & let by the Duchess of Devonshire.—About the same period of time you had so expressed yourself on the subject of my separation from Lady B. that my friends deliberated—whether they ought not to inform me of your language—& desisted only on the representation of Ld. Holland that you were so notoriously imprudent in your general conversation that nobody thought it worth notice.——— This may be a good reason for their not to have informed me of your lies, but none for me not to notice them when aware of you having taken me for yr. subject which I only became in 1817.———In July 1816, you wrote a letter to M[adam]e de Stael desiring her not to interfere between Lady Byron & myself as the breach was irreparable— thereby exceeding your function as legal adviser the business having been settled in April—& never having been before a Court.———At Rome & elsewhere you went about shrugging & whispering & malignantly countenancing every report to my disadvantage.—In England after your return all reports to my disadvantage have arisen from you—according to information which your negative will not neutralize. From all these and other circumstances too long to detail you have proclaimed yourself my personal enemy & I treat you accordingly. I was not acquainted with these things till the Alps were between us—or I should not have delayed my present demand to be made the first time we became near enough, it is with considerable regret that I have been compelled by distance to forego for a time requiring the only satisfaction which you can give or I receive. The bearer of this &c. &c. will settle the remaining preliminaries.[1]

B

[TO JOHN MURRAY]   *Ravenna. May 8th. 1820*

Dear Murray—From yr. not having written again, an intention which yr. letter of ye. 7th. Ulto. indicated, I have to presume that "the Prophecy of Dante" has not been found more worthy than it's immediate precursors in the eyes of your illustrious Synod—in that case you will be in some perplexity—to end which—I repeat to you that you are not to consider yourself as bound—or pledged to publish any thing, because it is *mine*, but always to act according to your own views—or opinions—or those of your friends; & to be sure that you will in no degree offend me "by declining the article" to use a technical phrase.—The *Prose* observations on J[oh]n Wilson's attack—I do *not*

---

[1] Byron had intended to challenge Brougham to a duel when he planned to go to England in November or December, 1819, and he so wrote to Kinnaird. Why he wrote this challenge at this date is not certain. If he sent it to Kinnaird, it is probable that his banker friend quietly ignored it as he did Byron's challenge later to Southey. This paper is headed: "Copy of Message to Brougham to be sent on arriving in England."

intend for publication at this time—and I sent a copy of verses to Mr. Kinnaird (they were written last year—on crossing the Po) which must *not* be published either;—I mention this because it is probable he may give you a copy—pray recollect this—as they are mere verses of Society—& written upon private feelings & passions.—And moreover I cannot consent to any mutilations or omissions of *Pulci*—the original has been ever free from such in Italy—the Capital of Christianity—and the translation may be so in England—though you will think it strange that they should have allowed such *freedom* for so many centuries to the Morgante—while the other day—they confiscated the whole translation of the 4th. Canto of Childe Ha[rol]d & have persecuted Leoni the translator[1]—so he writes me—& so I could have told him—had he consulted me—before his publication.— This shows how much more politics interest men in these parts— than religion.—Half a dozen invectives against tyranny confiscate C[hil]d[e] H[arol]d in a month & eight & twenty cantos of quizzing Monks & Knights & Church Government—are let loose for centuries. I copy Leoni's account.—

"Non ignorerà forse che la mia versione del 4° Canto del Childe Harold fu confiscata in ogni parte: ed io stesso ho dovuto soffrire vessazioni altrettanto ridicole quanto illiberali; ad onta che alcuni versi fossero esclusi dalla censura. Ma siccome il divieto non fa d'ordinario che accrescere la curiosità così quel carme sull' Italia è ricercato più che mai, e penso di farlo ristampare in Inghilterra senza nulla escludere.—Sciagurata condizione di questa mia patria! se patria si può chiamare una terra cosi avvilita dalla fortuna, dagli uomini, da se medesima."[2]—

Rose will translate this to you—has he had his letter? I enclosed it to you months ago.—This intended piece of publication—I shall dissuade him from—or he may chance to see the inside of St. Angelo's— The last Sentence of his letter—is the common & pathetic sentiment of all his Countrymen—who execrate Castlereagh as the cause by the conduct of the English at Genoa.—Surely that man will not die in his

[1] See May 30, 1818, to Leoni, note 1 (Vol. 6, p. 42).
[2] "You are probably not unaware that my version of the 4th Canto of Childe Harold has been confiscated everywhere; and I myself have been obliged to suffer vexations both ridiculous and absurd in spite of the fact that some verses were excluded by the censor. But as prohibition usually increases curiosity, so that ode [poem] on Italy is more sought after than ever, and I am thinking of having it reprinted in England without excluding anything.—Wretched condition of this nation of mine! if one can call a nation a land so debased by fortune, by men and by its very own self."—(Translation by Professor Nancy Dersofi.)

bed, there is no spot of the earth where his name is not a hissing and a curse.—Imagine what must be the man's talent for Odium who has contrived to spread his infamy like a pestilence from Ireland to Italy—and to make his name an execration in all languages.

Talking of Ireland—Sir Humphrey Davy was here last fortnight—and I was in his company in the house of a very pretty Italian Lady of rank—who by way of displaying her learning in presence of the great Chemist then describing his fourteenth ascension of Mount Vesuvius—asked "if there was not a similar Volcano in *Ireland?*"—My only notion of an *Irish* Volcano consisted of the Lake of Killarney which I naturally conceived her to mean—but on second thoughts I divined that she alluded to *Ice*land & to Hecla—and so it proved—though she sustained her volcanic topography for some time with all the amiable pertinacity of "the Feminie." She soon after turned to me and asked me various questions about Sir Humphrey's philosophy—and I explained as well as an Oracle—his skill in gases—safety lamps—& in ungluing the Pompeian M.S.S.—"but what do you call him?" said she "A great Chemist" quoth I—"what can he do?" repeated the lady—almost any thing said I—"Oh then mio Caro do pray beg him to give me something to dye my eyebrows black—I have tried a thousand things and the colours all come off & besides they don't grow—can't he invent something to make them grow?" All this with the greatest earnestness—and what you will be surprized at—She is neither ignorant nor a fool but really well educated & clever but [they speak] like Children—when first out of [their] convents—and after all this is better than an English blue-stocking.—I did not tell Sir [Humphry] of this last piece of philosophy—not knowing how he might take it;—He is gone on towards England.—Sotheby has sent him a poem on his undoing the M.S.S. which Sir H. says is a bad one.—Who the devil doubts it?—Davy was much taken with Ravenna—& the *primitive Italianism* of the people who are unused to foreigners but he only staid a day.—Send me Scott's novels—& some news.—

[scrawl]

P.S.—I have begun and advanced into the second Act of a tragedy on the subject of The Doge's Conspiracy—(i.e. the story of Marino Faliero) but my present feeling is so little encouraging on such matters —that I begin to think I have mined my talent out—& proceed in no great phantasy of finding a new vein.——

P.S.—I sometimes think (if the Italians don't rise) of coming over to England in the Autumn after the coronation (at which I would not appear on account of my family Schism with "the feminie") but as yet I can decide nothing—the place must be a great deal changed since I left it now more than four years ago. May 9th, 1820. Address directly to Ravenna.—

[TO JOHN CAM HOBHOUSE]   *Ravenna. May 11th. 1820*

My dear H.—You were not *"down"*—but 700 a head in the *poll* when I lampooned you.—I had scrawled it before the election began—but waited till you were—or at least appeared, sure (in the *Gazettes*) before I sent to *you* ⟨what I⟩ what would have been a sorry jest had you *failed,*—it would then have been ill-natured—as it is—it was buffoonery—& this you know has been all along our mutual privilege. —When I left England *you* made those precious lines on Murray & Douglas Kin[nair]d & yr. humble Servt.—and in 1808—you put me into *prose* at Brighthelmstone about Jackson—& W[edderburn] W[ebster] & Debathe, and wrote mock epitaphs upon my poor friend Long when he was lost at Sea—all for the Joke's sake. Do you remember Capt. Bathurst['s] nautical anecdote of the boatswain shooting the Frenchman who asked for quarter while running down the hatchway "no—no you b-g—r *you* fired first"?——As for the Moray, he had no business whatever to put the lines in peril of publication. I desired him to give them to *you*—and their *signature* must have showed you in what spirit they were written.—And I am very glad that you have given him a rimproversation on the subject—having the greatest delight in setting you all by the ears.——

If you *will* dine with Bristol Hunt—& such like—what can you expect? but—never mind, you are in—and I can assure you that there is not a blackguard among your constituants half as happy as I am—in seeing you triumph.—.—I never would have forgiven you the use of such instruments, except in favour of success.—And pray don't *mistake* me—it is not against the *pure* principle of reform—that I protest, but against low designing dirty levellers who would pioneer their way to a democratical tyranny; ⟨it is against such men⟩ putting these fellows in a parenthesis—I think as I have ever thought—on that point—as it *used* to be defined—but things have changed their sense probably—as they have their names—since my time.—Four years ago *Radical* was unknown as a political watch-word.——

I am sorry to hear what you say of Scrope—it must have been *sore* distress—which made that man forget himself.—Poor fellow, his name seems not fortunate—there was Goose Davies, and now there is a Captain (who has planted his servant & run away for mistaking signatures)—of the same nomenclature, but what can have become of Scrope?—does nobody know? he could hardly remain at Bruges, it is sad that he should "point a moral and adorn a tale"[1] unless of his own telling; and his loss is the most "ill-convenient for my Lord Castlecorner"[2] that could have occurred—I shall never hear such jokes again; what fools we were to let him go back in 1816—from Switzerland.—He would at least have saved his credit—& money,—and then *what* is he to do? he can't *play*—and without play—he is wretched.—You will have by this time seen all my *prose* and poeshie,—I don't think of publishing the *former*—but I wish you to read it.———From Murray I have heard nothing lately. ———I sometimes think of going to England in autumn, but it is a project so repugnant to my feelings that my resolutions fade as the time approaches.

yrs. ever truly
B

[TO HARRIETTE WILSON]   *Ravenna, May 15th. 1820*

I enclose a bill for a thousand francs, a good deal short of fifty pounds; but I will remit the rest by the very first opportunity.[1] Owing to the little correspondence between Langle [Longhi?], the Bologna banker, I have had more difficulty in arranging the remittance of this paltry sum, than if it had been as many hundreds to be paid on the spot. Excuse all this, also the badness of my handwriting, which you find fault with and which was once better; but, like everything else, it has suffered from late hours and irregular habits.

The Italian pens, ink and paper are also two centuries behind the like articles in other countries.

Yours very truly and affectionately,
BYRON

I should have written more at length, in reply to some parts of your letter; but I am at "this present writing" in a scrape (not a pecuniary one, but personal, about one of your ambrosial sex), which may probably end this very evening seriously. Don't be frightened. The

[1] Johnson's *Vanity of Human Wishes*, line 222.
[2] Unidentified
[1] See March 30, 1820, to Harriette Wilson.

Italians don't fight: they stab a little now and then; but it is not that, it is a divorce and separation; and, as the aggrieved person is a rich noble and old, and has had a fit of discovery against his moiety, who is only twenty years old, matters look menacing.

I must also get on horseback this minute, as I keep a friend waiting. Address to me at Ravenna as usual.

[TO DOUGLAS KINNAIRD AND JOHN AND CHARLES HANSON]

Ravenna. May 20th. 1820

Gentlemen,—After mature consideration I decide in favour of the Mortgage & request your assistance & good offices to bring it to bear without further delay, or impediment.—*This Consent* you are to consider as definitive.—I have the honour to be Gentlemen

your friend & Sert.

Byron

P.S.—I trust that this will be considered as decisive;—I have no more to say upon the Subject.——

[TO JOHN HANSON] [*May 20, 1820?*]

P.S.—I request that this letter may be considered as definitive;— I know not how to express my consent in stronger terms.—

[Byron]

[TO JOHN MURRAY (*a*)] *Ravenna. May 20th. 1820*

Murray my dear—make my respects to Thom[a]s Campbell—& tell him from me with faith & friendship three things that he must right in his Poets.[1]—*Firstly*—he says Anstey's Bath Guide Characters are taken from Smollett—tis impossible—the Guide was published in *1766* and Humphrey Clinker in *1771*—*dunque*—tis Smollett who has taken from Anstey. *Secondly*—he does not know to whom Cowper alludes when he says that there was one who "built a church to *God* and then blasphemed his name"—it was "Deo erexit *Voltaire*" to whom that maniacal Calvinist & coddled poet alludes.[2]

---

[1] Campbell's *Specimens of the British Poets*, with biographical and critical notices, was published in 1819.

[2] Cowper's *Retirement* has the lines: "Nor he who, for the bane of thousands born, Built God a church, and laugh'd His word to scorn." He alluded, as Byron said, to Voltaire.

——Thirdly—he misquotes & spoils a passage from Shakespeare—
"to gild refined gold to paint the lily &c."[3]—for *lily* he puts the *rose*
and bedevils in more words than one the whole quotation.——Now
Tom is a fine fellow but he should be correct—for the 1st. is an
injustice (to Anstey) the 2d. an *ignorance*—and the third *a blunder*—
tell him all this—and let him take it in good part—for I might have
rammed it into a review & vexed him—instead of which I act like a
Christian.—

[scrawl]

[TO JOHN MURRAY (*b*)]   *Ravenna. May 20th. 1820*

Dear Murray—First and foremost you must forward my letter
to *Moore* dated *2d.* January—which I said you might open—but
desired *you to forward*—now—you should really not forget these
little things because they do mischief among friends;—you are an
excellent man—a great man—& live among great men—but do
pray *recollect* your absent friends—and authors.——

I return you the packets—the prose (the Edin. Mag. answer) looks
better than I thought it would—& *you may publish it*—there will be a
row—but I'll fight it out—one way or another.—You are wrong—I
never had those "*two* ladies"[1]—upon my honour! never believe but
half of such stories.—Southey was a damned scoundrel to spread such a
lie of a woman whose mother he did his best to get—& could not.—
So—you & Hobhouse have squabbled about my ballad—you should
not have circulated it—but I am glad you are by the ears, you both
deserve it—he for having been in Newgate—& you for not being
there.—Excuse haste—if you knew what I have on hand, you
would.——

In the first place—*your packets*—then a letter from Kinnaird on the
most urgent business—another from Moore about a communication
to Lady B[yron] of importance—a fourth from the mother of Allegra—
and fifthly at Ravenna—the Contessa G[uiccioli] is on the eve of being
divorced on account of our having been taken together quasi in the
fact—& what is worse that she did not deny it—but the Italian public
are on our side—particularly the women—and the men also—because
they say—*he* had no business to take the business up now after a year
of toleration.——The law is against him—because he slept with his

[3] *King John*, Act IV, scene 2.
[1] See Nov. 11, 1818 (Vol. 6, p. 76).

wife after her admission—all her relatives (who are numerous high in rank & powerful) are furious *against him*—for his conduct—& his not wishing to be cuckolded at *three*score—when every [one] else is at *one*.——I am warned to be on my guard as he is very capable of employing *"Sicarii"*—this is Latin—as well as Italian—so you can understand it—but I have arms—and don't mind them—thinking that I can pepper his ragamuffins—if they don't come unawares—& that if they do—one may as well end that way as another.—and it would besides serve *you* as an advertisement.— —

> "Man may escape from rope or Gun" &c.
> But he who takes Woman—Woman—Woman" &c.[2]

yrs.
[Scrawl]

P.S.—I have looked over the press—but Heaven knows how— think what I have on hand—& the post going out tomorrow—Do you remember the epitaph on Voltaire?

> ["]Cy git l'enfant gaté["] &c.
> "Here lies the spoilt Child
> Of the World which he spoil'd"

The original is in Grimm & Diderot &c. &c. &c.[3]

[TO RICHARD BELGRAVE HOPPNER] *Ravenna. May 20th. 1820*

My dear Hoppner—Let Merryweather be kept in for *one week*—& then let him out for a Scoundrel.[1]—Tell him that such is the lesson for the ungrateful, & let *this* be a warning—a little common feeling— & common honesty would have saved him from useless expence & utter ruin.—Never would I pursue a man to Jail for a mere *debt* & never will I forgive one for ingratitude such as this Villain's. But let him go & be damned—(*once in though first*) but I could much wish *you* to see him—& inoculate him with a moral sense—by shewing him the result of his rascality.——As to Mother Mocenigo—we'll battle with her—& her ragamuffin—Castelli must dungeon Merryweather if it be but for a day—for I don't want to hurt only to teach him.——I

---

[2] *The Beggar's Opera*, Act II, scene 2.
[3] Grimm, *Correspondance Littéraire*, Partie IIme, tome IV, p. 355 (1812).
[1] See Aug. 22, 1819, to Alexander Scott (Vol. 6, p. 213).

write to you in such haste and such heat—it seems to be under the
dog (or bitch) Star that I can no more—but sotto-scribble myself

yrs ever
[scrawl]

P.S.—My best respects to the Consolessa & Compts. to Mr.
Dorville. Hobhouse is angry with me for a ballad & epigram I made
upon him—only think—how odd!——

[TO THOMAS MOORE]   *Ravenna, May 24th, 1820*

I wrote to you a few days ago. There is also a letter of January last
for you at Murray's, which will explain to you why I am here. Murray
ought to have forwarded it long ago. I enclose you an epistle from a
country-woman of yours at Paris, which has moved my entrails. You
will have the goodness, perhaps, to enquire into the truth of her story,
and I will help her as far as I can,—though not in the useless way she
proposes. Her letter is evidently unstudied, and so natural, that the
orthography is also in a state of nature.

Here is a poor creature, ill and solitary, who thinks, as a last
resource, of translating you or me into French! Was there ever such a
notion? It seems to me the consummation of despair. Pray inquire, and
let me know, and, if you could draw a bill on me *here* for a few hundred
francs, at your banker's, I will duly honour it,—that is, if she is not
an imposter. If not, let me know, that I may get something remitted
by my banker Longhi, of Bologna, for I have no correspondence,
myself, at Paris: but tell her she must not translate;—if she does, it
will be the height of ingratitude.[1]

I had a letter (not of the same kind, but in French and flattery)
from a Madame Sophie-Gail, of Paris, whom I take to to be the spouse
of a Gallo-Greek of that name.[2] Who is she? and what is she? and
how came she to take an interest in my *poeshie* or its author? If you
know her, tell her, with my compliments, that, as I only *read* French,
I have not answered her letter; but would have done so in Italian, if I

---

[1] After receiving Byron's letter Moore called on the lady, an Irishwoman
named Mahoney and found her respectable. When he offered her the fifteen
Napoleons Byron had sent, she refused to accept pecuniary assistance. (Moore,
Memoirs, III, 123.)

[2] She was the widow of Jean Baptiste Gail, Professor of Greek Literature at the
Collège de France. Madame Gail had written novels and an Opera, *Les Deux
Jaloux*, which had considerable success in 1813. But Byron confused her with
Madame Sophie Gay, who was in fact his correspondent. Madame Gail was dead
at the time he wrote to Moore.

had not thought it would look like an affectation. I have just been scolding my monkey for tearing the seal of her letter, and spoiling a mock book, in which I put rose leaves. I had a civet-cat the other day, too; but it ran away, after scratching my monkey's cheek, and I am in search of it still. It was the fiercest beast I ever saw, and like ** in the face and manner.

I have a world of things to say; but, as they are not come to a *denouement*, I don't care to begin their history till it is wound up. After you went, I had a fever, but got well again without bark. Sir Humphry Davy was here the other day, and liked Ravenna very much. He will tell you any thing you may wish to know about the place and your humble servitor.

Your apprehensions (arising from Scott's) were unfounded. There are *no damages* in this country, but there will probably be a separation between them, as her family, which is a principal one, by its connections, are very much against *him*, for the whole of his conduct;—and he is old and obstinate, and she is young and a woman, determined to sacrifice every thing to her affections. I have given her the best advice, viz. to stay with him,—pointing out the state of a separated woman, (for the priests won't let lovers live openly together, unless the husband sanctions it,) and making the most exquisite moral reflections,—but to no purpose. She says, "I will stay with him, if he will let you remain with me. It is hard that I should be the only woman in Romagna who is not to have her *Amico*; but, if not, I will not live with him; and as for the consequences, love, &c. &c. &c."—you know how females reason on such occasions.

He says he has let it go on, till he can do so no longer. But he wants her to stay, and dismiss me; for he doesn't like to pay back her dowry and to make an alimony. Her relations are rather for the separation, as they detest him,—indeed, so does every body. The populace and the women are, as usual, all for those who are in the wrong, vis. the lady and her lover. I should have retreated, but honour, and an erysipelas which has attacked her, prevent me,—to say nothing of love, for I love her most entirely, though not enough to persuade her to sacrifice every thing to a frenzy. "I see how it will end; she will be the sixteenth Mrs. Shuffleton."[3]

My paper is finished, and so must this letter.

Yours ever,

B

[3] *John Bull, or the Englishman's Fireside*, by George Colman the Younger, Act II, scene 2.

P.S.—I regret that you have not completed the Italian Fudges.[4] Pray, how come you to be still in Paris? Murray has four or five things of mine in hand—the new Don Juan, which his back-shop synod don't admire;—a translation of the first Canto of Pulci's Morgante Maggiore, excellent;—a short ditto from Dante, not so much approved: the *Prophecy of Dante*, very grand and worthy, etc., etc., etc.:—a furious prose answer to Blackwood's Observations on Don Juan, with a savage Defence of Pope—likely to make a row. The opinions above I quote from Murray and his Utican senate;—you will form your own, when you see the things.

You will have no great chance of seeing me, for I begin to think I must finish in Italy. But, if you come my way, you shall have a tureen of macaroni. Pray tell me about yourself and your intents.

My trustees are going to lend Earl Blessington sixty thousand pounds (at six per cent.) on a Dublin mortgage. Only think of my becoming an Irish absentee!

[TO RICHARD BELGRAVE HOPPNER]   *Ravenna. May 25th. 1820*

My dear Hoppner—A German named Rupprecht has sent me heaven knows why several Deutsche Gazettes of all which I understand neither word nor letter.—I have sent you the enclosed to beg you to translate to me some remarks—which appear to be Goethe's upon Manfred[1]—& if I may judge by *two* notes of *admiration* (generally put after something ridiculous by us) and the word *"hypocondrisch"* are any thing but favourable.—I shall regret this—for I should have been proud of Goethe's good word—[but] I shan't alter my opinion of him even though he should be savage.—Will you excuse this trouble—and do me this favour—never mind—soften nothing—I am literary proof—having had good and evil said in most modern languages.—

believe me ever & truly yrs.

BYRON

P.S.—If Merryweather's *in*—let him out—if *out*—put him in—for a week—merely for a lesson[2]—and lecture him in *your best style*—

---

[4] Moore had been successful with his *Fudge Family in Paris* (1818) and had proposed to continue with the Fudge family in Italy, but he gave up the idea. A sequel, *The Fudges in England*, appeared in 1823.

[1] Goethe's review of *Manfred* appeared in *Kunst und Alterthum*.

[2] Merryweather was imprisoned for one day on June 7, 1820. See Marchand, II, 859, note.

by G-d you are worse than a year's imprisonment—when there's a Sirocco—& you take a sermon in hand.—

P.S.—Will you have the goodness to return the original with the translation.——

[TO COUNTESS TERESA GUICCIOLI (*a*)]   [*June? 1820*]

[Parts of a letter] . . . Io non ebbi il minimo sospetto—ma la tua premura—la tua *violenza* mi rendeva *non il sospetto*—ma la *certezza*.— Il motivo debbe essere ben forte—per spargere del sangue nella defese di una cosa generalmente indifferente ed esposta a tutto il mondo.—Credi tu che io sono come—— . . . a vanità—e indegn . . . . fa arrossire ciò che ho sofferto—ciò tu m'hai veduto soffrire per te—. . . . . Italia sempre perfida . . . . -sata nascondere. . . . . come——Ebbi la debolezza di amarti, trovarò la forza per superare un' amor del'quale tutti anticipavano le conseguenze.—Non son' sorpreso—ma ben' avvilito—[several words crossed out] Addio—un' giorno tu saprai cosa era quello che tu sacrificasti. [on other side of the page]: Questo era scritto jersera—lo mando per mostrarvi a quel' stato mi avete ridotto———se non eravate accorta prima;—anche in presenza di A[lessandro] io non poteva più reggere.——. . . . . .

[TRANSLATION (*a*)]   [*June? 1820*]

I had not the slightest suspicion, but your *anxiety*—your violence— awakened in me not *suspicion*, but *certainty*. The motive must be very strong—to shed *blood* in defence of a matter generally indifferent and known to all the world . . . Do you think that I am like[1]. . . . . vanity and indign. . . . I blush for what I have suffered—for what you have seen me suffer on your account. . . . . Ever perfidious Italy . . . . to hide. . . .

I had the weakness to love you—I shall find strength to overcome a love of which everyone anticipated the consequences. I am not surprised, but feel degraded. [five words erased] Farewell, one day you will know what you sacrificed. . . . .

[on the back of the page]

This was written last night—I am sending it to show you to what a

---

[1] Teresa cut several passages out of this letter and put the remaining fragments in a folder marked: "Unjust letter—to be destroyed".

state you have brought me. Even in A.'s presence I could not control myself. . . .

Amor Mio+—La mia condotta sincere e gli miei consigli furono *tali*, perche non volevo *precipitarti*—e metterti in una situazione dove bisognerebbe reciprocamente dei più grandi sagrifizi.—Si vuole in una donna del' molto carattere, della più vera amicizia, del' amore 'più sviscerato—ed' *instancabile*, e spesso e lungamente provato, per decidere per un partito così asvantaggio so in tutti gli sensi—ed *irrevocabile* per tutto il rimanente della vita. Ma se in detto ed in fatto quel'uomo ti perseguita per dei torti ai quali nessuno ha *contribuito*—nessuno ha dato la *protezione* più de[di] lui—allora io non posso esitare di più—egli può abbandonarti—*ma io mai.*——Io ho degli *anni* più di te—in età—ed altritanti *secoli* nella trista esperienza, prevedo dei dispiaceri e dei sagrifizi per te—ma saranno *participati*;—il mio amore—il mio dovere—il mio onore—il mio cuore—tutto e tutti mi renderebbero in eterno ciò—che sono *adesso*, il tuo amante amico (e quando le circonstanze permettesene) *marito!*

[Scrawl]

P.S.—Non *precipitare* niente per *delle ragioni*—che in parte ti ho spiegato a *voce*, ma se egli va avante—io non ti mancaro!—*Parla a papa prima.*

My Love +—My honest behaviour and my advice were what they were because I did not wish to hurry you—and put you in a situation where the greatest reciprocal sacrifices would be needed. A woman requires a great deal of character, the truest friendship, and the profoundest—and *untiring* love—proved often and for long—to decide on a course so disadvantageous in every way, and irrevocable for all the rest of her life. But as that man has persecuted you in words and deeds for injuries to which no one has *contributed*, and which no one has protected—more than he—now I can hesitate no longer.—He may abandon you—but I *never.*—I have *years* more than you in age—and as many *centuries* in sad experience; I foresee troubles and sacrifices for you, but they will be *shared*; my love—my duty—my honour—[my heart—] all these and everything should make me forever what I am. *now,* your lover friend and (when circumstances permit) your *husband.*[1]

P.S.—Don't commit yourself for *several reasons*—which I have explained to you in part by word of *mouth,* but if he goes ahead I shall not fail you.

Speak to Papa first.

Amor Mio + —Si—spero vederti questa sera—e risanata ben' presto.—Calmati—e credi che ciò che ho sempre detto—era un vero sagrifizio per me—ma che nonostante era il mio dovere di farti vedere le conseguenze della tua risoluzione.—Ho avuto due lettere una da Parigi—l'altra da Bologna. L'indirizzo della lettera francese ti fara ridere.—Eccole.—

Sempre e tutto il tuo amantiss.o amico

Bn

My Love + —Yes,—I hope to see you this evening—and very quickly recovered—calm yourself—and believe what I have always said. It was a real sacrifice for me—but nevertheless it was my duty to show you the consequences of your resolution.

I have two letters—one from Paris, the other from Bologna. The address of the French letter will make you laugh. Here they are.

Always and entirely your most loving friend.

Bn

A. M. + —In *20 minuti* sarò in liberta—& tu puoi fare ciò che ti pare meglio.——Io non so cosa più dirti—tu non vuoi sentire la ragione—& voi precipitarti per sempre. Ma—sono

[Scrawl]

My Love + —In *20 minutes* I shall be free—and you can do what you think best.

---

[1] With this letter is a note by Teresa: "Promesse!!!! d'être mon Époux!!"

I don't know what else to say to you—you will not hear reason and
are committing yourself, for ever.

But—I am

A. M. + + + —Ti ho sempre detto—che io non voleva precipitar
niente—ma che la cosa una volta decisa—*tu potevi disporre di me.*
Ora che siamo in questo punto,—vedrai che io non temo nè vacillo—
e non ho mai esitato se non principalmente per *causa tua.*—P ti avrà
raccontato ciò che io ho detto sul' tuoi affari.— —Io non vado al' Corso—
questoggi—perche non voglio prendere nessun divertimento quando
la mia amica ha il più piccolo disturbo.—A rivederti quando tu vuoi—
credimi—sempre tutto—tuo

[Scrawl]

[TRANSLATION (e)]   [*June? 1820*]

My Love + + + —I have always said to you—that I did not wish
to hurry things—but that once the matter was settled—you could
command me. Now that we have reached this point, you will see that
I have no fear or hesitation—and never have hesitated, except on
your account.[1] P. will have told you what I said about your affairs. I am
not going to the Corso today—for I do not want to enjoy any diver-
sion while my friend still is in the slightest trouble. Au revoir when
you wish.

Believe me ever entirely yours

[TO DOUGLAS KINNAIRD]   *Ravenna. June 1st. 1820*

Dear Douglas—Ecco the bonds!—You must fill up the dates,
they are signed—Last week or weeks I sent you my consent—my
"facilis *consensus Averni*"[1]—for what I know—but pray sell out at as
good a time as you can.— —You don't say a word of Rochdale or an
accommodation for which Hanson touched in the letter he sent me—

[1] On the folder containing this letter Teresa wrote: "Après la décision" (i.e.,
the decision to seek a separation?).

[1] Adapted from Virgil's *Aeneid*, VI, 126: "Facilis descensus Averno" ("The
way to Avernus [the infernal regions] is easy").

which I enclosed to you long ago.—I am glad that Hobhouse succeeds—and don't wonder—but why don't he write?

> You and he were my debtors
> For two or three letters.
> *You* have answered with proper precision;
> But Hob, (damn his eyes)
> Makes a speech about Spies,
> And is busy in quoting *"Domitian."*

By Murray's demur—I suppose his bookselling leaven is uppermost,
and that he wants to shirk—because the poems have not a popular
cant—let him—but let me know—I *don't pin* him to his own offers
about Don Juan, and as to the others you can read & pronounce upon
their estimate—I have named none, and am docile.——I suppose you
will hardly sell out of the funds before *my fee becomes due* which pray
remit—and the extraction from Murray—if there be any—at any
rate let me hear from you.——You may give any copies you like of
the Lines to the Po (damn your quibble) since you think them so fine—
even to Murray. I wrote them this *very day* last year June 1st.

yrs.
[scrawl]

[TO THOMAS MOORE] *Ravenna, June 1st, 1820*

I have received a Parisian letter from W[edderburn] W[ebster],
which I prefer answering through you, if that worthy be still at Paris,
and, as he says, an occasional visitor of yours. In November last he
wrote to me a well-meaning letter, stating, for some reasons of his
own, his belief that a reunion might be effected between Lady B. and
myself. To this I answered as usual; and he sent me a second letter,
repeating his notions, which letter I have never answered, having had
a thousand other things to think of. He now writes as if he believed
that he had offended me by touching on the topic; and I wish you to
assure him that I am not at all so,—but on the contrary, obliged by
his good-nature. At the same time acquaint him *the thing is impossible.*
You know this, as well as I,—and there let it end.

I believe that I showed you his epistle in autumn last. He asks me
if I have heard of *my* "laureat" at Paris,[1]—somebody who has written

---

[1] Byron's laureate at Paris was the poet Lamartine, whose "L'Homme—à Lord
Byron" was one of the poems in his *Premières Méditations Poétique* (1820).

"a most sanguinary Epitre" against me; but whether in French, or Dutch, or on what score, I know not, and he don't say,—except that (for my satisfaction) he says it is the best thing in the fellow's volume. If there is anything of the kind that I *ought* to know, you will doubtless tell me. I suppose it to be something of the usual sort;—he says, he don't remember the author's name.

I wrote to you some ten days ago, and expect an answer at your leisure.

The separation business still continues, and all the world are implicated, including priests and cardinals. The public opinion is furious against *him*, because he ought to have cut the matter short *at first*, and not waited twelve months to begin. He has been trying at evidence, but can get none *sufficient*; for what would make fifty divorces in England won't do here—there must be the *most decided* proofs. ✻✻✻

It is the first cause of the kind attempted in Ravenna for these two hundred years; for, though they often separate, they assign a different motive. You know that the continental incontinent are more delicate than the English, and don't like proclaiming their coronation in a court, even when nobody doubts it.

All her relations are furious against him. The father has challenged him—a superfluous valour, for he don't fight, though suspected of two assassinations—one of the famous Monzoni of Forli. Warning was given me not to take such long rides in the Pine Forest without being on my guard; so I take my stiletto and a pair of pistols in my pocket during my daily rides.

I won't stir from this place till the matter is settled one way or the other. She is as femininely firm as possible; and the opinion is so much against him, that the *advocates* decline to undertake his cause, because they say that he is either a fool or a rogue—fool, if he did not discover the liaison till now; and rogue, if he did know it, and waited, for some bad end, to divulge it. In short, there has been nothing like it since the days of Guido di Polenta's family,[2] in these parts.

If the man has me taken off, like Polonius "say he made a good end,"[3]—for a melodrame. The principal security is, that he has not the courage to spend twenty scudi—the average price of a clean-handed bravo—otherwise there is no want of opportunity, for I ride about the wood every evening, with one servant, and sometimes an acquaintance, who latterly looks a little queer in solitary bits of bushes.

Good bye.—Write to yours ever, &c.

[2] Guido di Polenta was the father of Francesca da Rimini.
[3] *Hamlet*, Act IV, scene 5.

[TO JOHN MURRAY] *Ravenna. June 7th. 1820*

Dear Murray—Enclosed in something which will interest you—
(to wit) the opinion of *the* Greatest man of Germany—perhaps of
Europe—upon one of the great men of your advertisements—(all
"famous hands" as Jacob Tonson used to say of his ragamuffins) in
short—a critique of *Goethe's* upon *Manfred.*—There is the original—
Mr. Hoppner's translation, and an Italian one—keep them all in
your archives—for the opinions of such a man as Goethe whether
favourable or not are always interesting—and this is moreover
favourable.—His *Faust* I never read—for I don't know German—but
Matthew Monk Lewis in 1816 at Coligny translated most of it to me
viva voce—& I was naturally much struck with it;—but it was the
Staubach & the *Jungfrau*—and something else—much more than
Faustus that made me write Manfred.——The first Scene however &
that of Faustus are very similar.—Acknowledge this letter—

yrs. ever
[scrawl]

P.S.—I have received *Ivanhoe*;—*good.*—Pray send me some tooth
powder & *tincture* of Myrrh.—by *Waite* &c.—Ricciardetto should
have been *translated literally or not at all.*—As to puffing *Whistlecraft*—
it won't do[1]—I'll tell you why some day or other.——Cornwall's a
poet[2]—but spoilt by the detestable Schools of the day.—Mrs. Hemans
is a poet also—but too stiltified, & apostrophic—& quite wrong[3]—
men died calmly before the Christian æra—& since without Christianity—witness the Romans—& lately Thistlewood[4]—Sandt[5]—&
Louvel[6]—*men who ought to have* been weighed down with their crimes
—even had they believed.——A deathbed is a matter of nerves &
constitution—& not of religion;—Voltaire was frightened—Frederick
of Prussia not.—Christians the same according to their strength rather

[1] An article on *Whistlecraft* in the *Quarterly Review* (Vol. XXI, p. 503) main-
tained that Frere's poem was superior to his model, the *Ricciardetto* (1738), by
Niccolò Forteguerri. That poem was a burlesque of Ariosto.
[2] Bryan Waller Procter, who took the pen name of Barry Cornwall, had been at
Harrow with Byron.
[3] Mrs. Felicia Hemans, in *The Sceptic* (1820) argued for the truth of religion
because of man's misery without it—expecially at the moment of death.
[4] Arthur Thistlewood, a revolutionary who finally plotted to assassinate the
ministers, but was apprehended and hanged. He was defiant to the last.
[5] Charles Sandt assassinated Kotzebue.
[6] Louvel was the assassin of the Duc de Berri.

113

than their creed. What does Helga Herbert[7] mean by his *Stanza?* which is octave got drunk [or gone] mad.—He ought to [have] his ears boxed with Thor's hammer, for rhyming so fantastically.——

[TO JOHN MURRAY] *Ravenna. June 8th. 1820*

Dear Murray—It is intimated to me that there is some demur & backwardness on your part to make propositions with regard to the M.S.S. transmitted to you at your own request.—How or why this should occur when you were in no respect limited to any terms—I know not—& do not care—contenting myself with *repeating* that the two cantos of Juan were to reckon as *one* only & that even in that case *you are not to consider* yourself as bound by your former proposition—particularly as your people may have a bad opinion of the production—the which I am by no means prepared to dispute.——With regard to the other M.S.S. (the *prose* will *not* be published in any case) I named nothing—& left the matter to you and to my friends.—If you are the least shy—(I do not say you are wrong) you can put the whole of the M.S.S. in Mr. Hobhouse's hands—& there the matter ends—your declining to publish will not be any offence to me.

yrs. in haste

[B]

[TO JOHN CAM HOBHOUSE] *Ravenna. June 8th. 1820*

My dear Hobhouse—You are right—the *prose* must not be published—at least the merely *personal part*;—and how the portion on Pope may be divided I do not know.[1]—I wish you would ferret out at Whitton—the "Hints from Horace". I think it (the Pope part) might be appended to that Popean poem—for publication or no—as you decide. I care not a damn.——Murray was in a violent hurry for poetry—I sent it—& now he is reluctant.——I don't *pin* him—I am quite equal upon the subject—I do not even require his own offers.

---

[7] The Hon. William Herbert, third son of the 1st Earl of Carnarvon, was one of the early *Edinburgh* reviewers. He published a poem called *Helga* in 1815, and another called *Hedin, or the Spectre of the Tomb* in 1820. The latter had a peculiar metre.

[1] Part of Byron's reply to the article in *Blackwood's Edinburgh Magazine* was an attempt to refute the accusation that he was cruel to his wife and to women in general. The rest was a defence of Pope against the disparagement by such "Lake Poets" as Wordsworth.

About Don Juan—as I said before;—you may lock up the whole—Dante and all—in your desk—it is to me the same.——The only thing that mattered was the "conscription"—lawyer Scout's object of respect—his fee—but I won't dispute about dirty elements in such matters—least of all with Murray;—anything disagreeable is his own fault—he bored me for something all the winter—& I sent him what I had—but I am not at all persuaded of the merits of aught but the translation from Pulci—which is verse for verse—and word for word—an't it?—I am tired of scribbling—& nothing but the convenience of an occasional extra thousand pounds would have induced me to go on—but even that will not weigh with me—if it is to be cavilled upon.——I don't know whether the *Danticles*[2] be good or no—for my opinions on my poeshie are always those of the last person I hear speak about them.—Murray's costivity—is a bad sign of their merits—& your notion is probably the right one;—for my own part I don't understand a word of the whole four cantos—& was therefore lost in admiration of their sublimity.——

Tell Dougal—that by this post I expedite a *full* & *unconditional* consent to the Mortgage—he is sullen—but must cheer up.—If I quarrel with my banker as well as the bookseller—it would be troppo.——It is quite unlikely that the poeshies should be popular—but in case of Non publication you can take care of the M.S.S. they will do for a posthumous—someday or other.——I can't promise to be in England in Autumn or at all—I don't much affect that paese.——You say the Po verses are fine—I thought so little of them—that they lay by me a year uncopied—but they were written in *red-hot Earnest*—& that makes them good.——The best news you could send me—would be the translation of Lady N[oel]—the adjustment & sale of Rochdale—the conclusion of the Irish Mortgage—and though last—not least—your own *Succes* (as Madame D. had it) which will be ensured by *"delicaci"*.[3] I have quite lost all personal interest about anything except money to supply my own indolent expences, and when I rouse up to appear to take an interest about anything—it is a temporary irritation—like Galvanism upon Mutton.——The life of an Epicurean—& the philosophy of one are merely prevented by "that rash humour which my Mother gave me"[4] that makes one restless &

[2] *The Prophecy of Dante*, a poem in four cantos, was published with *Marino Faliero* in 1821.

[3] See *LJ*, V, 575. This was a pleasantry which Byron shared with Hobhouse about an "entremetteuse", a Frenchwoman, who assured him that "Delicaci ensure everi succès" with a girl.

[4] *Julius Caesar*, Act IV, scene 3.

nervous—& can overthrow all tranquillity with a Sirocco.——Surely you agree with me about the real *vacuum* of human pursuits, but one must force an object of attainment—not to rust in the Scabbard altogether.——

yrs. ever most truly

[scrawl]

[TO DOUGLAS KINNAIRD]   *Ravenna. June 8th. 1820*

My dear Douglas—Enclosed is *the full consent*—I make no further limitation about the price of Stocks—and must take my chance.—Of course you will endeavour to let me lose as little as you can help.—I had already sent you *one* full consent & suppose that one or both will be conclusive.——You say you can do *nothing* about Rochdale—you can *hear* and *judge*—& surely you have always found me disposed to follow your counsels.—I should like to see the matter accommodated & the Manor sold.——Hanson says they wish to settle without the law.——Tell Hobhouse that he is *right*—the *prose* [on] the Edin [burgh] Mag[azine]—must not be published.—With regard to the verse I am not very anxious—and I do not wish Murray to be forced to anything—it [is] his own fault—he was fiercely impatient for something to publish—& now he has got it—seems reluctant.—He will do as he likes.

yrs.

[scrawl]

P.S.—I presume that there will be in all events my half year's fee from the funds—but let me know—that I may look about me.—— Claughton *should pay.*—Say so to Hanson.—*Insist on Hanson's bill.*

[TO DOUGLAS KINNAIRD AND JOHN AND CHARLES HANSON]

Ravenna. June 8th. 1820

Gentlemen—I hereby give my *full and unconditional* consent to the terms of the Mortgage proposed by & on the part of Lord Blessington and request that you will without further delay complete the same.—

BYRON

P.S.—Let this be considered as my definitive consent to lend the Sum proposed on Mortgage to Lord Blessington—without cavil or delay—if there were any form of words stronger than this to express my Consent—I would use it.—

Galignani has just sent me the Paris edition of your works (which I wrote to order), and I am glad to see my old friends with a French face. I have been skimming and dipping, in and over them, like a swallow, and as pleased as one. It is the first time that I had seen the Melodies without music; and, I don't know how, but I can't read in a music-book—the crotchets confound the words in my head, though I recollect them perfectly when *sung*. Music assists my memory through the ear, not through the eye; I mean, that her quavers perplex me upon paper, but they are a help when heard. And thus I was glad to see the words without their borrowed robes;—to my mind they look none the worse for their nudity.

The biographer has made a botch of your life—calling your father "a *venerable old* gentleman," and prattling of "Addison," and "dowager countesses,"[1] If that damned fellow was to *write my* life, I would certainly *take his*. And then, at the Dublin dinner, you have "made a speech" (do you recollect, at Douglas K.'s., "Sir, he made me a speech?") too complimentary to the "living poets," and somewhat redolent of universal praise. *I* am but too well off in it, but * * * * * * * *

You have not sent me any poetical or personal news of yourself. Why don't you complete an Italian Tour of the Fudges? I have just been turning over Little,[2] which I knew by heart in 1803, being then in my fifteenth summer. Heigho! I believe all the mischief I have ever done, or sung, has been owing to that confounded book of yours.

In my last I told you of a cargo of "Poeshie," which I had sent to M. at his own impatient desire;—and, now he has got it, he don't like it, and demurs. Perhaps he is right. I have no great opinion of any of my last shipment, except a translation from Pulci, which is word for word, and verse for verse.

I am in the third act of a Tragedy; but whether it will be finished or not, I know not: I have, at this present, too many passions of my own on hand to do justice to those of the dead. Besides the vexations

---

[1] The biographical sketch of Moore in Galignani's edition of his works alluded to Moore's marriage to Miss Dyke and added that "the fate of Addison with his Countess Dowager" held "no encouragement for the ambitious love of Mr. Moore."

[2] Moore's early poems entitled *Poems of the Late Thomas Little,* first published in 1801.

mentioned in my last, I have incurred a quarrel with the Pope's carabiniers, or gens d'armerie, who have petitioned the Cardinal against my liveries, as resembling too nearly their own lousy uniform. They particularly object to the epaulettes, which all the world with us have on upon gala days. My liveries are of the colours conforming to my arms and have been the family hue since the year 1066.

I have sent a trenchant reply, as you may suppose; and have given to understand that, if any soldados of that respectable corps insult my servants, I will do likewise by their gallant commanders; and I have directed my ragamuffins, six in number, who are tolerably savage, to defend themselves, in case of aggression; and, on holidays and gaudy days, I shall arm the whole set, including myself, in case of accidents or treachery. I used to play pretty well at the broad-sword, once upon a time, at Angelo's; but I should like the pistol, our national buccaneer weapon, better, though I am out of practice at present. However, I can "wink and hold out mine iron."[3] It makes me think (the whole thing does) of Romeo and Juliet—"now, Gregory, remember thy *swashing* blow."[4]

All these feuds, however, with the Cavalier for his wife, and the troopers for my liveries, are very tiresome to a quiet man, who does his best to please all the world, and longs for fellowship and good will. Pray write.

I am yours, etc.

[TO RICHARD BELGRAVE HOPPNER]   *Ravenna, June 12th. 1820*

My Dear Hoppner,—The accident is very disagreeable, but I do not see why *you* are to make up the loss, until it is quite clear that the money is lost; nor even then, because I am not at all disposed to have you suffer for an act of trouble for another. If the money has been *paid*, and not accounted for (by Dorville's illness), it rests with me to supply the deficit, and, even if not, I am not at all clear on the justice of your making up the money of another, because it has been stolen from your bureau. You will of course examine into the matter thoroughly, because otherwise you live in a state of perpetual suspicion. Are you *sure* that the *whole sum came from the Bankers*? was it *counted* since it passed to you by Mr. Dorville or by yourself? or was it kept unmixed with any cash of your own expences?—in Venice and with

---

[3] *Henry V*, Act II, scene 1.
[4] *Romeo and Juliet*, Act I, scene 1. [Moore has: "smashing blow."]

Venetian servants any thing is possible and probable that savours of villainy.

You may give up the *house* immediately and licentiate the Servitors, and pray, if it likes you not, sell *the Gondola*, and keep that produce and in [sic] the other balance in your hands till you can clear up this matter.

Mother Mocenigo will probably try a bill for breakables, to which I reckoned that the new *Canal posts* and *pillars*, and *the new door* at the other end, together with the year's rent, and the house given up without further occupation, are an ample compensation for any cracking of crockery of her's in *aflitto*. Is it not so? how say you? the Canal posts and doors cost many hundred francs, and she may be content, or she may be damned; it is no great matter which. Should I ever go to Venice again, I will betake me to the Hostel or Inn.

I was greatly obliged by your translation from the German; but it is no time to plague you with such nonsense now, when in the full exasperation of this vexatious deficit.

Make my best respects to Mrs. Hoppner, who doubtless wishes me at the devil for all this trouble, and pray write.

And believe me, yours ever and truly,
BYRON

P.S.—Allegra is well and obstinate, much grown and a favourite. My love to your little boy.

[TO CHARLES HANSON]   *Ravenna. June 15th. 1820*

My Dear Charles—After a mature consideration I decided to agree to the mortgage—and sent my consent addressed jointly to Mr. Kinnaird with your father—a few days ago.—The contents of the January packet have not been returned—because I presume that *both* the witnesses must be Britons—and the only one here besides myself is my servant Fletcher.—Upon this point let me be avised.—It would have given me pleasure that the Rochdale suit could have been terminated amicably & without further law but by arbitration—but since it must go before a Court—I resign myself to the decision—& wish to hear the result.——I shall not return to England for the present—but I wish you to send me (obtain it) my summons as a Peer to the Coronation (from curiosity) and let me know if we have any claims in our family (as connected with Sherwood Forest) to carry any part of the mummery[1]—that they may not lapse—but by being presented—be preserved to my Successors.—It will give me great pleasure to hear further from you on these points and I beg you to believe me with my best regards to your father & family

yrs. ever & truly
BYRON

[TO DOUGLAS KINNAIRD]   *Ravenna. June 19th. 1820*

My dear Douglas—Enclosed are two letters from Messrs. Hanson. —To the first I have replied that my consent has already been sent to you; to the second I have answered by requesting the earliest information; it refers to the Rochdale question now on the point it appears of being brought to a termination.—It is of course a subject of anxious reflection to me—though I fear rather than hope—but although I should have had more pleasure had it been closed by an amicable compromise or by arbitration—yet it will at any rate put an end to suspense one way or the other and settle the whole affair—— You can cast your eye over the business & let me have your opinion according to circumstances.—It seems to me—that gain or lose— the whole if obtained or the remnant if not should be brought to the hammer—at present the part not litigated is of as little advantage as the portion still before the Courts.——Pray—let me have my half year's income—I suppose you will not sell out till that can be secured. ——With regard to Murray I know nothing—he has not been very open—but I will not quarrel with him for his delays—nor for his shirking after his great eagerness—for it was his own eagerness that made me send the M.S.S. at his own express desire—last winter. ——If he declines the whole, you can offer them to Longmans, or some others of the Booksellers—as I fix no price—there can be little difficulty.—And tell Murray that I have no personal *coolness* whatever with him, but shall always be glad to hear of his well doing and to hear from him when he pleases.——Of course I allude to the *poesy*—I *do not mean on any account* to publish the *prose letter* at least for the present.——Give my regards to Hobhouse and believe me ever & truly

yr. obliged & affecte.
BYRON

P.S.—Pray let me hear from you.

[1] The coronation of George IV, originally scheduled for August 1, 1820, was postponed because of the Queen's trial, and did not take place until July 19, 1821.

My dear Hobhouse—The continuing silence of yourself and the
"high minded Moray" renders me again troublesome;—I am aware
of the pettiness of such things to a man who is arraigning judges, and
preparing constitutions—but trust to a spare moment from debate
and legislation to an arrangement with a bookseller on the part of an
absent friend—who has written a ballad upon you.——The matter
may be terminated thus;—since he demurs, put the M.S.S. into
Longman's hands or in those of any respectable publisher who will
undertake them—on their *own* terms—or on none—(till after
publication shall have stamped their failure or Success) of course the
prose (on Blackwood &c.) is not to be published except that part
which refers *to Pope*—& that *not* unless you please—perhaps the best
way to do with it—would be to print in some periodical publication
as an *"extract* from a letter &c. containing some opinion on the poetry
of the day".—You must premise that the third & fourth Cantos of Don
J[uan] must be published anonymously & this merely because in the
present state of Cant and hypocrisy in England—any freedom of
espression on Creeds or manners—would prevent the author from
asserting the guardianship of his own children—*this I know*—for on
this ground the Chancellor decided on Shelley's case—and would be
but too happy to do likewise by any other person obnoxious to the
present rulers.——The other poems will have my name prefixed.——
You may also state to the same publishers that I am now writing a
tragedy—which if I complete—would naturally pass through their
press.——

To Mr. Murray say thus:—I have no *personal* difference with him—
& shall continue an acquaintance and correspondence while he
chooses—but as publisher *that* leaf of his ledger will close for ever.
——It is not because he *declines* that I disapprove—but because he
hesitates and *shuffles*—why *not speak at once?*—*Why not have spoken
months ago?* I sent the M.S.S. months ago at his own eager request—
and so far from making hard terms—*I let him off from his own previous
offers*—but is this a reason to keep me month & month in a state of
suspense—neither announcing my letters—nor replying to my
friends?——Could he not have said yes or No? If he supposes that I
will permit him to treat me as he may in the plenitude of his Government connections & Quarterly review prosperity—treat his hacks—I
will show him the difference.——I require nothing but an answer—he
is to decide by his own opinion—& those of his parlour.—I neither

impugn nor oppose him nor his people;—I neither expect nor wish to find a publisher more instructed—or so liberal as he may have been—but I shall at least find one that will give me an answer.—*And so tell him from me.*—I forwarded my assent some time ago to Doug K. for the Dublin Mortgage—but suppose that he will not sell out till my half-year's interest from the funds is received.—At least I hope this —Messrs. Hanson write that the Rochdale Cause is to be called on in the Court of Exchequer immediately—& therefore it may perhaps be settled by this time one way or the other.—I am by no means sanguine but would wish to be out of suspense.——It would have given me more pleasure that it should have been settled amicably & by arbitration—but at this distance I am a puppet in the hands of every body.—Still I hate the idea of returning so much that I submit in preference to such inconveniences. Let me know that you are prosperous and believe me

yrs. ever & truly
[scrawl]

P.S.—The papers announce the Queen's arrival and it's consequences.—They have sent a message to our house. What the opinion in England may be, I know not—but *here* (and we are in her late neighbourhood) there are no doubts about her and her blackguard Bergami.——I have just asked Madame la Comtesse G[uiccioli] who was at Pesaro two years ago—& she answers that the thing was as public as such a thing can be.——It is to me subject of regret—for in England she was ever hospitable & kind to me.—I have never seen her since.—If you see the Davys—give my regards—& tell Lady Davy that I shall answer her letter—the moment I am aware of her arrival in England.——

[TO JOHN CAM HOBHOUSE]   *Ravenna. July 6th. 1820*

My dear Hobhouse—You do not tell me if the Rochdale cause is judged—you may know perhaps that it has been harangued—& that the Chief Baron must soon decide—if he has not already pronounced sentence.—So Hanson writes, but leaves me in suspense—Judgement not having been past—when he wrote on the 12th. Ult.o.——I am [in] the 4th. act of Marino Faliero—you may keep back the rest of the trash till I have shaped the new Sooterkin.——I regret nothing but the *fee*—but even the fee in such cases should be a secondary consideration. "The Adversary"—(Vittoria Corombona the White

122

Devil[1] that is) *there* I grant you I am vulnerable—& when a bitch has made you pass through the pretty reports that this has strewed my path with you will sympathize with my insanity upon that topic; why don't you also take such another wife?——How is my *Shild?* you never name her.——I have got a motto for my Doge Conspirator—Eccolo—"*Dux* inquieti turbidus Adriae"[2]—an't it a good one?——I see by the papers you prosper in Parliament—go on. —As to Autumn & Switzerland that is as hereafter it may be "*who knows?*"—The *Mortgage* eh?—and the suit with the Counsellors at law?—tell me—my respects to Dougal.—I am in a Scrape on all sides at home and abroad—

yrs. very truly
[Scrawl]

P.S.—When the *Pope* has decided on Madame Guiccioli's business —(it is actually before him) I will tell you whether I can come to England (via Switzerland) or not—the relations *for* her—& the husband against her are stirring up the whole Conclave—you may suppose—as pugilistic Jackson says—that I have "a pretty time of it." —I can't settle any thing till I know the result—which will probably be a separation—he is trying to prove the Adultery—which in Italy is no easy matter to prove to a tribunal. There has not been such a row in Romagna these hundred years on private matters—& we expect on one side or the other a few Stillettate—or Scrippettate.——It is the fashion—they killed a Carabineer the other day—and wounded another—that is some country gentleman did—because they had been shut out of the theatre.——I have taken no precautions except pistols when I ride in the Pigneta which is a solitary forest.——All this will appear little to you who have a green bag—& a queen to deal with—but *here* it is noised about.—Let us hope the best

[yrs. ever?]

Forse ci rivedremmo [pronto?]—ma scrivi pure.—

---

1 In John Webster's play *The White Devil*, Vittoria Corombona, "the famous Venetian Curtizan", tried for murder, pleads her case with such art that she wins the love of the Duke of Florence who tries her. In the end Vittoria, "the white Devil" is murdered in revenge for her intrigues. Byron saw a parallel with his wife, who pleaded a bad cause so speciously that she won the sympathy of all those at her "trial".

2 This motto from Horace (Odes, III, iii), "the unquiet lord of Hadria's surge", appeared in the Latin on the title page of *Marino Faliero* when it was published in 1821.

[TO JOHN MURRAY]   *Ravenna. July 6th. 1820*

Dear Murray—My former letters will prove that I found no fault with your opinions nor with you for acting upon them—but I do protest against your keeping me *four months* in suspense—without any answer at all.—As it is you will keep back the remaining trash till I have woven the tragedy of which I am in the 4th act.—With regard to terms I have already said that I named & *name* none—they are points which I leave between you and my friends—as I cannot judge upon the subject,—neither to you nor to them—have I named any sum—nor have I thought of any—nor does it matter.——But if you don't answer my letters—I shall resort to the *Row*—where I shall not find probably good manners or liberality—but at least I shall have *an answer of some kind.*—You must not treat a blood horse as you do your hacks otherwise he'll bolt out of the course.—Keep back the stuff till I can send you the remainder—but recollect that I don't promise that the tragedy will be a whit better than the rest.—All I shall require then will be a *positive* answer but a *speedy* one & not an awkward delay.—Now you have spoken out are you any the worse for it?—& could not you have done so five months ago?—Do you think I lay a stress upon the merits of my "poeshie"—I assure you I have many other things to think of.—At present I am eager to know the result of the Colliery question between the Rochdale people and myself—the cause has been heard—but as yet Judgement is not passed—at least if it is I have not heard of it.——Here is one thing of importance to my private affairs.—The next is that I have been the cause of a great conjugal scrape here—which is now before the *Pope* (seriously I assure you) and what the decision of his Sanctity will be no one can predicate.—It would be odd that having left England for one Woman ("Vittoria Corombona the White Devil" to wit) I should have to quit Italy for another.—The husband is the greatest man in these parts and with 100000 Scudi a year—but he is a great Brunello[1] in politics and private life—& is shrewdly suspected of more than one murder.—The relatives are on my side because they dislike him—we wait the event

yrs. truly
[scrawl]

[1] In *Orlando Furioso* Brunello is a leader of the Saracen army, a misshapen dwarf, "Most leud and false, but politike and wise."

[*Ravenna, July 9? 1820*] [On Cover]: *July 13th 1820*

[Appended to a note by Lega Zambelli, dated 9 Luglio 1820]

Dear Sir—I have to thank you for yr. letter received this morning. The above is Lega's statement with whom the papers ought to be found if not consigned to Mr. Hoppner to whom I beg my compts. &c. —I sent by Vicenzo 60 Francs—to pay for two lottery tickets of Frankfort—which I request Mr. H[oppner] to purchase for me.—I am very desirous to remit the M[ocenigo] palace to it's owner and have already explained myself on that head to Mr. H[oppner].——There will be probably some attempt at imposition on the part of Mme. Mocenigo's people—to which I will not submit.——They may go to law if they like—and as long as they like.—

yrs. very truly
BYRON

[TO THOMAS MOORE] *Ravenna, July 13th, 1820*

To remove or increase your Irish anxiety about my being "in a wisp,"[1] I answer your letter forthwith; premising that, as I am a "*Will* of the wisp," I may chance to flit out of it. But, first, a word on the Memoir;—I have no objection, nay, I would rather that *one* correct copy was taken and deposited in honourable hands, in case of accidents happening to the original; for you know that I have none, and have never even *re*-read, nor, indeed, *read* at all what is there written; I only know that I wrote it with the fullest intention to be "faithful and true"[2] in my narrative, but *not* impartial—no, by the Lord! I can't pretend to be that, while I feel. But I wish to give every body concerned the opportunity to contradict or correct me.

I have no objection to any proper person seeing what is there written,—seeing it was written, like every thing else, for the purpose of being read, however much many writings may fail in arriving at that object.

With regard to "the wisp," the Pope has pronounced *their separation*. The decree came yesterday from Babylon,[3]—it was *she* and *her*

---

[1] "An Irish phrase for being in a scrape" (Moore, II, 335).

[2] *Revelations, XIX*, 11.

[3] The Pope issued his decree granting Teresa a separation from Count Guiccioli on July 6. She was not officially notified until July 14, but Byron learned of it by July 12, probably from Count Alborghetti, secretary to the Papal Legate in Ravenna.

friends who demanded it, on the grounds of her husband's (the noble Count Cavalier's) extraordinary usage. *He* opposed it with all his might because of the alimony,[4] which has been assigned, with all her goods, chattels, carriage, etc., to be restored by him. In Italy they can't divorce. He insisted on her giving me up, and he would forgive every thing,—even the adultery, which he swears that he can prove by "famous witnesses." But, in this country, the very courts hold such proofs in abhorrence, the Italians being as much more delicate in public than the English, as they are more passionate in private.

The friends and relatives, who are numerous and powerful, reply to him—"*You*, yourself, are either fool or knave,—fool, if you did not see the consequences of the approximation of these two young persons,—knave, if you connive at it. Take your choice,—but don't break out (after twelve months of the closest intimacy, under your own eyes and positive sanction) with a scandal, which can only make you ridiculous and her unhappy."

He swore that he thought our intercourse was purely amicable, and that *I* was more partial to him than to her, till melancholy testimony proved the contrary. To this they answer, that "Will of *this* wisp" was not an unknown person, and that "clamosa Fama" had not proclaimed the purity of my morals;—that *her* brother, a year ago, wrote from Rome to warn him, that his wife would infallibly be led astray by this ignis fatuus, unless he took proper measures, all of which he neglected to take, &c. &c.

Now he says, that he encouraged my return to Ravenna, to see "*in quanti piedi di acqua siamo*," and he has found enough to drown him in. In short,

> "Ce ne fut pas le tout; sa femme se plaignit—
> Procès—La parenté se joint en excuse et dit
> Que du *Docteur* venoit tout le mauvais ménage;
> Que cet homme étoit fou, que sa femme étoit sage.
> On fit casser le mariage."[5]

It is best to let the women alone, in the way of conflict, for they are sure to win against the field. She returns to her father's house, and I can only see her under great restrictions—such is the custom of the country. The relations behave very well:—I offered any settlement, but they refused to accept it, and swear she *shan't* live with G. (as he

[4] The decree required Count Guiccioli to grant his wife an allowance of 100 scudi a month (about £1000 a year).
[5] From La Fontaine's "Le Roi Candaule et le Maître en Droit".

has tried to prove her faithless), but that he shall maintain her; and, in fact, a judgment to this effect came yesterday. I am, of course, in an awkward situation enough.

I have heard no more of the carabiniers who protested against my liveries. They are not popular, those same soldiers, and, in a small row, the other night, one was slain, another wounded, and divers put to flight, by some of the Romagnuole youth, who are dexterous, and somewhat liberal of the knife. The perpetrators are not discovered, but I hope and believe that none of my ragamuffins were in it, though they are somewhat savage, and secretly armed, like most of the inhabitants. It is their way, and saves sometimes a good deal of litigation.

There is a revolution at Naples. If so, it will probably leave a card at Ravenna in its way to Lombardy.

Your publishers seem to have used you like mine. M. has shuffled, and almost insinuated that my last productions are *dull*. Dull, sir!— damme, dull! I believe he is right. He begs for the completion of my tragedy of Marino Faliero, none of which is yet gone to England. The fifth act is nearly completed, but it is dreadfully long—40 sheets of long paper of 4 pages each—about 150 when printed; but "so full of pastime and prodigality" that I think it will do.

Pray send and publish your *Pome* upon me; and don't be afraid of praising me too highly. I shall pocket my blushes.

"Not actionable!"—*Chantre d'enfer!*[6]—by * * that's a speech," and I won't put up with it. A pretty title to give a man for doubting if there be any such place!

So my Gail is gone—and Miss Maho*ny* won't take *money*.[7] I am very glad of it—I like to be generous, free of expense. But beg her not to translate me.

Oh, pray tell Galignani that I shall send him a screed of doctrine if he don't be more punctual. Somebody *regularly detains two*, and sometimes *four*, of his Messengers by the way. Do, pray, entreat him to be more precise. News are worth money in this remote kingdom of the Ostrogoths.

Pray, reply. I should like much to share some of your Champagne and La Fitte, but I am too Italian for Paris in general. Make Murray send my letter to you—it is full of *epigrams*.

Yours, &c.

---

6 A phrase from Lamartine's poem "L'Homme- à Lord Byron".
7 See May 24, 1820, to Moore.

R[avenna]—Luglio—15. 1820

Amor Mio +—Appena partita tutta la Città ha saputa la tua partenza.—Io sono stato fare la solita trottata e al' mio ritorno son' informato che il P[orco] di San Stefano (tu sai che Sant' Antonio ebbe un' altro simile ma beato e più pulito del' ⟨animale⟩ N. N di cui si tratta) è sortito con un' muso rispettabilmente burbero ed offuscato— il quale credo non sarà molto cambiato in allegria dimane quando saprà le conseguenze *quatrinesche.*—Egli è adesso al' teatro il suo sollievo—e diletto.—Ti mando Valeriano—pregandoti per ora ritenerlo con te—per *soddisfazione mia* assieme con Luigi—finche sapiamo qualche cosa. Non disturbarti per rispondere ma non mortificarmi con rimandare V[aleriano] in cui fido molto.——Aspetto le tue nuove ed *ordini superiori.*—Io farò ciò che tu vuoi—ma spero che in fine *saremo felice*—del' amor mio tu non puoi dubitare—continua il tuo,— mi raccommando al Sr. C. G. il tuo Genitore e sono sempre il tuo più

[Scrawl]

P.S.—Si dice che *A[lessandro]* fa' una cattiva figura. Scrivimi nel più bel Stile di Santa Chiara. Pessimo O. + + + + + + + Guardati bene.

Ravenna, July 15th, 1820

My Love +—Hardly had you left than the whole town knew of your departure.[1]—I went for my usual ride and upon my return was informed that the Pig of St. Stephen[2] (you know that St. Anthony had a similar one, but blessed, and cleaner than the animal[3] in question) had appeared with a fairly black and surly snout, which I do not think will become any more cheerful tomorrow, when he learns the consequences to his pocket. He is now at the theatre—his solace and delight. I send you Valeriano, begging you to keep him with you for the present—for *my satisfaction*—as well as Luigi—until we know something more. Don't trouble yourself to answer, but do not humiliate

---

[1] As soon as she got the official news of the separation, and before her husband knew of it, Teresa left the Palazzo Guiccioli and joined her father, Count Gamba and went to their country house at Filetto, about fifteen miles from Ravenna.

[2] Byron refers to Count Guiccioli who was a Cavaliere di San Stefano, and to the legend of San Antonio Abate who was always pictured in the company of a pig.

[3] Teresa later apparently tried to erase the words "pig" and "animal", writing the letters "N N" to cover up what Byron had written.

me by sending back Valeriano, whom I trust very much. I am expecting your news and *superior orders.*—I will do what you wish—but I hope that in the end *we may be happy.*—Of my love you cannot doubt— let yours continue.—Remember me to Count G[amba] your father and I am always your most

P.S.—It is said that *A[lessandro]* cuts a poor figure. Write to me in the finest style of Santa Chiara. Very naughty O. + + + + + + Be very careful!!

[TO COUNTESS TERESA GUICCIOLI] *Ravenna Luglio 17. 1820*

Amor mio + + + —La tua carissima m'è stata consegnata da *P.* jeri sera—Egli partirà quasi subito—dunque non ho che pochi momenti per risponderti ma tu mi perdonerai.——Cosa si pensa— cosa si dici—sarebbe difficile per me indovinare poiche non sorto— nè sortirò mai (se non alle mie solite trottate a Cavallo) finche noi due non siamo in uno stato di essere insieme nella Società.—Ho rifiutato di andare al' teatro—come feci quando tu eri qui ancora.—Papa ti saprà dire le nuove del' mondo private e politiche, delle ultime non sapiamo più niente—la Gazzetta di Lugano dice che la nostra Regina avendo rigettato ogni proposizione di pace—la camera dei Lord— ha già cominciato il processo.——non ti avrei seccato cosi tanto se tu non avesti domandato delle *nuove "politiche".*——P. ti dirà cosa Egli pensa sopra le *visite* per ora—ma se tu non sei persuasa ti ubbidirò— come debbe fare.——Ti scrivo in grandissima fretta.—Tieni Val- [erian]o—senza rimorso—ho trovato un *Vici*-Coco provisorio il quale riesce a meraviglia—in tartufoli—*anitre* (senza cipolle pero tu lo dici credo per ridere) ed anche in bocca di dama—dunque non faccio magro.——Ho compito la tragedia—adesso viene il lavoro delle correzioni—e non ho copista.——Intanto mi occupo—e colla speranza di ritrovarti con un amor ancora non molto inferiore al' mio sarò sempre il tuo BYRON + + +

P.S.—*Sandri* dice che il decreto *"è un decreto bestiale"* ecco le conseguenze di non aver' accordato a quel Sciagurato—gli 60 Scudi di sua domanda,—così sono gli uomini—se non si fa' del' bene a loro— vi odiano—e se lo fate vi odiano di più per aver avuto il potere e la facoltà.—Luigi 14.o di Francia diceva bene che quando egli accordava qualche favore—"fece cento malcontenti—ed *un'* ingrato."——Per Sandri però troverò una maniera—di castigarlo.——C'è un certo——?

no?—mi pare di sentirlo—"ricordati di me che son' la Pia"——Lega ti saluta umilmente—egli viene strappazato discretamente secondo il solito del'amabile Padrone.—Elisei gira i palchi senza esser più vicino al' *disiato nido*; si fa'qualche feste per Donzelli—ma non come si fece per la Morandi e la Cortesi.——Ho mandato la medicina al' Cardinale la quale se egli la prende come si deve—lo gioverà—credo.— Ma l'ho detto di far' venire il Chirurgo Rima prima di prenderla.—— Jeri è stato amazzato un Prete di Faenza—e un fattore di Alessandro. ——Domani termina il teatro—ma tu lo sapevi prima di partire.—— Addio + + +

[TRANSLATION]   *Ravenna, July 17th, 1820*

My Love, + + + —Your dearest letter was brought to me by P. yesterday evening.—He is leaving almost at once—so I have only a few minutes in which to answer you; but you will forgive me.—

What people are thinking—what they are saying—it would be difficult for me to guess, as I do not go about, nor shall I do so, except for my usual rides on horseback, until we two are able to go into Society together.—I have refused to go to the theatre—as I did when you were still here.—Papa will be able to give you private and political news; of the latter we know nothing more.—The Lugano Gazette says that, our Queen having rejected every peace proposal, the House of Lords has begun the trial.[1] I would not have troubled you with so much had you not asked for *"political news"*.—P. will tell you what he thinks about my *visits* just now—but if you are not convinced, I will obey you—as I should.—I write in very great haste.—Keep Valeriano without compunction—I have found a temporary under-cook who is marvellously successful with trifles—*ducks* (without onions—I expect you said it as a joke) and even with cakes—so I am not fasting.—

I have finished the tragedy—now comes the work of revision— and I have no copyist.—

Meanwhile I keep busy—and in the hope of finding you again with a love still not much inferior to mine, I shall always be your BYRON + + +

P.S.—*Sandri* says the decree "is a bestial decree"—this is the consequence of not having given that wretch the 60 scudi he asked for. That is what men are like—if you do not help them they hate you—

[1] The trial of Queen Caroline, wife of George IV, for adultery lasted until November when she was acquitted.

and if you do they hate you the more for having had the power and means of doing so. Louis XIV of France was right in saying that every time he granted a favour, "he made a hundred men discontented, and *one* ungrateful."

But as to Sandri—I shall find a way of punishing him. There is a certain. . . .? no?—I feel as if I could hear it. *Ricordati di me che son la Pia.*

Lega greets you humbly—he is being scolded a good deal by his amiable master. Elisei makes the round of the boxes without getting any nearer to the "desired nest"—some assemblies are being given for Donzelli, but not as good as they were for the Morandi and the Cortesi.[2]—I have sent the medicine to the Cardinal, and if he takes it properly it will do him good—I think. But I told him to send for the surgeon Rima before taking it.—

Yesterday a priest of Faenza was assassinated—and a factor of Alessandro's.—

Tomorrow the theatre ends—but you knew that before you left.— Goodbye + + +

[TO JOHN MURRAY] *Ravenna. July 17th. 1820*

Dear Murray—Moore writes that he has not yet received my letter of January 2d. consigned to your care for him—I believe this is the sixth time I have begged of you to forward it & I shall be obliged by your so doing.——I have received some books and quarterlies—& Edinburghs—for all which I am grateful—they contain all I know of England except by Galignani's newspaper.——The tragedy[1] is completed but now comes the task of copy and correction—it is very long (42 *Sheets* of long paper of 4 pages each), and I believe must make more than 140 or 150 pages—besides many historical extracts as notes which I mean to append.—History is closely followed.—Dr. Moore's account[2] is in some respects false and in all foolish and flippant— *none* of the Chronicles—(and I have consulted Sanuto[3]—Sandi—

[2] Opera singers.
[1] *Marino Faliero.*
[2] Dr. John Moore, author of the novel *Zeluco*, published in 1781 his *View of Society and Manners in Italy*, from which Byron had hoped to get some useful information about Faliero, the Doge of Venice, but he was disappointed in it.
[3] Marino Sanuto's Italian history of the Doges of Venice (first published by Muratori in 1733) was Byron's chief historical source for *Marino Faliero*. He also quoted from the other writers mentioned here in his preface.

131

Navagero—& an anonymous Siege of Zara—besides the histories of Laugier Daru—Sismondi &c.) state, or even hint that he begged his life—they merely say that he did not deny the conspiracy.—He was one of their great men—commanded at the siege of Zara—beat 80,000 Hungarians killing 8000—and at the same time kept the town he was besieging in order.—Took Capo d'Istria,—was ambassador at Genoa Rome and finally Doge—where he fell—for treason in attempting to alter the Government by what Sanuto calls a Judgement on him for— many years before (when Podesta and Captain of Treviso) having knocked down a bishop, who was sluggish in carrying the host at a procession.—He "saddles him" as Thwackum did Square "with a Judgement"[4] but does not mention whether he had been punished at the time—for what would appear very strange even now—& must have been still more so—in an age of Papal power & glory—Sanuto says— that Heaven took away his senses for this buffet—in his old age— and induced him to conspire.—"Pero fu permesso che il Faliero perdette l'intelletto, &c."——

I don't know what your parlour boarders will think of the drama I have founded upon this extraordinary event—the only similar one in history is the story of Agis King of Sparta[5]—a prince *with* the Commons against the aristocracy—& losing his life therefor—but it shall be sent when copied.—I should be glad to know why your Quater*ing* Reviewers—at the Close of "the Fall of Jerusalem"[6] accuse me of Manicheism?—a compliment to which the sweetener of "one of the mightiest Spirits" by no means reconciles me.——The poem they review is very noble—but could they not do justice to the writer— without converting him into my religious Antidote?—I am not a Manichean—nor an *Any*-chean.—I should like to know what harm my "poeshies" have done—I can't tell what [your] people mean by making me a hobgoblin.——This is the second thing of the same sort— they could not even give a lift to that poor Creature Gally Knight— without a similar insinuation about "moody passions" now are not the *passions* the food and fuel of poesy?—I greatly admire Milman;—but they had better not bring me down upon Gally for whom I have no such admiration.——I suppose he buys two thousand pounds' worth of

[4] In Fielding's *Tom Jones*.

[5] Agis IV, King of Sparta (244–240 B.C.). Byron relied on Plutarch's account.

[6] In his review of Henry Hart Milman's *The Fall of Jerusalem* Bishop Heber wrote (referring obviously to Byron) ". . . by a strange predilection for the worser half of Manicheism, one of the mightiest spirits of the age has, apparently, devoted himself and his genius to the adornment and extension of evil. . . ." (*Quarterly Review*, Vol. XXIII, p. 225.)

books in a year which makes you so tender of him—But he won't do—
my Murray—he's middling—and writes like a Country Gentleman—
for the County Newspaper—I shall be glad to hear from you—& you'll
write now because you will want to keep me in a good humour till you
can see what the tragedy is fit for.—I know your ways—my Admiral.

yrs. ever truly
[scrawl]

[TO COUNTESS TERESA GUICCIOLI]   *Ravenna. Luglio 18.0 1820*

Amor Mio+—In verità io non so niente; vedendo solamente
Elisei nelle solite cavalcate—ed Egli adesso è troppo occupato di una
sua disgrazia di jeri per pensare di noi o del'paese.—Nel' fare un
salto con me nei campi egli è caduto insieme col suo cavallo—e s'è
fatto male in un occhio—non gran male—ma abbastanza per farlo
sfigurare nel' bel mondo per alcuni giorni.—Il peggio è che essendo
Egli gran Cavallarizzo in sua propria opinione—(e con ragione poiche
cavalca bene) erano [pure] presenti per asardo molti spettatori in
carrozza &c. di questa sua avventura—e per conseguenza l'amor
proprio è stato non men ferito del' occhio.—La sua berretta—il
vestito—e tutta la montatura fin all [word blotted out] *speroni*—sono
anche mezzo rovinati nella caduta ch'era piuttosto forte.—Fortunata-
mente per lui v'era dell' erba—e nessun Sasso.——La tua lettera è
stata la mia prima informazione del' colloquia di A[lessandro] Col
Cardinale e col'Alborghetti.—Da questo tu saprai che io non so
niente di tutto ciò che tu dici e domandi.——Luigi e Valeriano furono
tuoi servitori prima di essere i miei—e queste sono ciarle che non
dureranno più di qualche giorni;—sarebbe bello che non puoi avere un'
domestico perchè egli m'ha servito prima di servirti.——Guiccioli ha
detto a Lega questa mattina che egli non vuole portare avanti la lite
per la casa—io ho risposto che resta con lui farla cessare.——
  Per la lontananza non so cosa dirti—tu sai cosa voglio—ma resta
con te e coi tuoi parenti decidere.—Per me (se vuoi) staremo insieme
e mandaremo A[lessandro] e il suo assegnamento a farsi s [word
illegible—page torn]——Io non son stato molto bene—jeri del'
gran' caldo—ma oggi sto meglio.——Ti ringrazio cordialmente delle
tue rose che erano fresche ancora—l'ho *baciate* e messe in acqua fresca
subito.——Tu temi per me—io non so perchè—ma cosa vuoi che ne
faccio? ciò che sarà sarà—e un' sito non è più sicuro di un' altro.—Pensa
guardarti bene.—ciò mi preme assai più di me a tutto ciò che può

accadere a mia persona.——Papa ti informerà delle dic[erie] (se lo sono) ma ricordate che finiscono sempre in un' mese—se siano buone o cattive.—Questa sera è la Serata di Donzelli—ma io non son' andato—ti prego amarmi e credermi il tuo più sincero ed amantissimo

+ + + + + [Scrawl] + + + +

[TRANSLATION]   *Ravenna, July 18th, 1820*

My Love +—Truly I know nothing, since I see no one but Elisei on my usual rides—and he is now too busy about an accident of his own to think about us or about his country. Jumping with me yesterday in the fields, he fell with his horse—and hurt an eye—not very badly—but enough to disfigure him in society for a few days. The worst of it is, that [Elisei][1] being a great horse-man in his own opinion (and rightly, for he rides well), by chance a great many spectators in carriages were present and witnessed his misadventure—consequently his pride has been no less injured than his eye.—His cap— his clothes—and all his equipment down to [illegible—paper torn]— his spurs were also half-spoiled by the fall, which was rather heavy. Fortunately for him there was some grass and no stones.

Your letter has given me the first news about A[lessandro]'s conversation with the Cardinal and Alborghetti.—From this you will realize that I know nothing about what you say and ask—this is all gossip that will not last more than a few days.—It would be a fine thing if you could not have a servant because he served me before going to you![2]

Guiccioli told Lega this morning that he did not want to pursue the lawsuit about *the house*—I have replied that it was for him to bring it to an end.

About our separation I don't know what to say to you—you know what I want—but the decision must depend on you and on your family. For my part (if you will) we will live together and send A. and his alimony to [page torn]

I have not been very well these days, owing to the great heat, but I am better today.

Thank you *very* much for your roses which are still fresh—I *kissed* them and at once put them in fresh water.

You are afraid for me—I don't know why—but what can I do

---

[1] See Aug. 12, 1820, to Teresa, note 1.
[2] Teresa was concerned because she had heard gossip criticizing her for taking two of Byron's servants with her when she left the Guiccioli Palace.

about it?—What will be, will be—and one place is not safer than another. Look after yourself well—this matters much more to me than myself, or anything that can happen to me. Papa will keep you informed about the gossip (if there is any) but remember that it will be over in a month, whether it is good or bad.—This evening is Donzelli's benefit night, but I have not gone to it—pray love me and believe me your most sincere and loving

+ + + + + [scrawl] + + + +

[TO RICHARD BELGRAVE HOPPNER]   *Ravenna, July 20th, 1820*

My Dear Hoppner,—On Vincenzo's return I will send you some books, though the latter arrivals have not been very interesting you shall have the best of them.

You do not mention that *Vincenzo* delivered to you a paper with *sixty francs*; he had it; did you get it? they were for the tickets.

Lega tells me that the Mocenigo *Inventory* was delivered last week; is it so? I made him send to Venice on purpose.

With regard to Mrs. Mocenigo, I am ready to deliver up the palace directly; with respect to *breakables* she can have no claim till *June next*, the rent being stipulated as prior payment (and paid), but not the articles missing till the whole period was expired. I have replenished three times over, and made good by the equivalent of the doors, and Canal posts (to say nothing of the exorbitant rent), any little damage done to her pottery. If any articles are taken by mistake, they shall be restored or replaced; but I will submit to no exorbitant charge, nor imposition. You had best state this by Seranzo, who *seduced* me into having anything to do with her, and who has probably still something of the gentleman about him. What she may do, I neither know nor care: if they like the law, they shall have it for years to come, and if they gain, what then? They will find it difficult to "shear the Wolf" no longer in Lombardy. They are a *damned infamous set*, and, to prevent any unpleasantness to you with that nest of whores and scoundrels, *state my words as my words*; who can blame *you* when you merely take the trouble to repeat what I say, and to restore what I am disposed to give up,—that is her house,—a year before it is due, thereby losing a year's rent?

I can hardly spare Lega at this moment, or I would willingly send him. At any rate you can give up the house, and let us battle for her crockery afterwards.

135

I regret to hear what you say of yourself, if you want any cash, pray use any balance in your hands (of course) without ceremony. I am glad the Gondola was sold at any price as I only wanted to get rid of it.

I am not very well, having had a twinge of fever again; the heat is 85 in the Shade.

I suppose you know that there is a Revolution at Naples.

Yours ever and truly, in haste,
BYRON

P.S.—I have finished a tragedy in five acts, *Marino Faliero*; but now comes the bore of copying, and in this weather too.

Compts. to Madame Hoppner.

[TO DOUGLAS KINNAIRD] *Ravenna. July 20th. 1820*
11 o'Clock at Night

Dear Douglas—Some weeks ago you will have received my consent to the Mortgage to be lent to Ld. Blessington—what have you done upon it?—my half year's fee from the funds where is it?—Messrs. Hanson write that the Rochdale Cause has been heard—is it decided? —I shall be glad to hear on these and other points at your imperial leisure.——There is a Revolution at Naples and one is expected throughout Italy daily.—I have completed (but have to copy out) a tragedy in five acts—on Marino Faliero Doge of Venice.——The fever has attacked me again but slightly—I caught it riding in the Forest part of which is agueish & marshy.——

Madame Guiccioli has been separated from her husband who has been sentenced (by the Pope) to pay her twelve hundred crowns a year of alimony—a handsome allowance for a lone woman in these parts—almost three hundred pounds sterling a year and worth about a thousand in England.——The story is a long one—he wanted to bully and failed with both lady and gentleman—they say here that he will have me taken off—it is the custom—there were two perished last week—a priest—and a factor—one by a political club—and the other by a private hand for revenge;—nobody fights—but they pop at you from behind trees, and put a knife into you in company—or in turning a corner—while you are blowing your nose—he may do as he pleases—I only recommend to him not to miss—for if such a thing is attempted—and fails—he shan't have another opportunity— "Sauce for the Goose is sauce for the Gander" it would be easy to know the quarter whence it came and I would pistol him on the spot on my return from the escape.——I have taken no precautions (which indeed would be useless)—except taking my pistols when I ride out in the woods every evening—you know I used to be a pretty good shot—and that if the rogues missed that I should probably hit.—— All these fooleries are what the people of the place say (who detest him by the way) and whether true or not—I shan't stir a step out of my way;—a man's life is not worth holding on such a tenure as the fear of such fellows and what must be will—if it be decreed but not otherwise.——

While I am in *the very act of writing* to you—my Steward Lega has come to tell me that this moment—a quarter of an hour past—a brigadier of the Gens d'armes has been shot in the thigh (I heard the pistol and thought it was my servants cleaning my own and firing them first) by no one knows who—all we know is that they had a quarrel with the populace two weeks ago—who warned them—and had already wounded two before.—They had also a squabble (the Gens d'armes) with my Servants about the lace of my liveries as resembling their uniforms—but they were reduced to order by the decision of the police in favour of the liveries.—I hope none of my ragamuffins have been in this matter.———Here is a state of society for you! it is like the middle ages—Grand Uncertainty—but very dramatic.

> yrs. ever
> [scrawl]

P.S.—*all fact* I assure you[;]. it is Moonlight. A fortnight ago a similar thing happened to these soldiers—but they were only wounded (two of them) with knives—one lost his hat in the Scuffle.

[TO JOHN MURRAY]   *Ravenna. July 22d. 1820*

Dear Murray—The tragedy is finished but when it will be copied is more than can be reckoned upon.—We are here upon the eve of evolutions and revolutions.—Naples is revolutionized—& the ferment is among the Romagnoles—by far the bravest and most original of the present Italians—though still half savage.—Buonaparte said the troops from Romagna were the best of his Italic corps and I believe it.— The Neapolitans are not worth a curse—and will be beaten if it comes to fighting—the rest of Italy—I think—might stand.—The Cardinal is at his wit's end—it is true—that he had not far to go.—Some papal towns on the Neapolitan frontier have already revolted.—Here there are as yet but the sparks of the volcano—but the ground is hot—and the air sultry.—Three assassinations last week—here & at Faenza—an anti-liberal priest, a factor, and a trooper last night—I heard the pistol-shot that brought him down within a short distance of my own door.—There had been quarrels between the troops and people of some duration—this is the third soldier wounded within the last month.—There is a great commotion in people's minds—which will lead to nobody knows what—a row probably.——There are secret Societies all over the country as in Germany—who cut off those obnoxious to them like the Free tribunals—be they high or low—and then it becomes impossible to discover or punish the assassins their measures are taken so well.—

You ask me about the books. Jerusalem[1] is the best.—Anastasius[2] good but no more written by a Greek—than by a Hebrew—the diary of an Invalid[3] good and true bating a few mistakes about "Serventismo" which no foreigner can understand or really know—without residing years in the country.—I read that part (translated that is) to some of the Ladies in the way of knowing how far it was accurate and they laughed particularly at the part where he says that "they must not have children by their lover"—"assuredly (was the answer) we don't pretend to say that it is right—but *men* cannot conceive the repugnance that a *woman* has to have children *except by the man she loves*.["]—they have been known even to obtain abortions when it was by the *other*—but that is rare—I know one instance however of a woman making herself miscarry—because she wanted to meet her lover (they were in two different cities) in the lying-in month (hers was [or] should have been in October) she was a very pretty woman—young & clever & brought on by it a malady which she has not recovered [from] to this day;—however she met her Amico by it at the proper time—it is but fair to say that he had dissuaded her from this piece of amatory atrocity—and was very angry when he knew that she had committed it—but the "it was for your sake—to meet you at the time which could not have been otherwise accomplished" applied to his Self love—disarmed him—and they set about supplying the loss.——

1 *The Fall of Jerusalem*, 1820, a dramatic poem by Henry Hart Milman.
2 *Anastasius, or Memoirs of a Greek, written at the close of the Eighteenth Century* (1819), by Thomas Hope. Byron expressed admiration for the book later. He told Lady Blessington that "he would have given his two most approved poems to have been the author of *Anastasius*."
3 *Diary of an Invalid*, by Henry Matthews, whose brother, Charles Skinner Matthews, was the friend of Byron and Hobhouse.

I have had a little touch of fever again but it has receded.—The heat is 85 in the Shade.—I remember what you say of the Queen—it happened in Lady O[xford]'s boudoir or dressing room if I recollect rightly, but it was not her Majesty's fault—though very laughable at the time—a minute sooner she might have stumbled over something still more awkward.—How the *Porcelain* came there I cannot conceive—and remember asking Lady O[xford] afterwards—who laid the blame on the Servants.—I think the Queen will win—I wish she may—she was always very civil to me.——You must not trust Italian witnesses—nobody believes them in their own courts—why should you? For 50 or 100 Sequins you may have any testimony you please—and the Judge into the bargain

yrs. ever
B

Pray forward my letter of January to Mr. Moore.

[TO COUNTESS TERESA GUICCIOLI]   *Ravenna Luglio 23.o 1820*

Amor mio + + + —Mi pare non troppo ben'fatto l'aver mandato Luigi nelle circonstanze attuali—ma però non serve molto.——Io lo faccio partire questa sera—non dovreste aver' paura di violenza contra di me—*tu stesso* hai assai più di temere da tuo marito, questo lo *so* —e perciò ti raccommando di tenere i vostri servitori sempre vicini a tua persona—quando tu sorti.—Per le nuove Luigi ti porterà tutte, domestiche e politiche.—Io non so niente.—Un' Carabiniere è stato ferito—una commedia è venuta—ecco tutto che ho imparato in questi giorni.——Ti scrivo in gran' fretta—per non far' aspettare il servitore. —Elisei è guarito di sua ferita ma non del' suo amor proprio.—— Non saprei cosa dirti di più senonche *ti amo*—e *ti amerò sempre*—ma quando ci rivedremmo non resta con me a decidere.—Con un' *raggiratore* come il Cavaliere non si può sapere niente—nè calculare niente.—Egli gira come un buffone e coll' istesso effetto.——Io sto' bene—fuorche un piccolo dolor in una mano—per aver sbarrato [sparato?] una pistola troppo caricata l'altro jeri in Pigneta.——Ti mando dei altri libri—e sono sempre il tuo più sincero ed amantissimo

[Scrawl]

[TRANSLATION]   *Ravenna, July 23rd, 1820*

My Love: + + + —I don't think you have done right in present circumstances in sending Luigi back—and it won't be much use—I shall send him off again this evening.

139

You need not be afraid of violence against me—you *yourself* have more to fear from your *husband*, this I *know*—and therefore I beg you to keep your servants always about your person—when you go out.— As to the news, Luigi will give you all of it—domestic and political.— I don't know anything.—A Papal guard has been wounded, a comedy has arrived, that is all that I have learnt in these days.

I am writing in a great hurry, so as not to keep the servant waiting. —Elisei has recovered from his wound, but not from his wounded pride.—I do not know what else to say, except that *I love you—and I shall always love you*—but when we shall see each other again, it is not in my power to decide.—With a twister like the Cavaliere one can know nothing—and count on nothing—He turns round and round like a clown, and as effectively.

I am well, except for a little pain in one hand—from having fired an over-primed pistol the day before yesterday in the Pine-forest.—

I am sending you some other books—and am always your most sincere and loving.

[TO COUNTESS TERESA GUICCIOLI] *Ravenna. Luglio 24.o 1820*

Amor mio + + + —Non temere—ti assicuro che fosse solamente per divertimento che scaricai le pistole miei in Pigneta e non per difesa contro un' assassino—i miei servitori l'avevano troppo caricati e ho sofferto un poco di dolore in una mano—il quale è già passato. ——Io licenziai tre servitori perche in vece di far' loro dovere si trovono all' osteria—poco prima di mezza notte—una cosa insop- portabile—lasciare a quell' ora 8 cavalli[,] finimente[,] tre carrozzi &c. senza nessuno per custodirli.——Ma se vuoi—bisogna che li perdono.——Tu non sei obbligata, amor mio + leggere tutti quei libri—io creddi che tu fosti come me—mi piace leggere ora un' libro ora l'altro, poche pagine alla volta—e cambiare spesso—*ciò* vuole dire cangiare *i libri*—ma nessun'altra cosa fuori della *biancheria*— essendo io l'estratto della fedeltà.——Ti scrissi jeri in mal' umore—il non vederti—e mille altre cose me disturbavano—piccole ma noiose, cose di casa—il caldo &c. &c.—Non ho nuove particolari dell' Inghilterra—le Gazzette sono piene della benedetta Regina—gran cosa in questo mondo che non si può farsi amare in pace—senza tutto questo chiasso.—La sua Maestà ha messo il morale del' mio moralis- simo paese in gran periglio e scandalo—mi pare già deteriorato, perche leg[g]o nelle gazzette di una dama Irlandese di 37 anni che è

scappata con un' giovane Inglese di 24,—piantando un' marito di 50—
e una figlia di 16.——Ti bacio 100000 + + + volte—e mi consolo
coll' idea che in ogni caso ci rivedremmo——Amami—sono sempre
il tuo

[Scrawl]

Ravenna, July 24th, 1820

My Love: Don't be afraid—I assure you that it was only for
amusement that I discharged my pistols in the Pineta and not in self-
defence against an assassin—my servants had overcharged them and I
suffered a little pain in one hand—which is already gone.—

I have sent away three servants, because, instead of doing their
duty, they went to the tavern—a little before midnight—an insuf-
ferable thing—leaving eight horses, harness, three carriages, etc., at
that time of night with nobody to look after them—But if you want
me to—I shall have to forgive them.—

You are not obliged, my love, to read all those books—I thought
you were like me—I like sometimes to read one book and sometimes
another, a few pages at a time,—and change frequently, that is, change
books—but nothing else except *linen*—since I am the essence of fidelity.
—I wrote to you yesterday in a bad humour;—not seeing you has
upset me—and a thousand other things—little things, but tiresome,
household matters; the heat, etc.

I have no particular news from England—the Gazettes are full of
our blessed Queen—it is a fine thing that in this world one cannot be
loved in peace—without all this fuss!—Her Majesty has put the
morals of my very moral country in great danger and scandal. They
seem deteriorated already, for I read in the Gazette of an Irish lady of
37 who has run away with a young Englishman of 24—leaving
behind a husband of 50 and a daughter of 16.

I kiss you one hundred thousand times and console myself with the
thought that in any case we shall see each other soon.

Love me—I am always yours

[TO JOHN MURRAY]   *Ravenna. July 24th. 1820*

Dear Murray—Enclosed is the account from Marin[o] Sanuto of
Faliero &c. You must have it translated (to append original and translation to the drama when published) it is very curious & simple in
itself and authentic—I have compared it with the other histories—that

blackguard Dr. Moore has published a false and flippant story of the transaction.—

yrs.
[scrawl]

P.S.—The first act goes by this post.—Recollect that without previously reading the *Chronicle*, it is difficult to understand the tragedy. —So—translate.——I had this reprinted separately on purpose.——

[TO JOHN MURRAY]   *Ravenna. July 25th. 1820*

Dear Murray—Enclosed is the first act of the tragedy.[1]—The rest shall be sent as copied.——

yrs.
[Scrawl]

[TO COUNTESS TERESA GUICCIOLI]   *Ravenna. Luglio 26.o 1820*

Amor Mio + + + + + —Ho mandato subito a Giulio Rasponi per la villeggiatura—ma egli dice che la Contessa Capra la vuole per se—e che egli non è padrone senza il di lei permesso.—Pessimo O + dunque tu sei divenuta cacciatrice, ma è un' principio piuttosto non buono ammazzare i poveri cani.—Tu non puoi desiderare a rivolermi quanto ti voglio io—l'amor mi punge moltissimo (senza contare la torta [word erased]—) speriamo però che fra poco tempo si può combinare tutto.—Il Cavaliere fa' spargere delle voci—che tu sei venuta qui per trovarmi (ma guai!) che egli ha trovato delle mie lettere le quali ha fatto *bollare* &c.—che vuole far' causa—e *mille altri sogni.*—Una cosa è certa—Egli cerca (e trova in alcuni) delle testimonianze di non averti in *apparenza mal trattato.*—Ma chi può mai sapere ciò! nè il pubblico nè gli amici—poiche sono cose di casa e di famiglia.——V'è qui la Commedia—ma non son' stato. Faccio delle trottate—e scarico delle pistole—leggo e scrivo—ecco tutto!— *La lontananza m'incommoda molto—m'intendi*——Lega mi dice che la Fanni l'ha fatto un' altro bastardo—un' maschio—del' quale credo— si farà regalo allo 'spedale di Venezia—io lo consigliai ci mandare anche *l'Aspasia,* sarebbe una brutta C——— di meno in quella sua non troppa bella famiglia.——Le altre *cadreghe* (questa non è parola di

[1] *Marino Faliero.*

Santa Chiara ma di San' Marco) sono venute da Forli—con dell' altra roba—bella—ma vogliono troppi *quatrini*, e Lega ha avuto di soffrire delle strappazate furiose.——Ti prego perdonarmi tutte queste sciocezze e credermi il tuo più [fedele] + + +

[Scrawl]

P.S.—Si Cocchina—ti ho inteso—con tutti i tuoi + + + povera piccinina!—spero che caveremo tutti questi nostri desiderii ben presto ancora un poco di pazienza.

[TRANSLATION]   *Ravenna, July 26th, 1820*

My Love + + + + + I at once sent a message to Giulio Rasponi about the villeggiatura[1] but he says that Countess Capra wants it for herself—and that he cannot do it without her consent.—Very naughty O+so you have become a huntress, but it is not a good beginning to kill the poor dogs.—You cannot desire me and want me back more than I do you—Love stings me very much, without counting the cake [word erased] but let us hope that we shall be able to arrange something—the Cavaliere is spreading rumours—that you have been here to visit me—(would it were so!)—that he has found some letters of mine that he has had impounded—that he wants to sue me—and a *thousand other* fantastic designs. One thing is certain—he is seeking (and in some people finding) witnesses to say that he did not seem to be *ill-treating* you.—But who can ever know! Neither the public nor one's friends—for these are family matters, at home.

The Play is here but I have not been to it. I have been riding—and firing pistols—I read and write—that is all!

This separation from you inconveniences me greatly—you understand.

Lega tells me that Fanny has produced another bastard—a boy—whom I believe she is to present to the Venice hospital—I advised him to send Aspasia too,—it would be one ugly C——— the less in that not over beautiful family.

The other "cadreghe"[2] (this is not a word of Santa Chiara's but of St. Mark's) have come from Forlì with some other stuff—fine—but they want too much money and Lega has had to take some furious scoldings.

Pray forgive all this nonsense and believe me your most + + +

[1] Teresa had been urging Byron to take a summer place in the country, for the sake of Allegra and to be nearer her at Filetto.

[2] "Cadreghe" is the word for *chairs* in the Venetian dialect.

P.S.—Yes, my Duck—I have understood you—with all your + + + poor child! I hope that we shall fulfil all these wishes of ours very soon —have a little more patience.

[TO DOUGLAS KINNAIRD]   *Ravenna July 27th. 1820*

Dear Douglas—I have received what you call the "fatal intelligence" of the Rochdale decision.—It is indeed a severe blow after fifteen years of litigation—and almost as many thousand pounds of law expences with two verdicts in my favour—but

> "Fortuna Saevo laeta negatio, et
> Ludum insolentem ludere pertinax
> Transmutat incertos honores
> Nunc mihi nunc aliis benigna
> Laudo manentem, si celeres quatit
> Pennas resigno quae dedit"[1]

A man has lived to little purpose—if he cannot sustain such things.— "Whom the Lord loveth he chasteneth."[2]——The only thing now to think of is what is best to be done.—I (were I on the spot) should immediately order the manor—& whatever rights are mine to be brought to the hammer—and sold to *any bidding* without consideration of price.—This will at least pay the law expences—and perhaps liquidate some part of the remaining debt—so pray my dear Douglas— let this be done directly.—I have tried the question and will have no more law—even supposing there was any further plea.—This is my order *peremptory* if you will see it fulfilled—indeed you must agree with me that the payment of debts must be now my only object.——. ——For the price it imports little—though it were only five—four— or three thousand pounds.—Being thus explicit—I trust that you will agree with me—and see this done without further delay.——Of the

---

[1] Horace's Ode 29, Book III, lines 49–54:

> "Fortune, her cruel trade quite to her mind,
> Persistent still her wanton game to play,
>   Transfers her favours day by day,—
>   To me, to others, kind.
>
> Stays she, I'm pleased, but if swift wings she shake,
> I drop her paltry gifts, wrapping my life
>   In its own worth; and Want for wife,
>   Undowered but honest, take."

[2] *Epistle to the Hebrews*, XII, 6.

144

Irish transfer you say nothing—is it done—or to be done?—You mention having sent £1100 in Circulars—but they are not yet arrived. ——Believe me

yours very truly & affectly.
BYRON

[TO JOHN HANSON]   *Ravenna. July 27th. 1820*

Dear Sir—I have received from Mr. Kinnaird the intelligence of the Rochdale decision. It has not surprized me—and there is no more to be said.—Even if a further question could arise—I am not disposed to carry it higher.—What I desire to be done and done quickly—is to bring the Manor—& my remaining rights immediately to auction—& sell it to the highest bidder without consideration of price;—it will at least pay the law expences—& part of the remaining debts.——Pray let this be done without delay—and believe me

yrs. very truly
BYRON

P.S.—I presume that you proceed in the transfer from the funds to the Irish Mortgage.——

[TO COUNTESS TERESA GUICCIOLI]   *Ravenna. Luglio 29.o 1820*

Amor Mio + + + —Il tuo fratellino mi piace molto—egli mostra del' carattere e del' talento—grandi sopraciglie!—e una statura di quale egli (mi pare) s'è arrichito a spese tua, almeno di *quelle*— m'intendi? La sua testa è un poco troppo riscaldato per le rivoluzioni— basta—che non si precipitata.—Si A[lessandro] vuole far' pace—spero che prima ti darà *una costituzione*—essendo la moda adesso dei tiranni. —Ti mando una lettera da Monaco—di una certa Baronessa Miltitz— che vuole la mia corrispondenza—sarà qualche pazza letterata—vuoi che ne rispondo?——V'è qualche speranza per la villa Columbani—io farò il possibile come tu ben sai per averla.——Ti scrivo nella più gran fretta—poiche Papa parte a momenti.——Lega è qui—lo faccio agire come un' dizionario—quando mi bisogna una parola—la dom- ando di lui.— Ti prego continuare il tuo amor per me—e credermi sempre il tuo più sincero ed amantissimo—

+ + + + + [Scrawl]

Ravenna, July 29th, 1820

My Love + + + + I like your little brother very much[1]—he shows character and talent—Big eyebrows! and a stature which he has enriched, I think, at your expense—at least in those— —[2]do you understand me? His head is a little too hot for revolutions—he must not be too rash.

If A[lessandro] wants to make peace, I hope he will give you a *constitution* first—that being now the fashion with tyrants.

I am sending you a letter from Monaco [Munich?], from a certain Baronessa Miltitz, who wants to correspond with me, she must be a mad literary lady—do you want me to answer her?—

There is some hope of Villa Colombani—I shall do everything possible, as you know, to get it.—I am writing in the greatest haste—for Papa is leaving in a few minutes.—Lega is here—I am using him as a dictionary—when I need a word—I ask him. Pray continue your love for me—and always believe me your most sincere and loving + + + +

[TO JOHN MURRAY] *[August, 1820 post mark]*

Dear Murray—Act Second—which you are requested to acknow-ledge—as also act 1st. sent by last post.—You will have heard that after fifteen years litigation—& two favourable verdicts—I have lost the Rochdale question—but never mind—If I live—I will right myself —or it shall go hard.—Neither that nor any other villainy shall beat me down.

[Scrawl]

[TO CHARLES HANSON] *Ravenna. August 2d. 1820*

Dear Charles—I have received your letter.—That being the case— I hereby authorize you to enter an *Appeal* immediately.[1] Inform me when & where the further proceedings will come on.———

yrs. truly & affectly
BYRON

---

[1] Teresa's brother, Pietro Gamba, had just returned from his studies in Rome.
[2] Byron probably referred to Teresa's legs which were rather short.
[1] Byron had earlier concluded that the cost of continuing legal action to recover his rights in the Rochdale "collieries", illegally leased by his great uncle, the 5th Lord Byron, was not worth while. See July 27, 1820, to Kinnaird.

Amor mio + + + —La mia figlia è ammalata.—Ho licenziato
la vecchia.—Lega ha preso in casa questa *Clara* di quale io non so
niente—Lega risponderà pei suoi proprii peccati—io posso rispondere
solamente pei miei—ed appena per quei.—Ho cercato e cerco per un'
casino, sinora non si trova.—Guiccioli non ebbe diritto di fare il *cieco*—
dopo la tua lettera del' anno scorso—di quale egli mandò la copia al
Conte Pietro.——Se egli non era accorto allora—non dovrebbe
esserlo mai più.—Quello era il momento di dire, "fate la vostra
scelta"—e non otto mese dopo—mi pare che il tuo sentimento fù
già spiegato.——Papa ti farà ridere della rottura fra *il tenente
Elisei—e me*—Quel' buffone ha fatto finalmente ciò che io ho desiderato
abbastanza—(ma non seppi come compirlo)—egli ha preso sopra di
lui di essere offeso perche io non voleva comprare una *scrivania* da un'
artista protetto di lui—povero Sciocco—che voleva fare il maestro di
casa—e non fù capace.——Ti scrivo in fretta e sono sempre il tuo
+ + + + + + +

[Scrawl]

P.S.—I miei rispetti al' Conte P[ietro]—Perdona il mal' umor in cui
ho scritto—la malattia della bimba mi ha disturbato assai. La figlia
del' Cocchiere Rasponi &c. è stata già ricevuta in casa mia per servizio
della bimba.—

[TRANSLATION]   *Ravenna, August 3rd.*[1] *1820*

My Love + + + My daughter is ill. I have sent away the old
woman—Lega has taken into the house a certain Clara of whom I·
know nothing.—Lega will answer for his own sins—I can only
answer for mine—and hardly for those.—

I have looked and am looking for a country house, but it cannot yet
be found.

Guiccioli has no right to sham *blindness*—after your last year's letter
of which he sent a copy to Count Pietro—If he did not notice anything
then,—he should never have done so—That was the moment to say,
"Make your choice"—and not eight months later—it seems to me
that your feelings were already evident.

Papa will make you laugh about the break between Lieutenant
Elisei and me—the buffoon has at last done what I hoped for often

---

[1] So printed by Origo, but the manuscript clearly shows Ag[ost]o 2d, and is so
given in her Italian transcript.

enough (but did not know how to accomplish)—he has taken upon himself to be offended because I would not buy a *writing-desk* from an artist protected by him.—Poor fool—he wanted to run my house and found he couldn't.

I am writing in a hurry, and am always yours + + ⊦ + + + +

P.S.—My respects to Count P[ietro]. Pardon the ill humour in which I have written—the illness of the little girl has disturbed me so much.

The daughter of Rasponi's coachman has already been taken into my house to look after the child.

[TO COUNTESS TERESA GUICCIOLI]   *Ravenna. Agosto 3. 1820*

"⟨rabbiosa?⟩ come in Convento—"

La malattia dell'Allegrina—si può verificare dal'medico Rasi—o dal'-Conte Ruggiero.—Sta male molto.——Per la Cameriera della bimba —Lega dovrebbe rispondere—tutto che tocca a me rispondere è che io *non sono mai stato abasso*—e che non è mio costume.——Jeri una lettera del'Signor Hobhouse mi prevenga che tutti i pari che si allontanano dal' processo della Regina—saranno condannati ad una *multa*— o alla *Torre* (una prigione di Stato) con tutto ciò io non pensai andare— ma non credeva di ricevere per il premio dei disgusti che vado soffrendo per causa di altrui—delle rimprovere della persona stessa che gli cagiona.——La serva della bambina dice (ti dimenticai dirlo) che non voleva servire in casa *Guiccioli*—perche il Signor Cavaliere gode poca opinione in *tutto* e *dappertutto*—in queste ragioni io non posso entrare—lasciando cose simili al' mastro di casa.—— La mia Lite va in Appello.——La villa Spreti è già presa—e si pensa andare la settimana ventura. Sono sempre il

[Scrawl]

[TRANSLATION]   *Ravenna, August 3rd, 1820*

[in a rage?] like [you] in the Convent.[1]

Allegrina's illness can be confirmed by Dr. Rasi and by Count Ruggero.—She is very ill.—As to the child's maid, Lega will answer you. All that I have to answer for—is that I have never been *below stairs* and that I am not in the habit of going there.———

---

[1] Written in the upper left hand corner of the page (partly torn).

Yesterday a letter from Hobhouse told me that all the Peers who are absent from the Queen's trial will be condemned to a *fine* or to the Tower (a State prison)—in spite of which I do not think of going—but I do not think I should be rewarded for the trouble I am facing for someone else's sake, by the reproofs of the very person who is causing it.

The child's maid says (I forgot to tell you) that she would not take service in Guiccioli's house—because a poor opinion is held of the Cavaliere everywhere and by everyone.—I cannot go into all the reasons—leaving such things to the steward.

My law-suit is going forward [is being appealed].

Villa Spreti is already taken—and we are thinking of moving in next week.

I am always yours.

[TO COUNTESS TERESA GUICCIOLI] *Agosto 5.o 1820*

A. M. Ho ricevuto i fiori—ed il libro—vi ringrazio per tutto.——
Jeri vi scriveva in risposta alla vostra. Se Luigi non vi conviene—prendete un' altro—solamente io non posso adesso riceverlo in mia famiglia—siamo già troppi—e se egli resta affatto senza impiego—voi conoscete cosa saranno le probabili conseguenze—essendo quell' uomo a giorno dei fatti nostri. Lega è andato quest' oggi—alla villa Spreti.——La bambina ha la febbre,—e piuttosto gagliarda.—Ho veduto papa jeri sera—sono sempre

[Scrawl]

[TRANSLATION] *August 5th. 1820*

My Love—I have received the flowers—and the book—and thank you for everything.—Yesterday I wrote to you in reply to yours.

If Luigi does not suit you—take another man—only I cannot receive him into my household—we are already too many—and if he remains without employment you know what the probable consequences will be—since that man knows about all our affairs. Lega has gone today to Villa Spreti—the child has a fever and rather high.

I saw Papa yesterday—I am always

[Scrawl]

Dear Murray—I have sent you *three acts* of the tragedy, and am copying the others slowly but daily.—Enclosed are some verses Rose sent me two years ago and more.—They are excellent description.— Pray desire Douglas K[innaird] to give you a copy of my lines to the Po in 1819—they say "they be good rhymes" and will serve to swell your next volume. Whenever you publish—publish all as you will— except the two Juans—which had better be *annexed* to a *new* edition of the two first as they are not worth separate publication—and I won't barter about them.—Pulci is my favourite—that is my translation—I think it the *acme* of putting one language into another.——I have sent you my Say upon yr. recent books—Ricciarda[1] I have not yet read.— having lent it to the natives—who will pronounce upon it.—The Italians have as yet *no tragedy*—Alfieri's are political dialogues— except Mirra.—Bankes *has* done *miracles* of research and enterprize— salute him.—

I am yrs.
[scrawl]

Pray send me by the first opportunity some of *Waite's red* tooth-powder.—

Amor mio + + + —*"Si dimentichi ciò che è fatto"* tu dici—la bella dimenticanza! cosa dunque era mai *fatto?* la donna è brutta come l'Orco—una roba di *Lega*—non giovanissima—non di cattiva con-dotta—non ornata con la minima qualità per eccitare un'cappriccio—e tu sei degnata essere gelosa—ciò che io non dimenticho[*sic*] cosi facil-mente come tu lo perdoni *generosamente* a ti stessa.—V'è un' pessimo O; lo sento.——Allegrina si è già abusata di tuo regalo—rompendo una delle carrozzine.—La sua febbre è un' poco cessata. Io non anderò in mio "bel paese" *di No*—se tu non sei gelosa delle Cameriere lercie, —altrimente si.——

La proposizione di G[uiccioli]—mi pare non da accetare nè da rifiutare senza aver' prima ben pensata sopra.—Forse se potrebbe far' così—rispondendo—che egli *dopo la sua morte* dovrebbe assicurarti *due mila scudi di assegnamento*—ed allora tu sarai disposta ceder 400 della 1200 decretate da quel' più giusto di tutti i papi. .—La libertà

---

[1] *Ricciarda, Tragedia* (in five acts), by Ugo Foscolo (1820).

sarebbe una gran' cosa non v'è dubbio—con quella tua testa—ma 400 scudi sono una somma rispettabili in questi paesi—e non essere abandonati senza qualche compensa.——Per il resto—se vuoi fidare in me—io ti renderò independente di tutti—almeno per la mia vita.——Ma tu vai in colera sul' idea—volendo essere independente da te e di scrivere delle *"cantate"* nelle lunghissime epistole alla moda di Santa Chiara,—il convento dove si dice che tu eri sempre *rabbiosa*.

Sto leggendo il secondo volume della proposta di quel' becco classico Perticari.—Sarà ben' scritto—nello stile degno di Santa Chiara e del' trecento—ma sarebbe più *apropos* se il Signor Conte in vece di provare che *Dante* fosse il più grande dei uomini—(ciò che nessuno vuole per ora disdire—essendo la moda del' tempo presente) potrebbe assicurare i suoi contemporanei che il Suocero *Monti non* è il più vile ed infame; e un' disonore tale al' talento stesso che un'uomo di ingegno debbe arrossire appartenere al'istesso secolo con' quel' Giuda di Parnasso.——Mi pare che questa è una *"cantata"* o almeno la sarebbe in Inglese—ma i miei pensieri cadono sotto l'effeminate parole della lingua dei musici.—Sono rabbiosa—come tu eri "in convento" questa sera.——Ti bacio ed abbraccio 1000000 + + + volte. —Amami

[Scrawl]

P.S.—C'è un certo o lo sento nel' biglietto stesso—e molto, si— si—Saluta i Signori G[amba] ambedue—mi preme di essere in loro bone grazie.——Si sta preparando questa benedetta villa—il più presto che sia possibile.—per causa delle due bambine—Allegra—e *tu*

[TRANSLATION]   *Ravenna, August 7th, 1820*

My Love "Forget what has happened", you say—a fine forgetful-ness—but what then did happen? The woman is as ugly as an ogre— a thing of Lega's—not very young—not of bad reputation—not adorned with the slightest quality that might arouse a caprice. But you have condescended to be jealous—which I shall not so easily forget, as you so *generously* forgive yourself. It is a very naughty O: I feel it.

Allegrina has already spoiled your present—breaking one of the little carriages. Her fever is a little better. I shall not go to my fair country of NO—unless you are jealous of filthy maids—in which case I shall.

I think you should neither accept nor refuse Guiccioli's proposal without thinking it over. Perhaps one could do this—reply that he should *assign you* 2000 *scudi* after his death, and in return you would be prepared to give up 400 of the 1200 decreed by the most just of all Popes. Freedom would be a great thing, no doubt—with that head of yours—but 400 scudi is a respectable sum in this country—and not to be given up without any compensation.[1] For the rest—you can trust me—I will make you independent of everyone—at least during my lifetime. But you are made angry by the mere idea—and want to be independent on your own and to write *"Cantate"* in lengthy epistles in the style of Santa Chiara—the convent where you were said to be always in a rage.[2]

I am reading the second volume of the proposal of that classical cuckold Perticari.[3] It may be well-written—in a style worthy of Santa Chiara and the *trecento*—but it would be more à propos if the Count, instead of proving that *Dante* was the greatest of men (which no one at present wishes to deny, as he is now all the fashion) could prove to his contemporaries that his father-in-law Monti is not the most vile and infamous of men, and such a dishonour to talent itself, that a man of ability ought to blush to belong to the same century as that Judas of Parnassus.[4]

This seems to have become a *cantata*, or at least would be in English, but my thoughts fail me when I must express myself in the effeminate words of the language of musicians. I am in a rage this evening— as you were in the convent.—I kiss and embrace you 1,000,000 + + + + times. Love me.

P.S.—There is a certain O—I feel it in the note itself—and very much—yes. Greet both the G[amba]s—I value their good graces. That blessed villa is being got ready—as quickly as possible on account of the two little girls—Allegra—and *you.*

---

[1] Count Guiccioli had offered to overlook the objects and valuables which Teresa had taken away with her when she left his house if she would consent to having her allowance reduced. On the advice of her father she finally signed such an agreement on August 17. See Origo, p. 207.

[2] Byron wrote "rabbiosa" (in a rage), which Teresa tried to change to "studiosa" (studious).

[3] "Count Giulio Perticari (1790–1822) the son-in-law of the poet Vincenzo Monti, whose wife was notoriously unfaithful to him, was one of the defenders of the classicists, against the new-fangled romantics. The work referred to is *Dell'amor patrio di Dante* (1820)." (Origo, p. 280n.)

[4] Monti was a political turncoat, first praising Napoleon, and then turning to the Austrians.

My dear H.—It is my intention to *appeal*, not to "Philip fasting" but
to the Judges drunk[1] (with power it should seem) being thereto encouraged by the advice of Counsel, and my own natural propensity to dis-
crepancy and litigation.—Avise therefore the Douglas of this mine
intent—after fifteen years law—ten more are trifling—perhaps the
Childer may be the better for't, and I shall be no worse—being probably
defunct or in a madhouse—before the Suit will terminate.—Having
already quoted Holy Writ and Horace to Doug. in a letter—I have no
more filosophy nor fine sentences to bring to bear upon the subject,
and so I will go to law again.——The *Queen's* defence is not reticent—
unless Bergamo's *rod* be with his "b—ll—s in the bottle" because in
Italy the women prefer the "*Musici*" for two reasons—first they do
not impregnate them—and next as they never ("sbor[s]avo? mai")
spend—they go on "in eterno" and serve an elderly lady at all times—
being constantly in line of battle, or ready to [per?]form—without
exhausting themselves.—To my own knowledge—Velati the Capon
carried off Aglietti's adopted daughter from an *entire* man—and
Chevalier—and Soldier of twenty nine who would *have married* her—
so the said discarded Cavalier with the testicles told me himself—
lamenting to be cut out by a codless [Hermogesser?].—You remember
Juvenal—satire ninth[2]—or Dryden's delicate version of

"With his *two pounders* to perfection grown["]3

the youth castrated to mount the matron of ancient Rome without
risk of pregnancy—or too rapid an emission?
   On her Majesty's part—I have done my best through some
acquaintance here—to get persuaded the Macchiarelli's (the first
family of Pesaro and nearly related to Count Gamba my Dama's
father) to repair to England—where they have been [remanded?]
to attest her Majesty's morality.——For myself I see not what good
I could do to her—as my first duty is to call out her Attorney General[4]
—which will be due the first time I come among you—to which I have
no inclination—not on account of the Scoundrel whom I desire of all

[1] *Valerius Maximus, Facta et Dicta memorabilia*, Book VI, Chapter 2 ("Appeal
from Philip drunk to Philip sober.")
[2] The Ninth Satire of Juvenal recounts the woes of a male prostitute.
[3] Dryden, *Works* (Oxford English Texts Edition, edited Kingsley, Vol. 2,
p. 599: California Edition, Vol. 4, p. 177). In Dryden's translation of the 6th
Satire of Juvenal. The passage refers to the preference of Roman women for
eunuchs.
[4] Henry Brougham was the chief defence counsel for the Queen.

things to destroy—at any personal peril—but because I hate the Country more than I do even that cowardly villain;—and I do not feel sure that anything could compensate to me the loathing I should feel to be in it.—I am glad to hear that you are doing well—continue to do so—I have always thought Parliament your element—and I [think] so still.—How much bet[ter for?] you to have started *then* t[han] ten years sooner—where and what are the Wards—and Mills's? (that poor creature) and Vernons[5]—and so forth—whose earlier elections and crude attempt, used to haunt you with a phantom of superiority?—I think you have "doubled up those beggars in brass" as the Life Guardsman said.——Fletcher reads you in Galignani—and comes grinning over your speeches to me—he has already noted Seventeen—a respectable number for a virgin Session—your maiden Speech—was like a widow's or a Spinning [house][6] maidenhead—so old Mansell is gone.—We expect a Revolution here daily by the diligence, it has worked at Naples.—There is little to say of this city—except—that like "Bob Acres"—they "kill a man a week"[7] it is the Romagnole fashion—however—they are decent savages—and made the best troops of B[uonaparte]'s Italian army—so he said himself—

I am yrs. [Scrawl]

[TO COUNTESS TERESA GUICCIOLI]   *Ravenna. Agosto 8.0 1820*

Amor mio + + + —Il tuo biglietto non è venuto che in questo punto—troppo tarde per permittere ch'io vado in campagna oggidi. ——Io ho già dato l'ordine a Lega fermare questa benedetta villa—ma finche mando la mia famiglia la—non sono stato nell' intenzione di venire a Filetto—non volendo nelle circonstanze attuali dare nessun' vantaggio al' Sig[no]r Cavaliere il quale correrebbe subito dal' Cardinale con' mila bugie e con' qualche *verità*.——Egli tiene delle Spie sopra di me—e jeri mancava poco che io non bastonassi un' uomo in Pigneta—che si mettava seguirmi dappertutto—fermarsi dove mi fermai e sempre tenersi vicino—finche io perdetti la pazienza e lo feci intendere che se egli non seguitava la sua strada—sarebbe peggio

---

5 John William Ward (1781–1833), later (1823) Viscount Dudley and Ward, and in 1827 first Earl of Dudley, was Tory M.P. for Downton in 1802 at the age of 23. Robert Pemberton Milnes (not Mills) left Trinity College in 1804 (a year before Byron entered) and became M.P. for Pontefract in 1806. Vernon, unidentified.

6 Cambridge University prison, where prostitutes were confined.

7 *The Rivals*, Act V, scene 3.

per lui—allora egli è 'scomparso.——Per il resto—amor mio+—ti ho scritto jeri—la lettera sarà già da papa.—Salutami il primogenito di casa Gamba—il *Quiroga* di Ravenna—e credimi sempre il tuo più fed[ele] + + +

[Scrawl]

P.S.—L'Allegrina sta meglio.——

[TRANSLATION]   *August 8th, 1820*

My Love + + + —Your note has not come until now, too late to permit me to go out to the country today————I have already given orders to Lega to retain this blessed Villa—but until I have settled my household there—it is not my intention to go to Filetto—as I do not wish, in these circumstances, to give an advantage to the Cavaliere, who would at once run to the Cardinal with a thousand lies and some *truths*—————

He has set spies upon me—and yesterday I nearly came to blows with a man in the pine-forest—who had begun to follow me every-where—stopping when I stopped—and always standing nearby—until I lost patience and made him understand that if he did not go on his way—it would be the worse for him—at that he disappeared.

As to the rest, my love I wrote to you yesterday, the letter must be already at Papa's. Greet the first-born of the Gambas for me—the Quiroga[1] of Ravenna—and believe me always your most faithful.

P.S.—Allegrina is better.

[TO AUGUSTA LEIGH]   *Ravenna. August 10th. 1820*

Dearest Augusta—Of the bond I know nothing—and of course *never had—nor could have*—any intention of acting upon it[1]—nor could Mr. Hanson do so without my orders.—I desire to be considered as *not* one of Col. Leigh's creditors.—I do not know how the bond came to be executed.—I am sure it was no wish of mine.—Whatever I can do to forward his disentanglement—shall be done—but what can I do? at this distance—and after four years' and as many months' absence?— If any assurance—or if *the destruction of the bond—will do it*—it shall

[1] Quiroga was a general at the head of the Spanish revolutionaries. The Italian Carbonari in the Romagna had adopted his name as a password.
[1] Byron gave Augusta and her husband £3,000 in 1814 to help clear up Colonel Leigh's debts. It was ostensibly a loan but was intended as a gift.

be done—but it seems to me that the Purchaser of 6 Mile B[ottom] is searching for *pretexts.*—Let this letter be your *warrant* to Messrs. Kinnaird—Hobhouse—or to Mr. Hanson.—I don't know how I can be more explicit.——It would give me the greatest pleasure to see you again—but I do not perceive any *immediate* prospect.—Pray excuse my rare epistles.—I have almost given up letter-writing except on absolute business.—Believe me

> ever & affectionately yours
>
> BYRON

[TO COUNTESS TERESA GUICCIOLI] *Ravenna. Agosto 11.o 1820*

Amor Mio + + + —Ti mando Lega, che ti dirà tutto che pensiamo fare per il casino &c. io verrò il più presto che si può combinare.—Io sono disposto di pensare in rapporto ai accomodamenti con A[lessandro] come la tua famiglia ne pensa per il tuo vantaggio.—Sono nella più gran' fretta il tuo più

> [Scrawl]

Scrivimi tutto che tu hai da dire contra E—si debbe dica [sic]

[TRANSLATION] *Ravenna. August 11th. 1820*

My Love + + + + —I am sending Lega to you, who will tell you everything that we are thinking of doing for the country house, etc. I will come as soon as it can be arranged.—I am disposed to think, in relation to the accommodations with A[lessandro], as your family thinks of it for your advantage.—I am in the greatest hurry your most

> [Scrawl]

Write me everything you have to say against E—[that can be said?][1]

[TO COUNTESS TERESA GUICCIOLI (*a*)] *Ravenna. Agosto 12.o 1820*

Amor Mio +—Bisogna che tu mi dici la tua *autorità*—per ciò che tu hai contato di E.—Non potrebbe venire nè dal' tuo padre nè dal tuo fratello—perche non ha confidenza con loro—dunque tu hai avuto delle visite—di quali non parli—ti prego—di dirmi il nome del' narratore altrimenti io *non* verrò in campagna. Se tu mi rispondi subito—io verrò la Settimana ventura—senza dubbio—ma per la

---

[1] Translated by Professor Nancy Dersofi.

156

domenica prossima—non posso promettere.—Son sempre e tutto tuo. Dimmi il nome di quello che dice che E. ha detto così

+ + + [Scrawl]

P.S.—Delle altre cose che tu domandi ti risponderò a voce.——

[TRANSLATION (*a*)]   *Ravenna. August 12th. 1820*

My Love +—It is necessary for you to tell me your *authority* for what you have told me about E.[1]—It could come neither from your father nor your brother—because he is not intimate with them—therefore you have had some visits—which you do not speak of—I pray you—tell me the name of the narrator, otherwise I will *not* come to the country. If you reply immediately—I will come next week—without fail—but for next Sunday—I cannot promise.—I am always and all yours. Tell me the name of the person who says that E. spoke thus + + +

P.S.—To the other things you ask about I will reply in person.[2]—

[TO COUNTESS TERESA GUICCIOLI (*b*)]   *Ravenna. Agosto 12.0 1820*

Amor mio + + + —Per La domenica non si può combinare—la bambina va' in campagna quel giorno—e vi sono mille cose di fare e disfare, tu conosci il numero di mia famiglia—&c. ti prego avere un' poco di pazienza—in due o tre giorni ci rivedremmo.—Prima di avere l'avviso formale del' intenzione dei Pari sopra ciò che la Gazzetta annunzia—io non so che risposta dare—quando l'avrò troverò una difesa nella malattia della bambina—e nella distanza.——io non so se la richiamata comprende anche quei via dal' paese—o solamente i *lords* ancora in Inghilterra.—Mi pare un' atto discretamente dispotico —e se veramente tocca a me di essere compreso in questo numero, non sarà senza una protesta delle più forti.——Ti bacio 10000 volte e sarò

+ + + + [Scrawl]

[TRANSLATION (*b*)]   *Ravenna. August 12th. 1820*

My love + + + —Sunday can't be managed—the child is going to the country that day and there are a thousand things to be done

---

[1] Probably Lieutenant Giovanni Battista Elisei, with whom Byron used to ride in the Pineta. He is mentioned frequently in earlier letters.

[2] Translated by Professor Nancy Dersofi.

and undone, you know the members [numbers?] of my household. Pray have a little patience—in two or three days we shall see each other again.

Before receiving the formal notice of the Peers' intention about the *Gazette's* announcement—I don't know what answer to give—when I get it I will find an excuse in the child's illness and the distance. I don't know if this call includes people who are out of the country—or only the Lords still in England. It seems to me a fairly despotic act—and if I really am included in the number, it will not be without the strongest of protests.—I kiss you 10000 times and shall be + + + +

[TO JOHN MURRAY]   *Ravenna. August 12th. 1820*

Dear Murray—Ecco—the fourth Act.—Received *powder—tincture —books.*—The first welcome—second ditto the prose at least—but no *more modern* poesy—I pray—neither Mrs. Hewoman's[1]—nor any female or male Tadpole of Poet Turdsworth's[2]—nor any of his ragamuffins.——Send me more *tincture* by all means—& Scott's novels—the Monastery.—We are on the eve of a *row* here—Italy's primed and loaded—and many a finger itching for the trigger.—So write letters while you can. I can say no more in mine for they open all.—

yrs. very truly,
[scrawl]

P.S.—Recollect that I told you months ago—what would happen—it is the same all over the *boot*—though the *heel* has been the first to kick—never mind these enigmas—they'll explain themselves.——

[TO JOHN MURRAY]   *Ravenna. August 17th. 1820*

Dear Moray—In t'other parcel is the 5th Act.—Enclosed in this are some notes—historical.——Pray—send me *no proofs*—it is the thing I can least bear to see.——The preface shall be written and sent in a few days.—Acknowledge the Arrival by return of post.—

yrs. [Scrawl]

P.S.—The time for the *Dante* would be now—(did not her Majesty occupy all nonsense) as Italy is on the Eve of great things.——I hear

1 Mrs. Felicia Hemans, a popular poetess of the day.
2 First two letters written over *Wo.*

158

Mr. Hoby says "that it makes him weep to see her[.] She reminds him so much of Jane Shore"

> Mr. Hoby the Bootmaker's soft heart is sore
> For seeing the Queen makes him think of Jane Shore—
> And in fact such a likeness should always be seen—
> Why should *Queens not be whores?* every *Whore* is a *Quean.*

this is only an epigram to the *ear.*——I think she will win—I am sure she ought—poor woman.——Is it true that absent peers are to be mulcted? does this include those who have not taken the oaths in the present parliament?—I can't come, and I won't pay.——

[TO AUGUSTA LEIGH]   *Ravenna. August 19th. 1820*

My dearest Augusta—I always loved you better than any earthly existence, and I always shall unless I go mad.——And if I did *not* so love you—still I would not persecute or oppress any one wittingly —especially for debts—of which I know the *agony by experience.*—Of Colonel Leigh's bond—I really have forgotten all particulars—except that it was *not* of *my wishing.*—And I never would nor ever will be *pressed* into the *Gang of his creditors.*—I would *not take the money*— if he had it.—You may judge if I would dun him having it not.—— Whatever measure I can take for his extrication—will be taken.— Only tell me how—for I am ignorant—and far away.—*Who does* and *who can* accuse *you* of "interested views"? I think people must have gone into Bedlam—such things appear to me so very incomprehensible[.] Pray explain—

yrs. ever & truly
BYRON

[TO COUNT ALESSANDRO GUICCIOLI]   *Ravenna. Agosto 21. 1820*

Illustrissimo Signore—Io sono stato informato che in una lettera da voi scritta a Roma in data delli 24 Giugno 1820 mi avete dichiarato uomo di *35* anni nel anno 1819—dal che risulterebbe che io ne avrei ora *36.*—Ciò mi sorprende assai, non potendo immaginare come nel ricoviere all Biografia degli uomini viventi per altre notizie riguardanti la mia persona per favorire le vostro circonstanze, vi sia Sfuggita poi solamente quel passo dove si parla della mia nascità come accaduta nell' anno *1788.*—il tutto al più mi fa' di anni ⟨*32*⟩ *trenta due.*—Vl ringrazio del lustro che mi avete generosamente regolato, ma non trovandomi in caso di accetarlo vi ne avverto,—e sono certo che un uomo a cui sta a cuore l'ordine in ogni cosa come voi siete, riceverà di buon grado questo mio avviso per corregere un errore che potrebbe un giorno notarsi ne' vostri archivi.—Se io nell' estendere un memoriale per la *vostra storia* vi facessi uomo di *Settanta* anni crescendo a voi pure un *Settimo* di età, credo non potrebbe piacervi, o per certo *io* non soffrirei di commettere questa ingiustizia che non è piccola toccando la verità: e voi sapete troppo bene essere tanto della natura umana il domandar anni da *Dio*; quanto il ricusarne degli *uomini*.—

> Ho l'onore di essere il vostro um[ilissim]o
> dev[otissim]o Servitore

BYRON

[TRANSLATION]   *Ravenna. August 21st. 1820*

Sir—I have been informed that in a letter written by you to Rome, dated June 24th, 1820,[1] you stated me to have been a man of 35 in 1819, which would now make me 36. This surprises me greatly, since I cannot conceive how, in consulting the *Biography of Living Men* for other information regarding my person, for your own purposes, you should have overlooked only the passage which refers to my birth as having taken place in the year 1788, which makes me at most *thirty-two*.

I thank you for the "lustrum" with which you have generously presented me, but not finding myself disposed to accept it, I cannot but tell you so; and I am sure that a man to whom correctness in everything is important, as it is to you, will receive my information in good part, so as to rectify an error which may some day be observed in your archives. If I, in drawing up a memorandum of *your history*, were to make you out a man of *seventy*, adding one seventh to your age, you would not assuredly be pleased, and I will certainly not bear this injustice—not a small one, since it affects the truth. You well know that it is as much in human nature to ask for additional years from *God*, as it is to refuse them from *Men*.

I have the honour to be your most humble and devoted servant

BYRON

[1] This letter was written after Byron had seen Count Guiccioli's letter to Pietro Gamba, then in Rome, complaining about his wife's lover. Byron perhaps took this way of letting Guiccioli know that he had seen that letter without mentioning its main subject, and at the same time took some delight in pointing up the difference in their ages.

Dear Murray—None of your *damned proofs* now *recollect*—print—paste——plaster—and destroy—but don't let me have any of your cursed printer's trash to pore over.—For the rest I neither know nor care.—

yrs.
[Scrawl]

[TO COUNTESS TERESA GUICCIOLI] *Ravenna. Agosto 24.o 1820*

Amor Mio + + + —Altro che deliquio!—la Fanni in idea—basta—la Fanni in persona sarebbe la Morte—per non dire l'inferno—in questa stagione—immagina pure la Signora Silvestrini e il caldo ensieme!—no—no—no. ——Scrivi—manda—fermala—liberami—altramente—non so cosa sarà di me—lo diceva—lo prevedeva—viene—se veramente arriva—mi faccio frate subito, e la Chiesa *guadagnerà* che ha perduta, perdendo Lega il [word torn out with seal] Sarò da te Lunedi—intanto ti mando un' certo libretto—Adolphe—scritto da un' antico amico della De Stael—di cui ho sentito la detta de Stael in 1816 dire delle *orrori* a Coppet—del suo cuore—e di sua condotta verso di lei[.] Ma il libretto è ben scritto e pur troppo vero. Amami—ricordami e sopra tutto—risparmiami la Fanni o vado in deliquio + + + + +

[TRANSLATION] *Ravenna, August 24th, 1820*

My Love + + + —Swoon, indeed! Fanny in theory is bad enough—Fanny in person would be Death—not to say Hell, in this weather.

Imagine Signora Silvestrini and the heat together! No—no—no. Write,—send—stop her—deliver me—otherwise I don't know what will become of me—I said it—I foresaw it—she is coming. If she really comes—I shall turn monk at once, and the Church will gain ——what she has lost in losing Lega, the [word torn out with seal].

I shall be with you on Monday;—Meanwhile I send you a little book, *Adolphe*[1]—written by an old friend of de Stael—about whom I heard de Stael say horrible things at Coppet in 1816, with regard to his feelings and his behaviour to her.—But the book is well-written

---

[1] Benjamin Constant's *Adolphe* was not a very tactful gift to Teresa, for, as Byron later told Lady Blessington, it was "The truest picture of the misery unhallowed liaisons produce."

and only too true. Love me—remember me and above all—deliver me from Fanny or I shall swoon. + + + + + +

[TO JOHN MURRAY] *Ravenna. August 24th. 1820*

Dear Murray—Enclosed is an additional *note* to the play sent you the other day.—The preface is sent too,—but as I wrote it in a hurry (the latter part particularly) it may want some alterations—if so let me know—& what your parlour boarders think of the matter;— remember—I can form no opinion of the merits of this production— and will abide by your Synod's.——If you should publish—publish them all about the same time,—it will be at least a collection of opposites.—You should not publish the new Cantos of *Juan separately*— but let them go in quietly with the first reprint of the others—so that they may make little noise—as they are not equal to the first. The Pulci—the Dante—and the Drama—you are to publish as you like if at all.—

[Scrawl]

[TO JOHN MURRAY] [*August 25? 1820*] *p.m. Sept. 14, 1820*

The Italian vespers are fixed for the tenth of Septr.[1]——You understand this for I dare not trust more to paper and scrawl this as unintelligibly as I can—if they strike you may or may not hear from me again—but that don't matter, write.——

[TO PERCY BYSSHE SHELLEY] *August 25th. 1820*

Dear Shelley—I should prefer hearing from you—as I must decline all correspondence with Claire who merely tries to be as irrational and provoking as she can be—all which shall not alter my regards to the Child—however much it contributes to confirm my opinion of the mother.—My respects to Mrs. S. believe me

yrs. v[er]y truly
[Scrawl]

[TO COUNTESS TERESA GUICCIOLI] *Ravenna. Agosto 26.o 1820*

Amor Mio + + + —Le circonstanze di "Adolphe" furono assai differente.—Ellenore non era mai *maritata*, ebbe molti anni più del'

---

[1] The date set for the supposed uprising of the Italian Carbonari against the Austrians.

162

Adolphe—non era amabile—&c. &c. Non pensare più sopra cose così dissimili in tutte le forme.—Per la lettera di A[lessandro] bisogna cominciare una risposta in nome *mio* il quale io sottoscriverò—facendo conoscere la verità della sua condotta con *me*—coi varj raggiri usati da lui per le interesse.—Non dimenticare anche l'*età*—perche mostra dal' principio—una sofistica determinazione di nascondere la verità.— Papa ha tutti i documenti—necessarj—nella representazione già fatta da lui al'Cardinale.—Dal' momento che io conobbi A[lessandro] Egli fece delle proposizioni strane—volendo ch' io sposassi l'Attilia—e che comprassi la *Casa Raisi* qui a Ravenna.—Per l'affare di Bologna e del resto—siete già informati.—Pensa a questo.——Lunedi ci rivedremmo—amami—mio solo amore + + + e credemi sempre tutto tuo +

[Scrawl]

[TRANSLATION]   *Ravenna, August 26th, 1820*

My Love + + + The circumstances of Adolphe are very different.[1] Ellenore was not married, she was many years older than Adolphe— she was not amiable—etc., etc.—Don't think any more about things so dissimilar in every way.—

As to Alessandro's letter you must begin an answer in my name, which I shall sign—telling the truth about his conduct to me—with the various *tricks* used by him in his own interest. Do not forget also the *age*, because it shows, from the beginning, a deliberate determination to conceal the truth. Papa has all the documents necessary for the statement which he has already made to the Cardinal. From the first moment that I knew A[lessandro], he began to make strange proposals to me—wanting me to marry Attilia[2]—and to buy the *Casa Raisi*[3] here in Ravenna. As to the Bologna affair and the rest, you already know about it.[4]—See to this.—On Monday we shall see each other again.

Love me—my only love + + + and believe me always your +

---

[1] Teresa was much hurt by Byron's sending her this book, imagining that he felt the unhappy love affair of Constant and Madame de Staël was similar to their own.

[2] Attilia was Count Guiccioli's daughter by a former marriage. She was then twelve years old.

[3] Count Pompeo Raisi, a historian of Ravenna, died in 1818. His palazzo was for sale.

[4] During the summer of 1819, while Byron was in Bologna with the Guicciolis, the Count asked him for a large loan, which Byron declined to make. (Origo, p. 116).

Amor Mio + + + —Papa ti scriverà la ragione più forte perche non vengo da te oggi come si era combinato, e Lega ti dirà un altra ragione.—Ti prego, a questi dispiaceri non aggiungere delle tue rimprovere—poiche io non ho colpa.—— Ho ceduto solamente alle ragione di papa—il quale mi pregò fortamente non andare adesso—— finche il Cardinale sia chetato.——Non ho avuto delle tue nuove oggi —dunque non dirò più senonche sono e sempre sarò il tuo più

+ + + [Scrawl]

[TRANSLATION]   Ravenna. August 27th. 1820

My Love + + + —Papa will write you the chief reasons why I am not coming today as we had arranged, and Lega will tell you another reason. Pray do not add to these troubles your reproaches— because it is not my fault—I have given way only to Papa's arguments —who begged me strongly not to come now—until the Cardinal has calmed down.—

I have no news of you today—So I shall not say any more, except that I am and always shall be your most + + +

[TO JOHN MURRAY]   August 28th. 1820

For the tragedy of Marino Faliero—Additions &c. Alterations &c. &c.

In the Doge's ⟨Speech it⟩ Soliloquy in act fourth—after—
                    "He is gone
And on each footstep moves a life.—["]
                    ___
                    Add
                    'Tis done.
Now the destroying Angel hovers oer
⟨Saint Marks⟩ Venice, and pauses ere he sounds the summons
                                        __
                                        or
                    ere he pours the Vial
Even as the Eagle overlooks his prey
                    __
                    or the serpent
And fixed, as 'twere, a moment in mid air
Suspends the motion of his mighty wings—

164

Then darts with his unerring beak.—
Thou Day!
That slowly walk'st the waters—March &c. &c.
And in act *5th.* in the Doge's concluding speech—for—
"Beggars for Nobles—*Lazars* for a people—
put   *Pandars* for a people.

[TO JOHN MURRAY]   *Ravenna. August 29th. 1820*

Dear Murray—I enclose to you for Mr. Hobhouse (with liberty to
read and translate or get translated—if you can—it will be *nuts* for
Rose) *copies* of the letter of Cavalier Commendatore G[uiccioli] to
his wife's brother at Rome—and other documents—explaining this
business which has put us all in hot water here. Remember—that
Guiccioli is *telling his own story*—true in some things—and very
false in the details—the Pope has decreed against him;—so also have
his wife's relations which is much.—No man has a right to pretend
blindness—after letting a girl of twenty travel with another man—
and afterwards taking that man into his house.——*You* want to
know *Italy*—there's more than Lady Morgan[1] can tell me—in these
sheets if carefully perused.

                                                    yrs.
                                                    [Scrawl]
The enclosed are authentic. I have seen the originals.—

[TO JOHN MURRAY]   [*August 30? 1820*] *p.m. Sept. 19, 1820*

The "Advice to Julia"[1] is excellent in gay poetry—& must have
been written by a Gentleman.—The Juan drawings are quite beautiful.[2]
—Ada—all but the mouth—is the picture of her mother—and I am
glad of it.—

---

[1] Lady Morgan's *Italy* was published in 1821.
[1] Henry Luttrell (1765?–1851), a natural son of the second Lord Carhampton,
noted as a wit and writer of society verse, published his *Advice to Julia, a Letter in
Rhyme* in 1820. Byron told Lady Blessington that Luttrell was "the best sayer of
good things, and the most epigrammatic conversationalist I ever met." And he
praised the *Advice to Julia* as "pointed, witty, and full of observation, showing in
every line a knowledge of society, and a tact rarely met with." (Blessington,
Lovell Ed., p. 76.)
[2] The painter R. Westall made 21 drawings for *Don Juan*. They were engraved
by C. Heath and published by Finden in 1820.

165

Ravenna. August 30th. 1820

My dearest Augusta—I have answered your two last letters—and at present I merely enclose you some *hair* which you may keep some of and throw the rest away—I have kept it for you some time.

ever dearest yrs.
[Scrawl]

[TO COUNTESS TERESA GUICCIOLI] *Ravenna. Agosto 30. 1820*

Amor mio + + + —Post dimani spero di essere con te.—Tu hai fatto benissimo nel strappazzare Papa in vece di me—prima perche non era colpa mia—e poi—perche una lettera lunga avrebbe fatto venire un forte *deliquio.*—Ciò che tu dici della bambina mi consola molto—fuori di quella disposizione di *canzonare* la quale può divenire un costume molto piacevole pei altri[,] ma che tosto o tardi porta del' danno a chi lo pratica.—Mi riservo per dirti a voce che penso della *R.*—per tante ragioni.—Guarda cosa tu scrivi sopra quel' proposito.— Ti dirò perche.——I miei rispetti a Papa—amami sempre come il tuo più sincero e amicissimo + + +

[Scrawl]

P.S.—Ti mando un libro francese dove troverai molto sopra Rousseau—e le sue relazioni con l'Epinay.—Quel' uomo era pazzo—e non ben trattato dai suoi amici.——Post dimani speriamo a rivederci —vi è un gran' o—+ lo sento—

[TRANSLATION] *Ravenna, August 30th, 1820*

My Love + + + —I hope to be with you on the day after tomorrow. You have done very well to scold Papa—instead of me—firstly because it was not my fault—and then—because a long letter would have made me *swoon.* What you say about the child comforts me very much—except for that tendency to mockery, which may become a habit very agreeable for others, but which sooner or later brings trouble to those who practice it.

I will wait to tell you by word of mouth what I think of R.—for many reasons. Be careful what you write on this subject. I will tell you why.

My respects to Papa—love me always as your most sincere and very friendly + + +

166

P.S.—I am sending you a French book in which you will find a lot about Rousseau and his relations with Mme. Epinay. That man was mad—and not well treated by his friends.

Let us hope we may see each other again the day after tomorrow—there is a big o———+I feel it———

[TO RICHARD BELGRAVE HOPPNER]   *Ravenna, August 31, 1820*

. . . Allegra has been ill but is getting better in the country where the air is much purer—the heat has been tremendous. Take care of your little boy. . . .

[TO DOUGLAS KINNAIRD]   *Ravenna. August 31st. 1820*

Important

Dear Douglas—If you did your wont—you would get me out of the funds before they fall—to zero or a war—if you knew what I *know* and you will all know soon enough—you would do this directly. Hanson *delays on purpose*—because he hates an Irish mortgage. You should use pretty *peremptory* manner which is excellent in business.— Do it now or never—a month hence it will be too late—I can't say *why*—by post.

I wish to advise you—that the Bankers Lunghi having lost their monopoly of Salt and Tobacco in Romagna have no further correspondence now at Ravenna—Ergo—I must draw a thousand or more pounds out of their bank—to lodge here—else I can have no cash but by a double per centage on the bills—Till now they had an agent at Ravenna and all went on as usual. You seem disturbed in England— and ready to present—here we are cocked—and it is but the drawing of a trigger.

yours
[Scrawl]

Murray has the play—which is at least as good as Mr. Turdsworth's Peter Bell. Imagine the state of things here—when yesterday they sent to know why I had such a quantity of Cartridges—The fact is that as you know pistol and rifle shooting has been always rather a pastime of mine—and I have hitherto indulged it —without rendering accounts to the Commander in Chief.

Dear Sir—I pray you to make haste with the title deeds—otherwise there will be a half year's interest lost—and the funds are falling daily. —See what you do by your confounded delays.——Pray—expedite— dispatch.—You have never sent me Counsel's opinion—on an appeal— as promised.—I am in favour of the appeal—if it shows a glimpse of ultimate success.—The deeds you sent me—in the winter cannot be signed for lack of *English witnesses.*——With my best remembrances to all your family believe me

yours very truly & affectly
BYRON

[TO JOHN MURRAY (*a*)]   *Ravenna. August 31st. 1820*

Dear Murray—I *have "put my Soul* into the tragedy" (as you *if* it) but you know that there are damned Souls as well as tragedies.— Recollect that it is not a political play—though it may look like it—it is strictly historical, read the history—and judge.——Ada's picture is her mother's—I am glad of it—the mother made a good daughter.—— Send me Gifford's opinion—& never mind the Archbishop—I can neither send you away—nor give you a hundred pistoles—nor a better taste.—I send you a tragedy and you ask for "facetious epistles" a little like your predecessor—who advised Dr. Prideaux to put "some more humour into his Life of Mahomet".[1]—The drawings for Juan are superb—the brush has beat the poetry——In the annexed proof of Marino Faliero—the half line "The law my Prince————["] must be stopped thus——as the Doge interrupts Bertuccio Faliero.—— Bankes is a wonderful fellow—there is hardly one of my School and College Contemporaries that has not turned out more or less cele-brated.—Peel—Palmerstone [sic]—Bankes—Hobhouse—Tavistock— Bob Mills [i.e. Milnes][2]—Douglas Kinnaird—&c. &c. have all of them talked and been talked of—then there is your Galley Knight— and all that—but I believe that (except Milman perhaps) I am still the youngest of the fifteen hundred first of living poets—as Wm Turdsworth is the oldest—Galley Knight is some Seasons my Senior—

---

[1] Humphrey Prideaux (1648–1724), Dean of Norwich, published *The True Nature of Imposture fully displayed in the Life of Mahomet* in 1697. It is said that when he offered it for publication, the bookseller wished that he had "put more humour" into it.

[2] See Nov. 9, 1820, to Murray, note 4.

pretty Galley! so *"amiable"*!!—you Goose you—such fellows should be flung into Fleet Ditch—I would rather be a Galley Slave than a Galley Knight—so utterly do I despise the middling mountebank's mediocrity in every thing but his Income.——

We are here going to fight a little next month—if the Huns don't cross the Po—and probably if they do—I can't say more now.—If anything happens—you have matter for a posthumous work—and Moore has my Memoirs in M.S.S.—so pray be civil.——Depend upon it there will be savage work if once they begin here—the French Courage proceeds from vanity—the German from phlegm—the Turkish from fanaticism & opium—the Spanish from pride—the English from coolness—the Dutch from obstinacy—the Russian from insensibility—but the *Italian* from *anger*—so you'll see that they will spare nothing.——What you say of Lady Caroline Lamb's Juan at the Masquerade[3] don't surprise me—I only wonder that She went so far as "the *Theatre*" for "*the Devils*" having them so much more natural at home—or if they were busy—she might have borrowed the bitch her Mother's—Lady Bessborough to wit——The hack whore of the last half century.——

[Scrawl]

[TO JOHN MURRAY (*b*)]   *Ravenna—August 31st. 1820*

Dear Murray—In the Doge's Soliloquy in Act fourth—after the lines—

He's gone—
with   falls
And on each footstep flits a life.—["]

Add

Tis fixed.—
Now the destroying Angel hovers oer
Venice—and pauses ere he pours the Vial
or
ere he sounds the Summons.
Even as the Eagle overlooks his prey
or
the Serpent

[3] Lady Caroline Lamb appeared at a masquerade at Almack's as Don Juan surrounded by a host of devils.

169

And for a moment poised in middle air
Suspends the motion of his mighty wings
Then darts with his unerring beak.—
          or
          swoops
                    Thou day—
          That slowly walk'st the waters &c. &c.

This version is altered since the one I sent last week—take which
Gifford thinks the best.—

                    In Act *5th*.
Instead of

          Beggars for Nobles—*Lazars* for a people—
          put   *pandars* for a people.

[TO THOMAS MOORE]   *Ravenna, August 31st, 1820*

D—n your "mezzo cammin"[1]—you should say "the prime of life,"
a much more consolatory phrase. Besides, it is not correct. I was
born in 1788, and consequently am but thirty-two. You are mistaken
on another point. The "Sequin Box" never came into requisition, nor
is it likely to do so. It was better that it had, for then a man is not
bound, you know.[2] As to reform, I did reform—what would you have?
"Rebellion lay in his way, and he found it."[3] I verily believe that nor
you, nor any man of poetical temperament, can avoid a strong passion
of some kind. It is the poetry of life. What should I have known or
written, had I been a quiet, mercantile politician, or a lord in waiting?
A man must travel, and turmoil, or there is no existence. Besides, I
only meant to be a Cavalier Servente, and had no idea it would turn
out a romance, in the Anglo fashion.

However, I suspect I know a thing or two of Italy—more than Lady
Morgan has picked up in her posting. What do Englishmen know of
Italians beyond their museums and saloons—and some hack * *,
en passant? Now, I have lived in the heart of their houses, in parts of
Italy freshest and least influenced by strangers,—have seen and be-
come (*pars magna fui*) a portion of their hopes, and fears, and passions,

---

[1] Moore had congratulated Byron on having arrived at the age of 33, the
"Mezzo cammin" (middle of our life's course) (*Dante, Inferno*, Canto I, stanza 1).
[2] Byron had already boasted of his "Sequin Box" to Kinnaird (see Jan. 27,
1819, Vol. 6, p. 98), and when Moore visited him in October, 1819, he observed
his "hoarding box".
[3] Henry IV, Part I, Act V, scene 1.

and am almost inoculated into a family. This is to see men and things as they are.

You say that I called you "quiet"—I don't recollect any thing of the sort. On the contrary, you are always in scrapes.

What think you of the Queen? I hear Mr. Hoby says, "that it makes him weep to see her, she reminds him so much of Jane Shore."

> Mr. Hoby the bootmaker's heart is quite sore,
> For seeing the Queen makes him think of Jane Shore;
> And, in fact, * * * * * * * * *[4]

Pray excuse this ribaldry. What is your Poem about? Write and tell me all about it and you.

Yours, &c.

P.S.—Did you write the lively quiz on Peter Bell?[5] It has wit enough to be yours, and almost too much to be any body else's now going. It was in Galignani the other day or week.

[TO COUNTESS TERESA GUICCIOLI]   *Ravenna.* ⟨*Ag.o*⟩ *Sette. 4.o 1820*

A. M. + + + —Sarò con te *Mercoledì* sera—domani vado al' mare.—Un' altra ragione per quale mi ritardo è—che il Porto *Corsini* (m'intendi?) non me pare in un' stato per *ingresso*—*domani*— se vuole almeno 4 giorni per il flusso e riflusso—no?—I Suoceri vivono ancora—forse—io non posso sapere niente sin' a Giovedì.— Ferdinando G[uiccioli] sta per morire—poveretto—Papa ti dirà come, e perche.—Amami sempre—post domani + + + —o! [several words cut off]

[TRANSLATION]   *Ravenna. September 4th. 1820*

My Love—I will be with you Wednesday evening—tomorrow I am going to the sea.—Another reason I am delaying is that Port *Corsini* (do you understand me?) does not seem to me to be suitable for *entrance*—*tomorrow*—if it takes at least 4 days for the flow and ebb [of the tide]—no?—The In-laws are still alive—perhaps—I cannot

---

4 See August 17, 1820, to Murray.
5 *Peter Bell*, a parody of Wordsworth, was written by John Hamilton Reynolds.

find out anything until Thursday.—Ferdinando G[uiccioli] is dying—poor fellow—Papa will tell you how, and why.—Love me always—[farewell until] day after tomorrow + + + —o!. . . .[1]

[TO JOHN MURRAY] *Ravenna. September 7th. 1820*

Dear Murray—In correcting the proofs—you must refer to the *Manuscript*—because there are in it *various readings.*—Pray—attend to this—and choose what Gifford thinks best.—Let me know what he thinks of the whole.——You speak of Lady Noel's illness—she is not of those who die—the amiable only do; and they whose death would DO GOOD—live.—Whenever she is pleased to return—it [may] be presumed that She will take her *"divining rod"* along with her[1]—it may be of use to her at home—as well as to the *"rich man"* of the Evangelists.——Pray do not let the papers paragraph me back to England[2]—they may say what they please—any loathsome abuse—but that.—Contradict it.——My last letters will have taught you to expect an explosion here—it was primed & loaded—but they hesitated to fire the train.—One of the Cities shirked from the league.—I cannot write more at large—for a thousand reasons.—Our *"puir hill folk"* offered to strike—and to raise the first banner.—But Bologna paused—and now 'tis Autumn and the season half over—"Oh Jerusalem! Jerusalem![''][3] the Huns are on the Po—but if once they pass it on their march to Naples—all Italy will rise behind them—the Dogs—the Wolves—may they perish like the Host of Sennacherib!—If you want to publish the Prophecy of Dante—you never will have a better time.—Thanks for books—but as yet No "Monastery" of Walter Scott's the *only* book except Edinburgh & Quarterly which I desire to see.—Why do you send me so much *trash* upon Italy—such tears—&c. which I know *must be false.*—Matthews is good—very good—all the rest—are like Sotheby's *"Good"* or like Sotheby himself—that old rotten Medlar of Rhyme.—The Queen—how is it?—prospers She?—

[1] Translated by Professor Nancy Dersofi.
[1] Lady Noel used a "divining-rod" to discover water.
[2] The *Morning Chronicle* of Aug. 18, 1820, announced Byron's arrival in London from Italy.
[3] *St. Matthew*, XXIII, 37.

Ravenna. ⟨August⟩ Septr. 8th. 1820

Dear Murray—You will please to publish the enclosed *note without* altering a word[1]—and to inform the author—that I will answer personally any offence to him.—He is a cursed impudent liar.—You shall not alter or [omit] a syllable—publish the [note at] the end of the play—and answer this—

[Scrawl]

P.S.—You sometimes take the liberty of *omitting* what I send for publication: if you do so in this instance I will never speak to you again as long as I breathe.

[TO COUNTESS TERESA GUICCIOLI] *Ravenna. Sett.e 9.o 1820*

A. M. + + + —La Pesca e la Pescatrice!!—Sempre qualche cosa di nuovo.——Sai che la Gazzetta di Milano dice che sono *arrivato* in Londra per affari della Regina!!—La gran' verità delle Gazette!— Quelle di Londra ripetono questa verità—e gli miei amici là la credono —dicendo che voglio essere per ora *incognito.*—Un' mio Amico mi scrive che molti sono venuti da lui—e andati via senza credere che non sono tornato, tra altri la *Lamb*—subito.—Ella è partita incredula. —Tutto questo ho trovato jeri per la posta.—Nulla dei Suoceri— *lerej*!——Ferdinando sta meglio.——Lunedi ci rivedremmo—sono *carico di Sentimento* ma non so come esprimarlo—o istenderlo in *quattro* pagine di parole—ma ti giuro che ti amo in una maniera che tutte le epistole di Cicerone non potrebbero spiegare mai[,] se anche l'*amor proprio* di quel' celebre Egoista fosse convertito in amore di altrui—e espresso con quell'eloquenza che fu il suo mestiere.—— Amami—mio *p.o.c.* + + +

[Scrawl]

P.S.—La Pesca—che *Pesce? B*?

[TRANSLATION] *Ravenna, September 9th, 1820*

My Love + + + Fishing and the Fisherwoman! Always something new.—Do you know that the Milanese *Gazette* says that I have *arrived* in London about the Queen's Business!! The veracity of Gazettes! The

---

[1] The note, printed at the end of *Marino Faliero*, is an attack on the author of *Sketches Descriptive of Italy . . .*, who said "I repeatedly declined an introduction" to Lord Byron "while I was in Italy." When he later discovered that the author was a woman, Byron asked Murray to cancel the note.

London papers report this—and my friends believe it, saying that for the present I want to be *incognito*.—One friend writes to me that many of them have been to see him—and went away again still not believing that I had not returned—among them the *Lamb*—without delay. She went away incredulous.—All this I found in yesterday's post.

Nothing from the filthy parents-in law[1]—Ferdinando is better——. On Monday we shall see each other again.——I am charged *with Sentiment,* but don't know how to express it—or spread it over four pages of words—but I swear that I love you in a way that all the letters of Cicero could not express—even if the *self-love* of that celebrated *Egoist* were converted into love of his neighbour—and expressed with all the eloquence of his profession——Love me—my p.o.c.

P.S.—Fishing——what *Fish*? B?

[TO RICHARD BELGRAVE HOPPNER]   *Ravenna. Septr. 10th. 1820*

My dear Hoppner—Ecco Advocate Fossati's letter.—No paper has nor will be signed.—Pray—*draw* on me for the Napoleons—for I have no mode of remitting them—otherwise. Missiaglia would empower some one here to receive them for you—as it is not a *piazza bancale.*—I regret that you have such a bad opinion of Shiloh[1]—you used to have a good one.—Surely he has talent—honour—but is crazy against religion and morality.—His tragedy is sad work[2]—but the subject renders it so.—His Islam had much poetry.—You seem lately to have got some notion against him.—Clare writes me the most insolent letters about Allegra—see what a man gets by taking care of natural children!—Were it not for the poor little child's sake—I am almost tempted to send her back to her atheistical mother—but that would be too bad;—you cannot conceive the excess of her insolence and I know not why—for I have been at great care and expence—taking a house in the country on purpose for her—she has *two* maids & every possible attention.—If Clare thinks that she shall ever interfere with the child's morals or education—she mistakes—she never shall—The girl shall be a Christian and a married woman—if possible.—As to seeing her— she may see her—under proper restrictions—but She is not to throw

---

[1] Teresa's grandparents (parents-in-law of Count Gamba?) were extremely illiberal, and Byron suspected them of disapproving of his liaison with Teresa.

[1] "Shiloh" was Byron's nickname for Shelley, derived from the name of the saviour to be born to Joanna Southcott, according to the fanatic prophets.

[2] *The Cenci,* Shelley's tragedy on the theme of incest, was published in 1819.

every thing into confusion with her Bedlam behaviour.—To express it delicately—I think Madame Clare is a damned bitch—what think you?

Ravenna. Sept. 11th. 1820

Dear Murray—Here is another historical *note* for you—I want to be as near the truth—as the Drama can be.——Last post I sent you a note fierce as Faliero himself—in answer to a trashy tourist who pretends that he could have been introduced to me.——Let me have a proof of it—that I may cut its lava into some shape.——What Gifford says is very consolatory—(of the first act) "English sterling *genuine English,*" is a disideratum amongst you—and I am glad that I have got so much left—though heaven knows how I retain it—I *hear* none but from my Valet—and his is *Nottinghamshire*—and I *see* none—but in your new publications—and theirs is *no* language at all—but jargon.——Even yr. "New Jerusalem" is terribly stilted and affected —with *"very very"*—so soft and pamby.——Oh! if ever I *do* come amongst you again I will give you such a "Baviad and Mæviad"[1] not as *good* as the old—but even *better merited.*—There never was such a *Set* as your ragamuffins—(I mean *not* yours only but every body's) what with the Cockneys and the Lakers—and the *followers* of Scott and Moore and Byron—you are in the very uttermost decline and degradation of Literature.—I can't think of it without all the remorse of a murderer—I wish that Johnson were alive again to crush them. I have as yet only had the first and second acts, & no opinion upon the second.——

Ravenna. S.e 14.0 1820

Amor Mio + + + —Prima di Lunedi non posso venire—ho tante lettere da scrivere e molte altre cose—dunque Lunedi ci rivedremmo. —Così avrai tempo di andare a Russi &c. cosa che io non me sento in caso di fare.—Avrei scritto jeri—ma non ho veduto alcuno di tuoi parenti.——Ferdinando è ancora molto ammalato—l'Allegra è venuta qui jeri—sempre colla febbre pero.—Ti scrivo in fretta e sono sempre + + + Amami

[Scrawl]

[1] Gifford's *Baviad* (1794) and *Maeviad* (1795) were satires on contemporary writers and were much admired by Byron. They served as models for *English Bards and Scotch Reviewers.*

175

Ravenna. September 14th. 1820

My Love + + + —I can't come before Monday—I have so many letters to write and a lot of other things—so on Monday we shall see each other. So you will have time to go to Russi[1] etc. which in any case I don't feel like doing—I would have written yesterday—but have not seen any of your relations.——

Ferdinando is still very ill[2]—Allegra came here yesterday, but still with some fever.—

I am writing in a hurry, and am always + + + Love me——

[Scrawl]

[TO JOHN MURRAY] *Ravenna. Septr. 14th. 1820*

What? not a line.—Well have it your own way.——I wish you would inform Perry that his stupid paragraph is the cause of all my newspapers being stopped in Paris—The fools believe me in your infernal country, and have not sent on their Gazettes—so that I know nothing of your beastly trial of the Queen.——I cannot avail myself of Mr. Gifford's remarks—because I have received none except on the first act.——

yrs.
[Scrawl]

P.S.—Do pray beg the Editors of papers to say anything black-guard they please but not to put me amongst their arrivals—they do me more mischief by such nonsense than all their abuse can do.——

[TO JOHN MURRAY] *Ravenna. Sept. 21st. 1820*

So you are at your old tricks again—this is the second packet I have received unaccompanied by a single line of good bad or indifferent.—It is strange that you have never forwarded any further observations of Gifford's—how am I to alter or amend if I hear no further?—or does this silence mean that it is well enough as it is—or too bad to be repaired?—If the last—why do you not say so at once

---

[1] A small town not far from Filetto.

[2] Lega Zambelli, Byron's steward, added a postscript: "Ferdinando, [Count Guiccioli's son by a former marriage] if not dead, is drawing his last breath. Poor boy, he has been sacrificed, owing to his family's lack of care." He died that night, and the next day Teresa wrote a long letter of condolence to Count Guiccioli. Byron was not pleased when he heard of it.

instead of playing pretty—since you know that soon or late you must out with the truth—

[Scrawl]

P.S.—My Sister tells me that you sent to her to enquire where I was—believing in my arrival—"driving a curricle," &c. &c. into palace yard: do you think me a Coxcomb or a madman to be capable of such an exhibition? My Sister knew me better and told you that *could not* be true—you might as well have thought me entering on "a pale horse" like Death in the revelations.—

[TO JOHN CAM HOBHOUSE]   *Ravenna. Septr. 21st. 1820*

My dear H.—If I could be of any real use to the Queen—or to anybody else I would have come long ago—but I see no advantage to her nor to others.—I have done my best to get the Pesaro Patricians to travel—which lies about tumults and ill treatment seemed about to prevent—but I made Count Gamba here write to the Machirelli's[1] (the first family in Pesaro, and his relatives) and he has set one of them agoing—who has letters from me for divers—and amongst others for *you*.——Be civil to the bearer when he arrives—he is a great man at Fano—and a witness for her Maestà.—Another thing that kept me here (besides my Serventismo) was that here we all expected—and had actually got on "our bandeliers" with "an unco band of blue bonnets at our backs" for a regular rising and all that—in which I amongst thousands was to have a part—being urged thereto by my love of liberty in general and of Italy in particular—and also by the good opinion which some of the confederates had of me as a coadjutor— but all of a sudden the *City of Sausages* (do you understand me?) withdrew from the league—and wanted to temper and to temporize— and so leave us in the lurch.—Of course without B[ologna]—the Romagnuole towns can do but little—with the Germans on the Po— and so here we are the principals liable to arrest every day—"'some taken and some left" like the "foolish virgins" (or some other parable) in the Evangelist.——In the meantime—there is a little stabbing and shooting—but in a small way—guards doubled—palace shut at ten o'nights—and the Cardinal praying to Saint Apollonari—the Patron

[1] The Countess Cecilia Machirelli Giordani was Teresa's maternal grand-mother.

177

Saint of the City, who should protect the city against the Austrians—
if he does his duty.—

I never was fool enough to think of having Brougham out—till
the Queen's settled.—But as "Nullum tempus occurrit regi"—so—
nullum tempus occurrit *honori*.—In Purefoy and Roper's business
seven years had taken place—in Tollemache (the Son's) *fifteen*—in
Stackpole and Cecil's *three*[2]—since the provocation.—All depends
upon the parties having met or no.—*You* know that I have never been
near Brougham since his insults, and was ignorant of them till long
after their occurrence—*keep this in mind as you yourself* were one of my
informants—and I am sorry to say—though (from a good motive) a
late one.——If I come to England now I must wait till his trial of the
Queen is over before I can have him out—but if his meeting me is
guaranteed me for the moment that's over—I will come and do my
best for her—otherwise not.—He would be sure at present to make
that a plea & an excuse—and I should be a fool to think of overruling
it—but neither that nor four nor five years—nor ten—nor twenty
do nor ought to prevent me from satisfaction whenever and wherever
we encounter.——My cartel and it's reasons I have already in writing
and have had since the hour I thought of returning to England.——
Sure I am that you and Douglas K[innaird] will approve it—when you
see them.—I have no other object nor view till this can be settled.——

Here at Ravenna—nobody believes the evidence against the Queen
—they say—that for half the money they could have any testimony
they please—this is the public talk.——The "Hints &c." are good are
they? As to the friends we can change their names unless they rhyme
well—in that case they must stand. Except Scott and Jeffrey and Moore
—Sir B. Burgess and a few more I know no friends who need be
left out of a good poem.—Has Murray shown you my play?—Pray
look at it—I want your opinion—you know I have taken it lately in

[2] Thomas Purefoy was an Ensign in the 66th Regiment under the command of
Major Roper on the Island of St. Vincent. The severity of his treatment for a
minor offence (a court martial and dismissal from the service) led to harsh words
and a challenge. The duel, in which Roper was killed, took place on December 21,
1788, a year after the quarrel and not seven years later as Byron supposed. The
confusion no doubt came from the fact that Purefoy was brought to trial in 1794,
following six years of exile and nine months of confinement. When the circumstances were brought before a jury, he was acquitted. John Tollemache, a Captain
in the Royal Navy, and son of the Earl of Dysart, was killed in a duel in or near
New York with Captain Pennington of the Guards in 1777. The duel grew out of
"a foolish quarrel about humming a tune". Of the duel of Stackpole and Cecil, it is
recorded that Stackpole when mortally wounded said with great sang-froid: "By
George, I've missed him."

such good part—that you need not mind being a little rough if necessary.——It is long enough an' that be all.—Murray told me that
Lady Noel was ill—he lied I believe—I suppose if she returns to
whence She came—she will take her "divining rod" with her, [it]
may be of use to her at home and to her neighbour the rich man
(Dives clothed in purple) mentioned in the play of Henry 4th. and by
the Evangelists.—But the Lady will not die—her living does too much
ill—You'll see she'll recover and bury her betters—the bitch!——

> write to yrs.
> [Scrawl]

P.S.—Pray make your motion—you make a great figure in Galignani—who by the way—has withheld his messengers since the paragraphs of my arrival in England—believing them.—Fletcher is ill and
has had three pounds of blood let since yesterday—for a sore throat.—
In his jacket and handkerchief—and foolish face he looks like Liston—
or much such a figure as he did in Albania in 1809 during the autumnal
rains in his jerkin and umbrella.—As Justice Shallow says "Oh the
merry days that we have seen!"[3]——

[TO JOHN MURRAY]   *Ravenna. Septr. 23d. 1820*

Dear Murray—Get from Mr. Hobhouse and send me a proof (with
the Latin) of my Hints from H[orace] &c.;—it has now the "*nonum
prematur in annum*" complete for its production[1]—being written at
Athens in 1811.—I have a notion that with some omissions of names
and passages it will do—and I could put my late observations *for* Pope
among the notes with the date of 1820, and so on.—As far as versifica-
tion goes it is good—and on looking back to what I wrote about that
period—I am astonished to see how *little* I have trained on—I wrote
better then than now—but that comes from my having fallen into the
atrocious bad taste of the times—partly.——It has been kept too
nine years—nobody keeps their piece nine years now a days—except
Douglas K[innaird]—he kept his nine years and then restored her to
the public.—If I can trim it for present publication—what with the
other things you have of mine—you will have a volume or two of
variety at least—for there will be all measures styles and topics—
whether good or no—I am anxious to hear what Gifford thinks of the

---

[0] *Henry IV*, Part 2, Act 3, scene 2: "Jesus, the days that we have seen".
[1] Horace's stipulation in the *Ars Poetica* (lines 388–89) that a writer should
keep his composition nine years before giving it to the public.

tragedy—pray let me know—I really do not know what to think myself.——

If the Germans pass the Po—they will be treated to a Mass out of
the Cardinal de Retz's *Breviary*[2]—Galley Knight's a fool—and could
not understand this—Frere will—it is as pretty a conceit as you would
wish to see upon a Summer's day.—Nobody here believes a word of
the evidence against the Queen—the very mob cry shame against
their countrymen and say—that for half the money spent upon the
trial—any testimony whatever may be brought out of Italy.——
This you may rely upon as fact—I told you as much before—as to what
travellers report—*what are travellers?*—now I have *lived* among the
Italians—not *Florenced* and *Romed*—and Galleried—and Conver-
sationed it for a few months—and then home again—but been of their
families—and friendships and feuds—and loves—and councils—and
correspondence in a part of Italy least known to foreigners—and have
been amongst them of all classes—from the Conte to the Contadino—
and you may be sure of what I say to you.——

yrs.
[Scrawl]

[TO JOHN CAM HOBHOUSE]   *Septr. 25th. 1820*

Dear H.—I open my letter to enclose you one which contains some
hints which may be useful to Queeney—and her orators—but mind
and don't betray the Writer H[oppner] or he will lose his place.——
When you wanted me to come—you forgot that absence during the
earlier part of the stages of the bill *precludes voting*—I see by the
papers that more than two days absence does.—Dunque?—or adunque
—argal—

yrs.

P.S.—Brougham says *"discorso"* is *not* Italian! Oh rare! it—and
"discorrere" are as common as *"cazzo"*,[1]—I suppose that fellow
thinks *"conversazione"* means *conversation*—Apropos of Italian

---

[2] Byron referred to a passage in Cardinal de Retz's *Mémoires* (ed. Geneva,
1777, tome II, p. 122), about one of the leaders in the Fronde, who was something
of a pacifist, but was forced to carry a poniard. One of the Guards perceiving it
sticking out of his pocket, remarked: "Voila la bréviare de M. le Coadjutor".
Byron meant to imply that there would be savage work if the Austrians crossed the
Po.

[1] A blow or punch on the head.

witnesses—since I have been in Italy I have had *six* law-suits—twice as plaintiff against debtors—once about horseflesh as plaintiff—twice about men's wives as defendant—and once as defendant against shop-keepers wanting to be paid *twice* over for the same bills—I gained them all but the horsedealer's, he diddled me.—In the Shopkeeper's one last Novr.—the fellow declared positively in a court that *I ordered in person the articles* in company with my secretaries—and when desired to describe me—described me as a *tall thin flaxen-haired man*!!!—Of course he was non-suited.—The fellow was reckoned one of the *most respectable negocianti* in Venice.———If you can quote this you may and I'll prove it if necessary.———

[TO JOHN MURRAY (*a*)]   *Septr. 28th. 1820*

Mr. J. Murray—Can you keep a Secret? not you—you would rather keep a w——e I believe of the two—although a moral man—and "all that—Egad"—as Bayes says.—However I request and recommend to you to keep the enclosed one[1]—viz—to *give no copies*—to permit *no publication*—[else] you and I will be two.—It [was written near]ly three years ago—upon the double-[faced] fellow—it's argument—in consequence of a letter ⟨from Italy⟩ exposing some of his usual practices.—You may *show* it—to Gifford—Hobhouse—D. Kinnaird and any two or three of your own Admiralty favourites—but don't betray *it*, or me, else you are the worst of men.———Is it like?—if *not*—it has no merit.—Does he deserve it?—if not—burn it.—He wrote to M[oore] (so M. says) the other day saying on some occasion—"what a fortunate fellow you are! surely you were born with a rose in your lips, and a Nightingale singing on the bed-top"—M[oore] sent me this extract as an instance of the old Serpent's sentimental twaddle.—I replied—that I believed that "he (the twaddler) was born with a Nettle in his a—e and a Carrion Crow croaking on the bolster", a parody somewhat *un*delicate—but such trash puts one stupid—besides the Cant of it—in a fellow who hates every body. Is this good? tell me and I will send you one still better of that black-guard Brougham;—there is a batch of them.—

                                                                    [Scrawl]

---

[1] The enclosed lines were the bitter rhymes on Rogers beginning, "Nose and chin that make a knocker".

181

[TO JOHN MURRAY (*b*)]   *Ravenna. Septr. 28th. 1820*

D[ea]r. M[urra]y—I thought that I had told you long ago—that it *never* was intended nor written with any view to the Stage.—I have said so in the preface too.—It is too long—and too regular for your stage.—The persons too few—and the *unity* too much observed.—It is more like a play of Alfieri's than of your stage—(I say this humbly in speaking of that great Man) but there is poetry—and it is equal to Manfred—though I know not what esteem is held of Manfred.——
I have now been nearly as long *out* of England—as I was *there*—during the time when I saw you frequently—I came home July 14th. 1811—and left again April 25th. 1816.—So that Septr. 28th. 1820—brings me within a very few months of the same duration of time of my stay—and my absence. In course I can know nothing of the public taste and feelings but from what I glean from letters &c.—Both seem to be as bad as possible.——I thought *Anastasius excellent*—did I not say so?—Matthews's Diary most excellent—it and Forsyth[1] and parts of Hobhouse—are all we have of truth or sense upon Italy.—Ye letter to Julia[2] very good indeed.—I do not despise Mrs. Heman[s]—but if [she] knit blue stockings instead of wearing them it would be better.——
You are taken in by that false stilted trashy style which is a mixture of all the styles of the day—which are *all bombastic* (I don't except my *own*—no one has done more through negligence to corrupt the language) but it is neither English nor poetry.——Time will show.—I am sorry Gifford has made no further remarks beyond the first act—does he think all the English equally sterling—as he thought the first?—You did right to send me the proofs—I was a fool—but I do really detest the sight of proofs—it is an absurdity—but comes from laziness. —You can steal the two Juans into the world quietly—tagged to the others.——The play as you will—the Dante too—but the *Pulci* I am proud of—it is superb—you have no such translation—It is the best thing I ever did in my life.—I wrote the play—from beginning to end—and not a *single scene without interruption* & being obliged to break off in the middle—for I had my hands full—and my head too just then,—so it can be no great shakes—I mean the play—and the head too if you like.——

[Scrawl]

[1] *Remarks on Antiquities, Arts, and Letters, during an excursion in Italy, in the years 1802 and 1803,* by Joseph Forsyth, was published in 1813.
[2] *Advice to Julia, a Letter in Rhyme,* by Henry Luttrell (1820).

182

P.S.—Send me proofs of "the Hints" get them from Hobhouse.

P.S.—Politics here still savage and uncertain—however we are all in "our bandaliers" to join the "Highlanders if they cross the Forth" i.e. to crush the Austrians if they pass the Po.—The rascals!—and that Dog Liverpool[3] to say that their subjects were *happy*—what a liar!—if ever I come back I'll work some of these [ministers].——

Dear Murray—
> You ask for a *"volume of Nonsense"*
> Have all your authors exhausted their store?
> I thought you had published a good deal not long since
> And doubtless the Squadron are ready with more.—
> But on looking again—I perceive that the Species
> Of "Nonsense" you want must be purely *"facetious"*—
> And as that is the case you had best put to press
> Mr. Sotheby's tragedies now in M.S.S.—
> > Some Syrian Sally
> > From common-place Gally—
> Or if you prefer the bookmaking of women—
> Take a spick and Span "Sketch" of your feminine *He-Man.*—

[Scrawl]

Why do you ask me for opinions of your ragamuffins—you see what you get by it—but recollect I never give opinions till required.——

Septr. *29th.*—I open my letter to say—that on reading more of the 4 volumes on Italy—where the Author says *"declined* an introduction" I perceive (horresco referens)[4] that it is written by a WOMAN!!![5] In that case you must suppress my note and answer—and all I have said about the book and the writer.—I never dreamed of it till now— in extreme wrath at that precious note——I can only say that I am sorry that a Lady should say anything of the kind.—What I would have said to a person with testicles—you know already.—Her book too (as a *She* book) is not a bad one—but she evidently don't know the Italians—or rather don't like them—and forgets the *causes* of their misery and profligacy (*Matthews* and *Forsyth* are your men of truth and tact) and has gone over Italy in *company always* a *bad* plan.—

---

[3] 2nd Earl of (1770–1828), Prime Minister, 1812–1827.
[4] Virgil, *Aeneid*, II, 204 ("I shudder to recall," etc).
[5] See Sept. 8, 1820, to Murray, note 1. The author, as Byron discovered, was Miss Jane Waldie (afterward Mrs. Watts).

You must be *alone* with people to know them well.—Ask her—who was the *"descendant of Lady M. W. Montague"* and by *whom*? by Algarotti?—I suspect that in Marino Faliero you and yours won't like the *politics* which are perilous to you in these times——but recollect that it is *not* a *political* play—& that I,was obliged to put into the mouths of the Characters the sentiments upon which they acted.—I hate all things written like Pizarro[6] to represent france England & so forth—all I have done is meant to be purely Venetian— even to the very prophecy of it's present state. Your Angles [English] in general know little of the Italians—who detest them for their numbers and their *Genoa*[7] treachery.——Besides the English travellers have not been composed of the best Company—how could they?— out of 100000 how many gentlemen were there or honest men?— ——Mitchell's Aristophanes is excellent[8]—send me the rest of it.—I think very small beer of Mr. Galiffe[9]—and his dull book.—Here and there some good things though—which might have been better.——

These fools will force me to write a book about Italy myself to give them "the loud lie"——They prate about assassination—what is it but the origin of duelling—and "a wild Justice" as Lord Bacon calls it—it is the fount of the modern point of honour—in what the laws can't or *wont* reach.—Every man is liable to it more or less—according to circumstances or place.—For instance I am living here, exposed to it daily—for I have happened to make a powerful and unprincipled man my enemy;—and I never sleep the worse for it—or ride in less solitary places,—because—precaution is useless—and one thinks of it as a disease which may or may not strike;—it is true—that there are those here who if he did—would "live to think on't" but that would not awake my bones;—I should be sorry if it would—were they once at rest.—

[6] Sheridan's *Pizarro* is set in Peru, but the action in the play on which it is based, Kotzebue's *Spaniards in Peru*, is supposed to represent a prospective French invasion of England.

[7] In 1814 Genoa rose against the French on the assurance of Lord William Bentinck, Commander of the British forces besieging the town, that the Allies would restore the town to independence. But it had been determined secretly at the Treaty of Paris that Genoa should be incorporated with the dominions of the King of Sardinia.

[8] Thomas Mitchell published the first volume of his translation of *The Comedies of Aristophanes* in 1820. Byron had met him when he went with Moore to visit Leigh Hunt in jail in June, 1813.

[9] *Italy and Its Inhabitants, in the years 1816 and 1817*, by James A. Galiffe of Geneva, was advertised by Murray in the *Literary Gazette* of June 10, 1820.

Amor Mio +—Don G. è impaziente per ritornare dunque non ho che un solo momento per risponderti.—Delle mie lettere non puoi aver' bisogna finche che sei (o *eri*) in correspondenza col' tuo marito— e della mia presenza nessuna premura—poiche sei stata in R[avenna] senza dire che ti venga trovare.——Pierino avrà forse esaggerato ciò che io dissi in un' momento di mal'umore sopra *le lettere*—o almeno io avrei esaggerato ciò che sentiva per l'istessa ragione. Questa stagione m'uccide di tristezza in tutti gli anni maggiormente in questo—tu sai la mia malinconia del' anno scorso—e quando ho quella malatia del'Spirito—è meglio per gli altri che mi tengo lontano. ——Però—il tempo solo mi ha trattenuto qui—per la prima occasione ci rivedremmo.—Credemi sempre il tuo più

[Scrawl]

P.S.—Ti ringrazio di cuore per le rose—amami. La mia anima è come le foglie che cadono nel autunno,—tutta *gialla*.—Una Cantata!!!

My Love + —Don G.[1] is impatient to return, so I have only a moment in which to answer you.—You cannot need my letters so long as you are (or were) in correspondence with your husband[2]—nor can you be in a hurry for my presence—since you have been to Ravenna without telling me to come and see you.

Pierino may perhaps have exaggerated what I said in a moment of ill-humour about *the letters*—or at least I may have exaggerated my feelings, for the same reason. This season kills me with sadness every year. You know my last year's melancholy—and when I have that disease of the Spirit—it is better for others that I should keep away. However—it is only the weather that keeps me here—at the first opportunity we shall see each other again.

Believe me always your most

P.S.—Thank you from my heart for the roses. Love me. My soul is like the leaves that fall in autumn—all yellow.—*A cantata*!

---

[1] Don Giovanni was the family priest at Filetto who, like Perelli earlier, was used as a messenger.

[2] See Sept. 14, 1820, to Teresa, note 1.

Amor Mio + + + —La tua Immaginazione ti porta troppo lontano.—Don Giovanni è un buffone coi suoi misteri.—Vi erano qui jeri due le[rcje]—una più brutta dell' altra per concorrere al'servizio—l'ho vedute in presenza di Lega per un solo momento—e poi non le ricevo—perche non mi paiono adattate a servire l'Allegrina.——Quando mi pareva necessaria cangiare la Governante—io mandai Lega dalla Vicari—in vece di andare in persona—per non darti ombra.——Cosa vuoi che ne faccio? io non conobbi altra Signora fuorche della tua amica—in cui potrei fidarmi per una tale raccomandazione.—Il momento che le strade saranno pratticabili verrò da te—e allora non saranno più questi sospetti—La mia lettera ti avrà spiegata la ragione perche non scrissi—io non ebbi altra ragione.—Per la mia *tristezza*—tu sai se non è nel' mio carattere—particularmente in certe stagioni.—E una vera malattia di temperamento—che mi fa' delle volte temere anche un' principio di pazzia—e per questa causa—mi tengo in quei momenti lontano da tutti—non volendo rendere infelici gli altri. E questo vero o no? o è la prima volta che tu m'hai veduto in quel stato?——Amami—e credi che ci rivedremmo—e ameremmo più che mai +

[Scrawl]

[TRANSLATION]   *Ravenna, September 29th, 1820*

My Love + + + —Your imagination carries you too far. Don Giovanni is a buffoon with his mysteries—Yesterday two filthy ladies were here, one uglier than the other—to try to enter my service.—I saw them in Lega's presence for just a minute—and then did not engage them—because they did not seem to me suitable for waiting on Allegrina.—When I thought it necessary to change the Housekeeper, I sent Lega to the Vicari instead of going in person,—so as not to annoy you. What did you want me to do? I don't know any other Lady but your friend, whom I could trust for advice of this kind.

As soon as the roads are practicable, I will come to you—then your suspicions will disappear. My letter will have explained to you why I did not write—I had no other reason.

As to my *sadness*—you know that it is in my character—particularly in certain seasons. It is truly a temperamental illness—which sometimes makes me fear the approach of madness—and for this reason, and at these times, I keep away from everyone—not wanting to make others unhappy.—Is this true or not? Is this the first time that you have seen me in this condition?

Love me and believe that we shall see each other soon again, and will love each other more than ever. +

[TO THE NEAPOLITAN INSURGENTS]   [*Oct.? 1820*]

Un' Inglese—amico della Libertà—avendo sentito che i Napolitani permettono anche ai stranieri di contribuire alla buona causa—bramerebbe l'onore di aver' accettata l'offerta di mille Luigi—la quale egli azzarda di fare.—Gia Testimonio oculare non molto fa della tirannia dei Barbari nei stati dei loro usurpati dell' Italia—Egli vede con tutto l'entusiasmo di un uomo ben nato la gloriosa determinazione dei N[apolitani] per confirmare loro ben' acquistata Independenza. Membro della Camera dei Pari della Nazione Inglese, Egli sarebbe un traditore ai principii che hanno posto sul' trono la famiglia regnante di Inghilterra—se non riconoscesse la bella lezione di bel nuovo cosi data ai popoli ed ai re.—L'offerta che egli brama di presentare [è] pocha in se stessa—come bisogna che sia sempre quella di un' individuo ad una nazione ma egli spera che non sarà l'ultima della parte dei suoi compatrioti.——

La sua lontananza dal'frontiere e il suo senso di sua poca capacità personale di contribuire efficacemente a servire la nazione, l'impedisce di proporsi come degno della più piccola commisione che domanda del' esperienza e del' talento—ma se come semplice volontario la sua presenza non sarebbe un' incommodo a quello che l'accettasse egli riparebbe a qualunque luogo indicato dal' Governo N[apolitano].—per ubbidire l'ordini e participare i pericoli—del suo Superiore, senza aver dei altri motivi che quello di dividere il destino di una brava nazione resistendo alla se-dicente Santa Allianza—la quale aggiunge l'ippocrisia al' despotismo.——

[TRANSLATION]   [*Oct.? 1820*]

An Englishman, a friend to liberty, having understood that the Neapolitans permit even foreigners to contribute to the good cause, is desirous that they should do him the honour of accepting a thousand louis, which he takes the liberty of offering. Having already, not long since, been an ocular witness of the despotism of the Barbarians in the States occupied by them in Italy, he sees, with the enthusiasm natural to a cultivated man, the [glorious] determination of the Neapolitans to

187

assert their well-won independence. As a member of the English House of Peers, he would be a traitor to the principles which placed the reigning family of England on the throne, if he were not grateful for the noble lesson so lately given both to people and to kings. The offer which he desires to make is small in itself, as must always be that presented from an individual to a nation; but he trusts that it will not be the last they will receive from his countrymen. His distance from the frontier, and the feeling of his personal incapacity to contribute efficaciously to the service of the nation, prevents him from proposing himself as worthy of the lowest commission, for which experience and talent might be requisite. But if, as a mere volunteer, his presence were not a burden to whomsoever he might serve under, he would repair to whatever place the Neapolitan Government might point out, there to obey the orders and participate in the dangers of his commanding officer, without any other motive than that of sharing the destiny of a brave nation, defending itself against the self-called Holy Alliance, which but combines the vice of hypocrisy with despotism.[1]

[TO JOHN MURRAY]   [October, 1820?]

[Extract]

I enclose you the stanzas which were intended for 1st. Canto,[1] after the line

"Who to Madrid on purpose made a journey:"

but I do not mean them for present publication, because I will not, at this distance, publish *that* of a Man, for which he has a claim upon another too remote to give him redress.

With regard to the Miscreant Brougham, however, it was only long after the fact, and I was made acquainted with the language he had held of me on my leaving England (with regard to the D[uche]ss of D[evonshire]'s house),[2] and his letter to Me. de Staël, and various

---

[1] The translation is from Moore, II, 389. According to Moore, the address, of which this is a first draft, was entrusted by Byron to a supposed agent of the Constitutional Government of Naples, who was really a spy of the Pontifical Government, so that it never reached its intended destination.

[1] See Dec. 7, 1818, to Murray (Vol. 6, p. 85). These were the stanzas on Brougham, for which Byron substituted others before publication. See *Poetry*, VI, 68–70.

[2] One of Brougham's offences was gossiping about Byron's failure to pay the rent to the Duchess of Devonshire for her house at 13, Piccadilly Terrace before he went abroad in 1816.

matters for all of which the first time he and I foregather—be it in England, be it on earth—he shall account, and one of the two be carried home.

As I have no wish to have mysteries, I merely prohibit the *publication* of these stanzas in *print*, for the reasons of fairness mentioned; but I by no means wish *him not* to *know* their existence or their tenor, nor my intentions as to himself: he has shown no forbearance, and he shall find none. You may show them to *him* and to all whom it may concern, with the explanation that the only reason that I have not had satisfaction of this man has been, that I have never had an opportunity since I was aware of the facts, which my friends had carefully concealed from me; and it was only by slow degrees, and by piecemeal, that I got at them. I have not sought him, nor gone out of my way for him; but I will *find* him, and then we can have it out: he has shown so little courage, that he *must* fight at last in his absolute necessity to escape utter degradation.

I send you the stanzas, which (except the last) have been written nearly two years, merely because I have been lately copying out most of the MSS. which were in my drawers.

[TO COUNTESS TERESA GUICCIOLI]   *R[avenna]. 8bre. 1.0 1820*

Amor Mio + + + —Ti risponderò a voce alla tua lettera *mercoledi* venturo—io non mi lagno delle circonstanze—nè della fortuna——la mia malinconia è una cosa di temperamento credita dalla famiglia di mia madre—particolarmente dal' *Nonno*—e poi non è costante— come tu sai—ma—non voglio seccarti con queste inezie.——Ti prego perdonarmi se non scrivo più in dettaglio—il tuo espresso vuol partire—ed io ho delle lettere da scrivere per Inghilterra.—Amami e credemi + + +

[Scrawl]

[TRANSLATION]   *Ravenna. October 1st. 1820*

My Love + + + —I will answer your letter myself when I see you on Wednesday—I do not complain about circumstances or Fortune. My melancholy is something temperamental, inherited from my mother's family—particularly from my *grandfather*—and it is not constant—as you know—but I don't want to bore you with these trifles. Pray forgive me if I do not write in greater detail—your

189

messenger wants to leave, and I have some letters to write for England.

Love me and believe me + + +

Dear Douglas—You send me no news of that damned Mortgage—though it is nearly a year since you proposed it.——Hanson has not sent me Counsel's opinion on the Appeal as I desired.——I have sent H[obhouse] some letters on the Queen's affairs (one goes by this post) has he got them[?]——I sent Murray a tragedy—(written *not* for the Stage) read it if you can——It is full of republicanism—so will find no favour in *Albemarle* Street.——They had got up as pretty a plot here as Hotspur's—when lo a City with sixty thousand men—*bilked* them and here we all are—in great confusion—some in arrest—some for flying to the Hills—and for making a Guerilla fight for it—others for waiting for better times—and both sides watching each other like hunting leopards—the fact is the Government is weak—for a Government—and the Constitutionals strong for such—but what will be the issue is doubtful;—my *voice* was like that of Sempronius—somewhat warlike—but the autumnal rains have damped a deal of military ardour.—In the mean time both sides embody and pay—*bands* of assassins—or *brigands* as they call them—at about ninepence a head—per diem—so you may suppose that I could soon whistle a hundred or two lads to my back—when I want them.——

Portugal and Spain as [are?] the whiteheaded boys after all.——Every thing was ready—and we were all in our bandaliers—what a pity to have missed such an opportunity—but it was all the bloody Austrians on the Po—if they do but ever get a grip of those fellows—you will hear strange things—the Huns will have enough of it at least such as fall into the hands of the natives. You may suppose that with such matters in possibility—it would be a satisfaction to know something of my worldly affairs—and be as decently in Cash as need be [so as] to take the field with fair forage as [words torn off with seal] every sixpence is a sinew of war.——[In] order to this—let me know how the Blessingtown goes on.—And when you have perpended the drama at Murray's—let me know at what you rate it.——I have not come to England—not feeling myself pious enough to decide whether the Queen fell [line crossed out] or no.—I wonder he did not tumble into it—it must have been like sleeping on the brink of a well—What trash your Parliament is———

yrs. [Scrawl]

8bre. 10.0

I wrote this letter on the first of the Moon and kept back ten days expecting to have a letter from you or Spooney—I have written twice to Hobby—ask him whether "Lankey has been into the Slaughter house yet"?[1] and whether there is not "too much *Tig*. and [*Tiri?*][2] in it?"—he will understand these questions—*you* won't—for you have not yet taken the [Dane's?] degree.—Give Murray the Po verses—and let me have some of your own prose.———

[TO RICHARD BELGRAVE HOPPNER]   *Ravenna. 8bre. 1.0 1820*

My dear Hoppner—Your letters and papers came very safely—though slowly—missing one post.—The Shiloh story is true no doubt[1]—though Elise is but a sort of *Queen's* evidence—you remember how eager she was to return to them—and then she goes away and abuses them.—Of the facts however there can be little doubt—it is just like them.—You may be sure that I keep your counsel.—I have not remitted the 30 Napoleons (or *what* was it?) till I hear that Missiaglia has received his safely—when I shall do so by the like channel.———What you say of the Queen's affair is very just and true—but the event seems not very easy to anticipate.—I enclose an epistle from Shiloh[2]—

yours ever & truly
BYRON

[TO JOHN MURRAY]   *Ravenna. 8bre. 6.0 1820*

Dear M[urra]y—You will have now received all the acts corrected of the M[arino] F[aliero]—What you say of the "Bet of 100 guineas"

---

[1] See Boswell's *Life of Johnson* (1780), Oxford Ed., II, 347. Bennett Langton was reading aloud to Johnson Dodsley's *Cleone, A Tragedy*. At the end of an act, Johnson said: "Come let's have some more, let's go into the slaughter-house again, Lanky. But I am afraid there is more blood than brains." The implication is a gibe at Hobhouse for having been in Newgate.

[2] Unidentified.

[1] This was the story told by Elise Foggi, who had been sent by the Shelleys to Byron with Allegra and who returned to the Shelleys. She had told the Hoppners that Claire Clairmont had a child by Shelley which they placed in a foundling hospital in Naples.

[2] i.e., Shelley. See September 10, 1820, to Hoppner.

191

made by some one who says that he saw me last week reminds me of what happened in 1810. You can easily ascertain the fact and it is an odd one.——In the latter end of 1811 I met one evening at the Alfred my old School and form-fellow (for we were within two of each other—*he* the higher—though both very near the top of our remove) *Peel* the Irish Secretary.—He told me that in *1810* he met me as he thought in St. James's Street, but we passed without speaking.—He mentioned this—and it was denied as impossible—I being then in Turkey.—A day or two after he pointed out to his brother a person on the opposite side of the way—"there"—said he "is the man I took for Byron"—his brother instantly answered "why it *is* Byron & no one else."—But this is not all—I was *seen* by somebody to *write down my name* amongst the Enquirers after the King's health—then attacked by insanity.—Now—at this very period, as nearly as I could make out —I was ill of a *strong fever* at Patras, caught in the marshes near Olympia—from the *Malaria.*——If I had died there this would have been a new Ghost Story for you.—You can easily make out the accuracy of this from Peel himself, who told it in detail.—I suppose you will be of the opinion of Lucretius—who (denies the immortality of the Soul—but) asserts that from the "flying off of the Surfaces of bodies perpetually, these surfaces or cases like the Coats of an onion are sometimes seen entire—when they are separated from it so that the shape & shadows of both the dead and absent are frequently beheld".[1]—But if they are—are their coats & waistcoats also seen?—— I do not disbelieve that we may be *two* by some uncommon process— to a certain sign—but which of the two I happen at present to be—I leave you to decide—I only hope that *t'other me* behaves like a Gemman.——I wish you would get Peel asked—how far [I] am accurate in my recollection of what he told me: for I don't like to say such things without authority.——I am not sure that I was *not spoken* with—but this also you can ascertain.——I have written to you such lots that I stop.—

yrs. [Scrawl]

P.S.—Send me proofs of the "Hints from H[orace][''] &c. &c.

P.S.—Last year (in June 1819) I met at Count Monti's at Ferrara— an Italian who asked me "if I knew Lord Byron?" I told him *no*— (no one knows himself *you* know) "then" says he—"I do—I met him at Naples the other day" I pulled out my card and asked him if that was the way he spelt his name—and he answered *yes*—I suspect

---

[1] Lucretius, *De Rerum Naturae*, Lib. IV, 35ff.

that it was a Blackguard Navy Surgeon named *Bury* or *Berry*—who attended a young travelling Madman about named Graham—and passed himself for a Lord at the Post houses—he was a vulgar dog— quite of the Cockpit order—and a precious representative I must [have] had of him—if it was even so—but I don't know. He passed himself off as a Gentleman and squired about a Countess Zinnani (of this place) then at Venice—an [ugly] battered woman of bad morals even for Italy.

[TO COUNTESS TERESA GUICCIOLI] *R[avenna] 8bre 7.o 1820*

Carissima Gaspara +—Penserò per la Settimana proposta—e tu puoi immaginare ben volontieri.——Jeri ho ricevuto delle nuove da Londra—le quali mi faranno preferire il rimanere qui—e limitare i miei servizj *patriottici* piuttosto alla parte Settentrionale del' *"bel' paese"*—che andare a scaldarmi a Monte Vesuvio—e dappiù non è necessario—poiche vi sono i *tuoi capelli*—color di fiamma —e la testa di sotto più calda della lava.—Poi sento certi rimorsi nel' idea di lasciarti—(se anche fosse per pochi mesi) i quali mi danno una cattiva idea dei piacere della lontananza.——*Papa* è qui con me—il Fattore parte—dunque Mia Carissima Gaspara + +

[Scrawl]

[TRANSLATION] *R[avenna]. October 7th. 1820*

Dearest Gaspara[1] + ——I shall think about the suggested week— and as you can imagine, very gladly.—Yesterday I received news from London—which makes me prefer to stay here and limit my *patriotic* services to the Northern part of the "bel paese"—rather than go and warm myself on Vesuvius—and then it is not necessary, since your flame-coloured hair is here and the head under it, hotter than lava. Besides, I feel a certain remorse at the idea of leaving you—(even if it were only for a few months) which gives me a poor notion of the pleasures of separation.

Papa is here with me—the Factor is leaving—so my dearest Gaspara + +

1 Byron used this name to tease Teresa. It was one of her names, it being the custom to give the name of one of the Magi to each of the children. He also added to the address: "born (Feb. 18th 1799) Gamba Ghiselli". Teresa tried to change the date to 1803.

Dear Moray—Foscolo's letter is exactly the thing wanted—
1[st]ly because he is a man of Genius—& next because he is an Italian
and therefore the best Judge of Italics.—Besides—

> "He's more an antique Roman than a Dane["]¹

that is—he has more of the antient Greek—than of the modern
Italian—Though "somewhat" as Dugald Dalgetty says "too wild
and Salvage"² (like "Ronald of the Mist"[)]—'tis a wonderful man—
and my friends Hobhouse and Rose both swear by him—and they are
good Judges of men and of Italian humanity.—

> "Here are in all *two* worthy voices gained"³

Gifford says it is good "sterling genuine English" and Foscolo says
that the Characters are right Venetian.——Shakespeare and Otway
had a million of advantages over me—besides the incalculable one of
having been *dead* from one to two Centuries—and having been both born
blackguards (which *are* such attractions to the Gentle living reader;)
let me then preserve the only one which I could possibly have—that—
of having been at Venice—and entered into the local Spirit of it—I
claim no more—I know what F[oscolo] means about Calendaro's
spitting at Bertram⁴—*that's* national—the *objection* I mean.—The
Italians and French—with those "flags of Abomination" their pocket
handkerchiefs—spit there—and here—and every where else—in your
face almost—and therefore *object* to it on the Stage as *too familiar.*—
But—we who *spit* nowhere—but in a Man's face—when we grow
savage—are not likely to feel this.—Remember *Massinger*—and
Kean's Sir Giles Overreach.

> "Lord! *thus* I *Spit* at thee and at thy Counsel!"—⁵

Besides—Calendaro does *not* spit in Bertram's face—he spits *at* him—
as I have seen the Mussulmans do upon the Ground when they are in a
rage.—Again—he *does not* in *fact despise* Bertram—though he affects
it—as we all do—when angry with one we think our inferior;—he is
angry at *not being* allowed to die in his own way——(though not
afraid of death) and recollect that he suspected & hated Bertram from

¹ *Hamlet,* Act V, scene 2.
² *A Legend of Montrose,* Chapter XIII.
³ *Coriolanus,* Act II, scene 3: "There is in all two worthy voices begged".
⁴ *Marino Faliero,* Act V, scene 1.
⁵ Massinger, *A New Way to Pay Old Debts,* Act V, scene 1.

the first.—Israel Bertuccio—on the other hand—is a cooler and more concentrated fellow—he acts upon *principle* and *impulse*—Calendaro upon *impulse* and *example.*——So there's argument for you.——The Doge *repeats*; *true*—but it is from engrossing passion——and because he sees *different* persons—and is always obliged to recur to the *cause* uppermost in his mind.—His speeches are long—true—but I wrote for the *Closet*—and on the French and Italian model rather than yours—which I think not very highly of—for all your *old* dramatists—who are long enough too God knows—*look* into any of them. I wish *you* too to recollect one thing which is nothing to the reader.——I never wrote nor copied *an entire Scene of that play*—without being obliged to *break* off—to *break* a commandment;—to obey a woman's, and to forget God's.—Remember the drain of this upon a Man's heart and brain—to say nothing of his immortal Soul.—*Fact* I assure you—the Lady always apologized for the interruption—but you know the *answer* a man must make when and while he can.—It happened to be the only hour I had in the four and twenty for composition or reading and I was obliged to divide even it, such are the defined duties of a Cavalier Servente, or Cavalier Schiavo.

I return you F[oscolo]'s letter—because it alludes also to his private affairs.——I am sorry to see such a man in straits—because I know what they are——or what they were.—I never met but three men who would have held out a finger to me—one was yourself—the other Wm Bankes—and the third a Nobleman long ago dead.——But of these the first was the only one who offered it while I *really* wanted it—the second from good will—but I was not in need of Bankes's aid—and would not have accepted it if I had (though I love and esteem him) and the *third*-[three lines crossed out] So you see that I have seen some strange things in my time.——As for yr. own offer it was in 1815—when I was in actual uncertainty of five pounds.—I rejected it—but I have not forgotten it although you probably have.——You are to publish when and how you please—but—I thought you and Mr. Hobhouse had decided *not* to print the whole of "*Blackwood*" as being *partly* unproducible—do as ye please after consulting Hobhouse about it.

P.S.—Foscolo's Ricciarda was lent with the *leaves uncut* to some Italians now in Villeggiatura—so that I have had no opportunity of hearing their opinion—or of reading it.—They seized on it as Foscolo's and on account of the beauty of the paper and printing directly —If I find it takes—I will reprint it *here*—the Italians think as highly of

Foscolo as they can of any man—divided and miserable as they are—
and with neither leisure at present to read, nor head nor heart to
judge of anything but extracts from French newspapers and the
Lugano Gazzette.——

We are all looking at one another like wolves on their prey in
pursuit only waiting for the first faller on—to do unutterable things.—
They are a great world in Chaos—or Angels in Hell,—which you
please;—but out of Chaos came Paradise—and out of Hell—I don't
know what—but the Devil went *in* there—and he was a fine fellow
once you know.——You need never favour me with any periodical
publications excepting the Edinburgh—Quarterly—and an occasional
Blackwood—or now and then a Monthly Review—for the rest I do
not feel curiosity enough to look beyond their covers.———To be sure
I took in the British Roberts finely—he fell precisely into the glaring
trap laid for him—it was inconceivable how he could be so absurd as
[to] think us serious with him.——Recollect that if you put my name
to ["Don] Juan" in these canting days—any lawyer might oppose my
Guardian right of my daughter in Chancery—on the plea of it's
containing the *parody*[6]—such are the perils of a foolish jest;—I was
not aware of this at the time—but you will find it correct I believe—
& you may be sure that the Noels would not let it slip—Now I prefer
my child to a poem at any time—and so should you as having half a
dozen.———Let me know your notions.—

[Scrawl]

If you turn over the earlier pages of the H[untingdon] peerage[7] story—
you will see how common a name *Ada* was in the early Plantagenet
days—I found it in my own pedigree in the reign of John and Henry,
and gave it to my daughter.—It was also the name of Charlemagne's
sister. It is in an early chapter of Genesis as the name of the wife of
Lameth, and I suppose Ada is the feminine of *Adam*. It is short—
antient—vocalic—and had been in my family—for which reason I
gave it to my daughter.——

[TO COUNTESS TERESA GUICCIOLI]   *Ravenna. Obre. 11.o 1820*

Carissima Gasparina+—Sarà stato un' fulmine per "incinerire il
Cameriere" come dice Don Magnifico.——Non v'è caduto niente—

---

[6] The parody of the Ten Commandments, *Don Juan*, Canto I, stanzas 205–206.
[7] Henry Nugent Bell in his *Huntingdon Peerage* (1820) mentions two ancestresses
of the Earl of Huntingdon with the name of Ada.

fù una buffonata dei servitori contra Luigi per spavantare la sua bella la degna dama di tua camera.—Ti prego non fare tanto macello delle *oche*—perche non posso venire per qualche giorni ancora.—Sarai prevenuta sempre un'giorno prima—Amor mio + non andare in colera. ——Mandami le stampe—perche voglio far fare delle cornici.—Ti mando una pessima traduzione in Francese di quel' libro che tu domandasti tempo fa.—Troverai nella notizia—(piena di Sioccezze e menzogne però) un' racconto ben diverso di quello dei amici Pierineschi—a Roma—della Causa della *divisione* colla moglie.—Vi è nel' primo tomo.——Se puoi favorirmi coi altri volumi della *biografia*— des hommes &c. &c. &c.—sarò riconoscente.—Sempre + + +

[Scrawl]

P.S.—I libri sono venuti—Grazie.

Si vuole qualche giorno ancora perche penso di venire a *cavallo*— e le strade saranno poco praticabili dopo la gran' pioggia.——

[TRANSLATION]   *Ravenna, October 11th, 1820*

Dearest Gasparina + —It must have been a stroke of lightning "to turn a lacquey to ashes" as Don Magnifico[1] says——Nothing has happened—it was a joke of the servants against Luigi to frighten his Lady, the fair dame of your chamber.

Pray do not have such a massacre of geese—as I cannot come for several days. You will always be warned the day before—My love— don't be angry.

Send me the prints—as I want to have some frames made. I send you a very bad translation in French of the book you asked for some time ago. You will find in it (full of foolishness and lies however) a very different account from that of my Pierinesque friends in Rome— about the cause of my *separation* from my wife.[2] It is in the first volume————If you can favour me with the other volumes of the *biography of famous men*, I shall be grateful. Always.

P.S.—The books have come. Thank you.

It will have to be in a few days as I want to come on horse-back and the roads won't be practicable after all that rain.

---

[1] A character in Rossini's *La Cenerentola*, which was being performed in 1820.
[2] Byron had sent Teresa a copy of his poems in French with a biographical sketch of the author. He refers to the people in Rome who told Pietro Gamba scandalous and untrue stories of Byron's treatment of his wife.

197

Dear Douglas—I presume that my affairs must go to the devil—
their own way—as Mr Hanson seems determined to have his—and no
one else is either willing or able to Check him.——Upon *one point*
however I insist—and that is that he *sends in his account*.——If not,
at all risks—losses—or hazards *I will withdraw my affairs out of his
hands*—and this I beg you to state for & from me—in plain and peremptory English.——I moreover refuse my consent to an Appeal unless
I have *Counsel's opinion*—particularly Chancery Bell's—as *this was
promised* & *has not been sent.*—The delay about the mortgage is the
more infamous—that it is evidently done on purpose—in the hope
that a war or some other affection of the funds may prevent my getting
out of them.——I enclose you two receipts sent me long ago by
Messrs. Hanson—it is some money due from Government to my
mother[1]—who was (as a limb of the Stuarts) a pensioner—you are to
receive it however before you give back the receipts.——I wish that
you would write a little peremptory to Mr. Hanson—else he will
finish by entirely destroying my affairs—and all for want of a proper
understanding—with him—*power* you can't want—as you represent
me—It is my wish also to know how *many years* an *Appeal* requires—
and the probable expence—before I plunge into it.—I would still
rather sell the undisputed part of the manor for what it would bring—
pray try it once more at the hammer.—

yrs. ever & truly
BYRON

[on envelope]: Perhaps the enclosed had better be obtained through
Messrs. H[anson] of Chancery Lane—[they] were sent by them for
[my] signature.—

Amor mio +—Forse tu hai ragione—di ciò discorreremo quando
siamo insieme.—per ora mi limiterò a dirti che nell' anno 1816
quando quei versi erano stampati—una *Signora Francese* allora in Londra
diceva appresso poco nelle tue parole—che "non poteva comprendere
come la più orgogliosa donna["] &c. &c. ["] poteva resistere["] &c.
["]e per me["] diceva—"qualunque che fosse stato il torto di mio
amante o di mio marito—non sarei ritenuto un momento dal' gittarmi

---

[1] See Feb. 26, 1806, to Mrs. Byron, note 2. (Vol. 1, p. 89).

fra le sue braccie" &c. questa opinione fu stampata nelle gazzette del'
giorno—io non conobbe mai la persona—oltrache fosse una donna
Francese.—E singolare che una Francese ed una Italiana se uniscono
in quel' sentimento—la difesa della beata *Matematica* era—"che non
fui sincero—ma che tutto questo fosse un' *Machiavelismo* mio—per
metterla lei in apparente torto—perche in *fatto* io desiderava di
separarmi["] &c. &c.—Tu puoi giudicare per te stessa—se io sono
cosi politico.——Ci rivedremmo in pochi giorni amami + mia
Gaspara.—

sempre [Scrawl]

[TRANSLATION]   *Ravenna, October 12th, 1820*

My Love + ——Perhaps you are right—we will talk about it when
we are together—for the present I will only tell you that in the year
1816, when these verses[1] were printed, a French woman then in London,
said, more or less in your words,—that "she could not understand
how the proudest woman", etc. etc., "could restrain herself", etc. etc.,
and "As for me," said she, "whatever had been the guilt of my lover
or husband, I could not have restrained myself a moment from flinging
myself in his arms." This opinion was printed in the daily gazettes—I
did not know the person—beyond that it was a Frenchwoman.—It
is singular that a Frenchwoman and an Italian agree in this feeling.
The defence of the blessed *Mathematician* was—"that I was not
sincere—that all this was *Machiavellism* on my part—to make her
seem in the wrong—because *in fact* I wished for a separation", etc. etc.
You can judge for yourself—if I am so politic.
We shall see each other in a few days—Love me + my Gaspara—
always

[TO JOHN MURRAY]   *Ravenna 8bre 12.o 1820*

D[ea]r Murray—By land and Sea Carriage a considerable quantity
of books have arrived—and I am obliged and grateful.—But 'Medio

---

[1] The poem which affected Teresa the most was Byron's "Fare Thee Well".
Teresa wrote that if it was sincere, "I cannot understand how the proudest, the
coldest, of Englishwomen could refrain from coming to throw herself into your
arms and beg for mutual forgiveness." But she also wrote, what Byron chose to
ignore in his answer, that the poem "might give the impression that in some
moments of your life you showed a certain weakness of character." (Origo, p. 229.)

de fonte leporum surgit amari aliquid["]¹ &c. &c.——— which being interpreted means—

> "I'm thankful for your books dear Murray
> But why not send Scott's Monastery?"

the only book in four *living* volumes I would give a baiocco [sic]² to see, abating the rest of the same author, and an occasional Edinburgh & Quarterly—as brief Chroniclers of the times.——Instead of this— here are Johnny Keats's *p—ss a bed* poetry³—and three novels by G—d knows whom—except that there is Peg Holford's name⁴ to one of them—a Spinster whom I thought we had sent back to her spinning.— Crayon⁵ is very good—Hogg's tales rough but *racy*⁶—and welcome— Lord Huntingdon's blackguard portrait may serve for a sign for his "Ashby de la Zouche" Alehouse⁷—is it to such a drunken half-pay looking raff—that the Chivalrous Moira is to yield a portion of his titles? into what a puddle has stagnated the noble blood of the Hastings? —and the bog-trotting barrister's advertisement of himself and causes!! upon my word, the house and the courts have made a pair of precious acquisitions?—I have seen worse peers than this fellow—but then they were *made not begotten*—(these Lords are opposite to *the Lord* in all respects)—but however stupid—however idle—and profligate— all the peers by inheritance had something of the gentleman look about them—only the lawyers and the bankers "promoted into *Silver* fish" looked like ragamuffins—till this· new foundling came amongst them.——

Books of *travels* are expensive—and I don't want them—having travelled already—besides they lie.——Thank the Author of "the Profligate"⁸ a comedy for his (or her) present.—Pray send me *no more* poetry but what is rare and decidedly good.——There is such a trash of Keats and the like upon my tables—that I am ashamed to look

---

¹ Lucretius: "Medio de fonte leporum surgit amari aliquid quod in ipsis floribus angat." ("From the midst of the fountain of delight something bitter arises to vex us even amid the flowers themselves.")

² A baiocco was a copper coin of the old Papal States worth about a halfpenny.

³ Keats's *Lamia, Isabella, The Eve of St. Agnes, and other Poems* was published in 1820.

⁴ Miss Margaret Holford published in 1820 *Warbeck of Wolfenstein*.

⁵ Washington Irving's *The Sketch-Book* was published under the name of Geoffrey Crayon.

⁶ *Winter Evening Tales* (1820).

⁷ The Huntingdon Arms at Ashby-de-la-Zouche was near Huntingdon Castle.

⁸ *The Profligate, a Comedy* (1820) was by George Watson, who afterward took the name of Taylor.

at them.———I say nothing against your parsons—your Smedleys[9]—and your Crolys[10]—it is all very fine—but pray dispense me from the pleasure, as also from Mrs. Hemans.— —Instead of poetry if you will favour me with a few Soda powders—I shall be delighted—but all prose (bating travels and novels *not by Scott*)—is welcome especially Scott's tales of My Landlord & so on.——

In the notes to Marino Faliero it may be as well to say—"Benintende" was not really of *the ten*—but merely *Grand Chancellor*—a separate office—(although important)—it was an arbitrary alteration of mine.—The Doges too were all *buried* in *Saint Mark's before* Faliero—it is singular that when his immediate predecessor *Andrea Dandolo* died—"the ten" made a law—that *all* the *future doges*— should be *buried with their families in their own churches—one would think by a kind of presentiment.*—So that all that is said of his *Ancestral Doges* as buried at Saint Johns & Paul's is altered from the fact— *they being in Saint Marks—Make a Note* of this and put *Editor* as the Subscription to it. As I make such pretensions to accuracy—I should not like to be *twitted* even with such trifles on that score.—Of the play— they may say what they please but not so of my costume—and dram. pers. they having been real existences. I omitted Foscolo in my list of living *Venetian authors in the Notes*—considering him as an *Italian* in general—and not a mere provincial—like the rest—and as an Italian I have spoken of him in the preface to Canto 4th of Childe Harold.——

The French translation of us!!!—Oime! Oime!—and the German— but I don't understand the latter—nor his long dissertation at the end about the Fausts.—Excuse haste—of politics it is not safe to speak— but nothing is decided as yet.——I should recommend your *not* publishing the *prose*—it is *too late* for the letter to Roberts and that to Blackwood—is too egoistical—and Hobhouse don't like it—except the part about *Pope*, which is truth and very good.——I am in a very fierce humour at not having Scott's Monastery.—You are *too liberal* in *quantity* and somewhat careless of the quality of your missives.— All the *Quarterlies* (4 in number) I had had before from you—and *two*

---

[9] The Rev. Edward Smedley had recently published two volumes of verse, *Religio Clerici, a Churchman's Epistle* (1818), and *A Churchman's Second Epistle* (1819). They were published anonymously, but Lord Holland gave Byron the name of the author and said that the poems had been ascribed to Crabbe but were much inferior.

[10] The Rev. George Croly wrote frequently for *Blackwood's Magazine* and for the *Literary Gazette* and was the author of numerous volumes of poetry. He had written a poem, *Paris in 1815* (1817) in imitation of *Childe Harold*, and after Byron's death (1846) he published *The Modern Orlando* in imitation of *Don Juan*.

of the Edinburghs—but no matter—we shall have new ones by and bye. No more *Keats* I entreat—flay him alive—if some of you don't I must skin him myself[;] there is no bearing the drivelling idiotism of the Mankin.——

I don't feel inclined to care further about "Don Juan"[;] what do you think a very pretty Italian lady said to me the other day?—She read it in the French, and paid me some compliments with due *drawbacks* upon it;—I answered that "what she said was true—but that I suspected that it would live longer than Childe Harold."—"Ah (but said She) I *would rather have the fame of Childe Harold for three years than an Immortality of Don Juan*"! The truth is that *it is too true*—and the women hate every thing which strips off the tinsel of *Sentiment*—& they are right—or it would rob them of their weapons.—I never knew a woman who did not hate *De Grammont's memoirs*—for the same reason.—Even Lady Oxford used to abuse them.—Thorwaldsen is in Poland, I believe; the bust is at Rome still—as it has been *paid* for these 4 years. It should have been sent—but I have no remedy *till* he returns.——Rose's work[11] I never received—it was seized at Venice. Such is the liberality of the Huns with their two hundred thousand men—that they dare not let such a volume as his circulate.—

[TO JOHN HANSON]   *Ravenna. 8bre. 12.0 1820*

D[ea]r. S[i]r—I can enter into no appeal without Counsel's opinion—this was promised & has *not* been sent.——I would still much rather sell the Manor—at any price than enter into a new & hopeless litigation. ——Your delay (which seems a purposed & unwarrantable one) in completing the Irish Mortgage—surprizes and distresses me—you will finish by causing me to lose many thousand pounds—you may delay as you please but the mortgage *must* be completed[;] for I would rather sell out at any loss than trust to the infamous bubble of the British funds—into which (had I been upon the spot) I could never have entered.—It is also surprizing that you have never sent in your account to Mr. Kinnaird[;] if it is not sent—how can we ever come to any final settlement?——In expectation of an answer on these points I remain

yrs. very truly
BYRON

11 William Stewart Rose's *Letters from the North of Italy* (1819).

My dear Hoppner—By the boat of a certain Bonaldo bound for
Venice—I forward ⟨to you⟩ certain Novels of Mrs. Opie and others—
for Mrs. Hoppner & you as you desired.—Amongst the rest there is a
German translation of *Manfred*—with a plaguy long dissertation
at the end of it; it would be out of all measure and conscience to ask
you to translate the whole—but if you could give me a short *sketch*
of it—I should thank you—or if you could make somebody do the
whole into *Italian*—it would do as well;—and I would willingly pay
some poor Italian German Scholar for his trouble.—My own papers
are at last come from Galignani—with many thanks for yrs.

I am yrs. very truly
BYRON

P.S.—I remit by *Missiaglia* 30—Napoleons—is *that* the Sum?—

[TO JOHN MURRAY (*a*)] *Ravenna 8bre. 16.o 1820*

D[ea]r M[urra]y—In act second to the line—
"there's much for me to do—
___
add
___
and the hour hastens"

___
then continue thus—

___
Angiolina

Remember what you were.—

___
Doge

It were in vain—
Joy's recollection is no longer Joy
And
or Sorrow's Memory is a Sorrow still.
While
___
Angiolina

⟨Yet ere you comm⟩
At least—whate'er ⟨betide⟩ may urge—let me implore—
That you will take some little pause of rest &c. &c.

And so on as before—inserting the above in the text.—The place is

towards the close of the Scene in Act 2d. between M. Faliero and the
Duchess.——

yrs. truly

B

Ravenna, 8bre 16th, 1820

Dear Moray,[1]—*The Abbot* has just arrived: many thanks; as also
for the *Monastery—when you send it*!!!

The Abbot will have more than ordinary interest for me; for an
ancestor of mine by the mother's side, Sir J. Gordon of Gight, the
handsomest of his day, died on a Scaffold at Aberdeen for his loyalty
to Mary, of whom he was an imputed paramour as well as her relation. His fate was much commented on in the Chronicles of the times.
If I mistake not, he had something to do with her escape from Loch
Leven, or with her captivity there. But this you will know better than
I.

I recollect Loch Leven as it were but yesterday. I saw it in my way
to England in 1798, being then ten years of age. My Mother, who
was as haughty as Lucifer with her descent from the Stuarts,
and her right line, from the *old Gordons, not the Seyton Gordons*, as
she disdainfully termed the Ducal branch, told me the story, always
reminding me how superior *her* Gordons were to the southern
Byrons,—notwithstanding our Norman, and always masculine descent,[2] which has never lapsed into a female, as my mother's
Gordons had done in her own person.

I have written to you so often lately, that the brevity of this will be
welcome.

Yours ever and truly,

BYRON[3]

Ravenna. 8bre. 17.o 1820

My dear Hobhouse—I hope that you have safely received my two
late letters—which contained *two* letters from H[*oppne*]r—relative to

---

[1] Prothero has supplied this salutation. It is not in Moore, which he gives as
his sole source for this letter.

[2] Prothero (*LJ*, V, 99) suggests that Mrs. Byron may have known of the bend
sinister cast on the Byron Escutcheon by the Sir John Byron who was the first
owner of Newstead Abbey. His natural son, "Little Sir John with the Great
Beard", was later knighted by Queen Elizabeth and carried on the Byron line.
The bend sinister was not put on the Byron arms perhaps because the first Sir John
later married the lady who bore his illegitimate son.

[3] Complimentary closing and signature supplied by Prothero.

the Queen's Concern.——D[ougla]s K[innair]d has written to me but he lets that legal Spooney go on as he pleases—so that the funds will fall & fall—and who knows what thousands of pounds may be lost by his dawdling.——Do pray Stir him up with a long pole—and make him a speech sharp as those you produce in Parliament.——Recollect that my distance makes me helpless.——Have you seen Murray? and read my "*Tig.*["] and ["]*Tiri*["]?[1] have you "gone again into the Slaughter House Lankey?"——Murray hath projects of publication—about the *prose* too—regarding which I will abide by *your opinion*—which was against publishing the *Blackwood* &c.—I will rest with yr. decision in that matter whatever it be.—Foscolo thinks the tragedy very good Venetian, and Gifford says it is Sterling English.— Now is a good time for the Prophecy of Dante;—Events have acted as an Advertisement thereto.—Egad—I think I am as good a vates (prophet videlicet) as Fitzgerald of the Morning Post.——

On politics I shall say nothing—the post being somewhat suspect. ——I see that you are still "campaigning at the King of Bohemy"[2]— your last Speech is at great length in Galignani—and so you were called to order—but I think that you had the best of it.——You have done your part very well in Parliament to my mind; it was just the place for you—keep it up and go on.—If ever I come home—I will make a speech too—though I doubt my extempore talents in that line—and then *our* house is not animating like the hounds of the commons— when in full cry.—Tis but cold hunting at best in the Lords.——I never could command my own attention to either side of their oratory —but either went away to a ball—or to a beefsteak at Bellamy's— and as there is no answering without listening—nor listening without patience—I doubt whether I should ever make a debater.——I think I spoke four times in all there[3]—and I did not find my facility encrease with practice.——D[ougla]s K[innair]d did not mention you in his letters—which are always filled with radical politics—all which I can have in the Newspapers.—I wish he was in Parliament again—which I suppose he wishes too.——

We have sad Sirocco weather here at present—and no very bright political horizon.——But on that I shall say nothing—because I *know*—that they have spies upon me—because I sometimes shoot

---

[1] Unidentified.

[2] Samuel Foote, *The Mayor of Garratt*, Act. II.

[3] There is record of only three speeches of Byron in the House of Lords; on the Frame Bill, on the Catholic Disabilities, and on Cartwright's petition. But he may have spoken informally on another occasion.

with a rifle.—The exquisite reason!——You will laugh and think of Pope and the Clerks of the Post Office, but a fact I assure you.— They are in such a state of suspicion—as to dread everything and every body—and though I have been a year here—and they know why I came here yet they don't think a woman a sufficing reason for so long a residence.—As for the Scoundrel Austrians they are bullying Lombardy—as usual.—It would be pleasant to see those Huns get their paiks[4]—and it is not off the cards that they may.—

yrs. [Scrawl]

They send an order from Rome to disarm my Servants—the best of it is that they were *not armed!*—

[TO JOHN MURRAY]   *Ravenna. 8bre. 17.0 1820*

D[ea]r M[urra]y—Enclosed is the dedication of Marino Faliero to *Goethe*—Query? is his title *Baron* or not?[1] I think yes.——Let me know your opinion & so forth.—

[Scrawl]

P.S.—Let me know what Mr. Hobhouse & you have decided about the two *prose* letters—& their publication.——I enclose you an Italian abstract of the German translation of "Manfred's" appendix in which you will perceive quoted what Goethe says of the *whole body* of English poetry (& *not* of one in particular) on this the dedication is founded as you will perceive[2]—though I had thought of it before for I look upon him as a Great Man.—

[TO THOMAS MOORE]   *Ravenna, October 17th, 1820*

You owe me two letters—pay them. I want to know what you are about. The summer is over, and you will be back to Paris. Apropos of Paris, it was not Sophia *Gail*, but Sophia *Gay*—the English word *Gay*—who was my correspondent.[1] Can you tell who *she* is, as you did of the defunct * *?

---

[4] Scottish for "firm blow".

[1] Byron addressed his dedicatory letter to "Baron Goethe", but Goethe though titled (with the *Von* before his name), was not a baron.

[2] Byron's somewhat facetious dedication was delayed in transit and was not published with *Marino Faliero*. Goethe saw it first in 1831. See *Poetry*, IV, 328.

[1] See May 24, 1820, to Moore, note 2.

Have you gone on with your Poem? I have received the French of mine. Only think of being *traduced* into a foreign language in such an abominable travesty! It is useless to rail, but one can't help it.

Have you got my Memoir copied?[2] I have begun a continuation. Shall I send it you, as far as it is gone?

I can't say any thing to you about Italy, for the Government here look upon me with a suspicious eye, as I am well informed. Pretty fellows!—as if I, a solitary stranger, could do any mischief. It is because I am fond of rifle and pistol shooting, I believe; for they took the alarm at the quantity of cartridges I consumed,—the wiseacres!

You don't deserve a long letter—nor a letter at all—for your silence. You have got a new Bourbon, it seems, whom they have christened "Dieu-donné"—perhaps the honour of the present may be disputed. Did you write the good lines on [Wordsworth], the Laker?[3] * * * * * *

The Queen has made a pretty theme for the journals. Was there ever such evidence published? Why it is worse than "Little's Poems" or "Don Juan." If you don't write soon, I will "make you a speech."

Yours, &c.

[TO AUGUSTA LEIGH]   *Ravenna. 8bre.* [18?].*o 1820*

My dearest Augusta—I suppose by this time that you will be out of yr. fidget—& that the dilatory Hanson will have set Colonel L[eigh] at rest upon the subject of the bond &c.——Ada's picture is very like her mother—I mean the prints—for I have not received the picture,— neither has Murray sent it—I presume.——She seems stout of her age—which is five years on the 10th. of 10bre.—is it not so?—It is almost as long since I have seen her—all but a month—what day of January was it when ⟨the Math⟩ Lady B—marched upon Kirkby?— which was the Signal of war.——Sir Walter Scott says in the beginning of "the Abbot" that ["]every *five* years we find ourselves another and yet the same with a change of views and no less of the light in which we regard them; a change of motives as well as of actions." This I presume applies still more to those who have past their *five* years in foreign countries—for my part I suppose that I am *two* others—for it seems that some fool has been betting that he

---

[2] Moore, with Byron's consent, had a copy made of the Memoirs in Paris, where he was then living. (See Moore, *Memoirs*, III, 116.)

[3] See August 31, 1820, to Moore, note 6.

207

saw me in London—the other day—in a *Curricle*—if he said a *Canoe* it would have been much more likely.——

And *you?* what have *your* "*five* years" done?—made your house like a Lying-in Hospital;—there never was such a creature except a rabbit—for increase & multiplication.—In short we are five years older in fact and I at least *ten* in *appearance*—the Lady B—I suppose retains her old starch obstinacy—with a deeper dash of Sternness—from the dint of time—and the effort it has cost her to be "magnanimous" as they called her mischief-making.—People accused somebody of painting her in "Donna *Inez*"—did it strike you so?—I can't say it did me—There might be something of her in the outline but the Spaniard was only a silly woman—and the other is a cut and dry made up character—which is another matter.——Time and Events will one day or another revenge her past conduct,—without any interference of mine.——So—Joe Murray is gathered to his Masters —as you say—the very Ghosts have died with him.—Newstead and he went almost together & now the B's must carve them out another inheritance.—If Ada had been a Son—I do not think that I should have parted with it after all—but I dislike George B[yron] for his behaviour in 1816.—and I am unacquainted with the others who may be in the line of the title—and being myself abroad—and at feud with the whole of the Noels—and with most of the B's except yourself—of course— these concurring with other & pressing circumstances—rendered the disposal of the Abbey necessary & not improper. Somebody said the other day—that "Lady Noel had been ill"—she is too troublesome an old woman ever to die while her death can do any good,—but if she ever does march—it is to be presumed that she will take her "water divining rod" with her—it may be a useful twig to her & the devil too —when she gets home again.——

I can say very little to you of Italy—except that it is a very distracted State.—In England the Queen has been bountiful to the Scandalmongers.—She has got the Noel batch of Counsellors—it seems (except Romilly—who cut his throat) you see who *those* sort of fellows *are*—and how they prey on a cause of this kind—like crows on carrion. —Her Majesty's innocence is probably something like another person's guilt.—However she has been an ill-used woman—that's the truth on't—and in the nature of things the woman ought to get the better. They generally do—whether they ought or not.——I did not come over for fifty reasons—and amongst others—that I do not think it a very creditable thing to be one of the Judges even, upon such matters. I have got a flourishing family (besides my daughter

Allegra)—here are two Cats—six dogs—a badger—a falcon, a tame Crow—and a Monkey.——The fox died—and a first Cat ran away.— With the exception of an occasional civil war about provisions—they agree to admiration—and do not make more noise than a well-behaved Nursery.——I have also eight horses—four carriage—and four saddle—and go prancing away daily—at present up to the middle in mire—for here have been the Autumnal rains—& drenched every thing—amongst others myself yesterday—I got soaked through cloak & all—& the horse through his skin—I believe.——I have now written to you a long family letter [a line cut out]

ever yrs. [Scrawl]

[TO COUNTESS TERESA GUICCIOLI]   *Ravenna. 8bre. 25.0 1820*

Amor Mio +—La Lettera della F[anni] è un' ritratto del' carattere di quella "Galeotta che la scrisse,"—Falsa—furba—arrogante—venale—pedantesca—adulante—bugiarda.—"*Franca* a Ravenna!"—franca al' inferno—che il diavolo paga il viaggio!—la sola cosa che mi piacerebbe un' istante sarebbe il vedere *l'affetto sopra Pierino*—sono certo che la gittarebbe per la finestra—il secondo giorno.——C[torn] coi suoi sforzati complimenti sul' riguardo [word torn out] la lercia!—ma io sono di [torn] apporto di lei!——Non ho tempo a dirti di più poiche il [torn] corriere è impaziente—saluta Papa e Pierino ed amami sempre + + +

[Scrawl]

P.S.—Non so se Lega sarà inteso colla Signora F[anni] ma io mi sono *inteso* con lui sopra quel' argomento.——

[TRANSLATION]   *Ravenna. October 25th. 1820*

My Love +—Fanny's letter is a portrait of "the procuress [Galleotto] who wrote it."[1] False, sly, arrogant, corrupt, pedantic, toadying and a liar. "*Frank* to Ravenna"—frank to Hell—let the devil pay the journey! The only thing I should like for a moment would be to see her effect on Pierino—I am sure he would throw her out of the window the second day.

---

[1] A reference to Dante's "Galeotto fu il libro e chi lo scrisse" (*Inferno*, V, v, 137).

[torn] with her forced compliments about me [torn] the bitch but I am [torn]

I have no time to say more for the [torn] courier is impatient. Greet Papa and Pierino and love me always. + + +

P.S.—I don't know if Lega has an understanding with Signora F[anny] but *I* have reached an understanding with *him* on the subject.

[TO LADY BYRON]   *Ravenna 8bre. 25.o 1820*

Mr. Kinnaird informs me that your trustees and advisers had opposed any present transfer from the 3 to 5 percents of the sum settled, in the interim of completing the examination of the Blessington papers.—This would be quite right if there was enough prospect of a rise in the funds—but I have reason to think this remote.———What your prospects may be at home—I know not—but here the Country is on the Eve of a great convulsion.—The Austrians are now on the Po—& the moment they pass it—your English funds will fall to sixty—at least.———I cannot for many reasons explain to you fully the *actual* state of Italy—at least of this part of it—where we are within a march of the Barbarians—but you may rely upon what I say to you.——— The Exasperation of men's minds is extreme and general—and too many are compromised not to render the war savage to a degree.— It is difficult to foresee how it will end—or even *tend*—for the Italians are *not*—like any other nation;—beaten and oppressed they will doubtless be in the beginning—for nothing but a Guerilla war can at all equalize unpracticed men with a regular army—but *would* they—or *could* they but unite—they would soon scatter the Barbarians.—But this is difficult—each province and district has all the prejudices of it's past history—without the power which made them then formidable to others, they are now more dangerous to each other by their weakness, than they once were by their Strength.—The Events I speak of are impending, and I request you to consider how far a foreign war is likely to affect your own funds—and to permit my trustees to place the remaining fortunes of my family upon a securer tenure than the Bank Bubble—even at the expence of some present loss.—It is *not* now as it was some months ago—the Spanish & Neapolitan revolutions have changed every thing.——Hanson will delay as long as he can— for the sake of his own opinions—or from other motives—for I do not understand him nor them—but my absence naturally places my affairs in all matters of legal investigation much in his power—but if your trustees united with mine—they would probably quicken him.— When I last wrote to you—I expressed my wish *not* to sell out at a loss—but there was then a prospect of an eventual rise—at present there is none—and I think you will agree with me *now* that the funds are not a desirable speculation for large sums.——

I have received two prints from Ada's picture—and although I cannot judge of the eyes and complexion from a print—I am well content. —"You bear a strong resemblance to your Mother" as Penruddock[1] says.—Murray has not sent the picture—and he has done *well* for if any accident had happened to it—I should have been very sorry.—Let me hope to see it & the original also some day or other—She is strikingly like yourself—I do not see much resemblance to me unless something in the bust I think.——There is a great deal of character in the head altogether—and very strongly marked for a Child of that age. —Pray let her be taught Italian,—I hope by the time she is twenty that Italy will be free and regenerated——Alas! at what a price of blood & butchery—must it be so—but anything is better than those Barbarians at the gate—if you had seen their infamous tyranny— their ignorant atrocity in Lombardy—& wherever they set their hoofs;—it would make even your temperate blood boil.—Imagine the effect it must have upon these "children of the Sun".——Their passage of the Po will be followed by confiscations and arrests and insurrection—besides the Neapolitan war.——The Suspicion of the government here is extreme—even of Strangers—(most of whom have retired) they sent an order the other day to *disarm my Servants* (who by the way *did not* carry arms) imagine what must be the state of things when a solitary stranger puts them upon such precautions?—I answered them that they might make what regulations they chose for such servants as were Papal—but they should not disarm *me*—unless by actual force—in a country where they "shoot a man a week" like Bob Acres "in the Country".—They said no more—but there is a general espionage—they seem to dread my influence on the younger men with whom they conceive me to be popular.—This is what they give out themselves.—They are mistaken however—I never was personally popular anywhere—and in Italy popularity at present is limited to *Opera Singers* and will continue to be so—till there is a renewed Rome.——

But I forget—and am wandering into politics when I should be treating of business- but the objects by which I am reminded must

---

[1] A character in Richard Cumberland's *Wheel of Fortune*. Byron played the role in amateur theatricals when a boy.

211

excuse it.——Let me request you to weigh how far what I have said of the funds & of the proposed transfer be well founded—and [do] not allow any secret aversion to whatever [comes] from me to bias you;—this is not [the] moment.——And if in these *"kittle* times" any accidents should occur which may throw the settlement into your own hands—be kind to my Sister and her children—as I have all along entreated you—though apparently to no great purpose.——I am yrs. &c. &c. &c.

BYRON

[TO JOHN MURRAY]   *Ravenna. 8bre. 25.o 1820*

D[ea]r Moray—Pray forward the enclosed to Lady Byron, it is on business.——In thanking you for the Abbot I made four grand mistakes.—Sir John Gordon was not of Gight—but of Bogagicht—and a Son of Huntley's.—He suffered—*not* for his loyalty—but in an insurrection.—He had *nothing* to do with Loch Leven having been dead some time at the period of the Queen's confinement.—And 4thly. I am not sure that he was the Queen's paramour or no—for Robertson does not allude to this—though *Walter Scott does*—in the list she gives of her admirers (as unfortunate) at the close of "the Abbot".—I must have made all these mistakes in recollecting my Mother's account of the matter—although she was more accurate than I am—being precise upon points of genealogy like all the Aristo-cratical Scotch.—She had a long list of ancestors like Sir Lucius O'Trigger's—most of whom are to be found in the old Scotch Chronicles—Spalding &c. in arms & doing mischief. I remember well passing Loch Leven as well as the Queen's Ferry——we were on our way to England in 1798.——Why do the papers call *Hobhouse young?* he is a year and a half older than I am—and I was thirty two last January.—Of Italy I can say nothing by the post—we are in instant expectation of the Barbarians passing the Po—and then—there will be a row of fury & extermination.—Pray write sometimes—the communications will not long be so open.

yrs. [Scrawl]

P.S.—Send me the *Monastery* and some Soda powders—You had better not publish Blackwood & the Roberts prose except what re-gards *Pope*—you have let the time slip by.——

212

Dear Douglas—By last post I consigned to Mr. Murray a letter on business to the Lady Byron.——In this I recommended strongly to her consideration (& to that of her trustees) the speedy removal of the settled property from the funds.—My motives are the almost immediate explosion which must take place in Italy in the impending event of the passage of the Po by the Barbarians now in great force on that river—and the fall further of the English funds in consequence—as your Tory Scoundrels will right or wrong take part in any foreign war.—*I wish you to write to her in aid of my representation*; for God sake —take advantage of any rise to sell out—otherwise it will ere long be too late.——I know better than any of you what is brewing in Italy— do not let the fortunes of my family be totally sacrificed at home— whatever I may be! Recollect that a month—a week—a day—may render all this abortive—and press upon this implacable woman & her trustees; as well as upon that dog Hanson—the necessity of selling out immediately.——If I did not abhor your Tory country to a degree of detestation, this would have been remedied,—I would last year have gone amongst you and settled my own business at least—but I prefer anything almost to making one of such a people, as your present Government has made of the present English.—Hanson has not sent *Counsel's opinion* on an *Appeal*—in that case—I revoke my consent—I have but one word for *him*—*his bill or a rupture.*—*Say so much in so many words.* I prefer almost any thing else to living amongst you English—but it is still my duty to represent as far as I can what ought to be done by my trustees in my absence.—

yrs. truly & affectly.

BYRON

P.S.—I have read lately several speeches of Hobhouse in taverns— his Eloquence is better than his company.—Tell him that if *Bergami* goes to England the Courier of the innocent Queen will beat him for *Westminster*.——To give you a hint of the doings *here*;—since I began this letter the news have arrived from *Forli* (the next & nearest city) that last night the liberals blew up by means of a mine the house of a "Brigand" (so they call here the Satellites of the tyrants) (during Comedy time or Opera time) but the master *was out* and so escaped. ——People were arrested [words torn out with seal] released them— & shot a blackguard [or one] of the Carabineers.——They have also intimated gently to his Eminence of Forli that if he continues to arm *assassins* (here they war in private in this way—there are bands in every

213

town at so much a head—for those who like such expences) they will throw him out of the palace windows—which are rather lofty.—If these things don't prelude "sword and gun fighting" you can judge for yourself.——Get me out of your funds—write in your *best manner* to the Mathematician—your letters of *business* are *models*—(your other letters somewhat brief and hasty) and persuade that excellent female to allow me to be an "Irish Absentee" before the three per cents are at no per cent.—If she don't, I will come over—be a radical—& take possession of the Kirkby Estate—before Lady Noel is in Hell—no long time—if people went there alive but the bitch will live forever to plague her betters.——Write to the trustees—press the matter—and prosper.——You should set up a radical Newspaper & call it "the Bergami"—it would beat Mr. Street's[1] now-a-days.——

[TO RICHARD BELGRAVE HOPPNER]   *Ravenna. 8bre 28.o 1820*

My dear Consul,—Your lines are good and true—too true to trust to the Barbarian post.—The Queen appears to triumph. Pray—was it 30 Napoleons that ought to have been or *more*? say so—for I am not a good accomptant.—Tell me when the books arrive—and if they are to your liking.——Let me know if I can send you any others—which I will willingly do.—I have Scott's *"Abbot"*—which is not his best—"a Sequel to the *Monastery*" which Murray[?] has not sent me.—Excuse haste—my best respects to Madame

yrs ever
BYRON

[TO COUNTESS TERESA GUICCIOLI]   *Ravenna. 8bre. 30.o 1820*

Amor Mio+—Posso ben credere qualunque cosa dei bigotti parenti—o del' governo che adesso sospetta di tutti e farebbe del' tutto—per allontanare o spaventare quelli che teme.—Non sarà pero solamente diretta a *me*—ma anche a *tua famiglia*—(Pierino per esempio) per essere stati sospettati in queste ultime cose patriotiche.—Ma

---

[1] Thomas George Street was long associated with Daniel Stuart, proprietor of the Tory *Morning Post* and *The Courier, The Courier,* edited by Street, had attacked Byron viciously after the publication in *The Corsair* of his "Lines to a Lady Weeping", which openly criticized the Prince Regent's conduct in deserting his Whig friends. Byron's suggestion for a radical newspaper to rival Street's *Courier* is based on the ironic fact that Bergami was Queen Caroline's "courier" and supposed lover. Street's *Courier* had been a leader in the press campaign against the Queen.

c'è un' ingiustizia nel' far' la guerra a una donna per le colpe di un' uomo.——Io aveva sperato (prevedendo queste cose) che la mia condotta dopo la tua separazione dal' marito—fu stata abbastantemente riservata (*in apparenza*) per allontanare ogni pretesta di prendere delle nuove misure, particolarmente dopo i patti con Guiccioli e la tua famiglia—per rilasciare tanto del' assegno. L'invidia dei bigotti naturalmente gli fa' sempre perseguitare gli altri per piaceri dei quali si privono loro stessi.—Per me—io non vedo—nè capisco nulla—senoche—per ogni piccolo mezzo—cercano di disfarsi della mia presenza nei stati pontifizj—e se non fosse per *certe speranze*——e *sentimento* (compreso *sopra tutto* l'amore per te) io ben presto gli leverei il disturbo.——Saluta papa e Pierino——Elisei è tornato e collocato a Faenza—ecco la sua lettera a me.——Io non conosco abbastantamente le circonstanze per dare dei consigli a *papa*—egli dovrebbe essere a giorno del' indole di suoi parenti—e di quanto il governo sarà o non sarà capace.——Del' amor mio tu hai avuto delle prove ed avrai—sono e sarò

[Scrawl]

Ravenna, October 30th, 1820

My Love +—I can well believe anything of those bigoted relatives (of yours)[1]—and of the Government, which now suspects everyone and would do anything—to send away or frighten those it fears—It will not, however, be directed only at *me*—but also at *your* family—(Pierino, for example) for being suspect in these recent patriotic matters.—But it is unjust to attack a woman for a man's misdoing———I had hoped, foreseeing all this, that my conduct after your separation from your husband had been sufficiently reserved (*in appearance*) to remove any pretext for taking fresh measures, particularly after the agreement between Guiccioli and your family—to give up a part of the allowance.

The bigots' envy naturally always makes them persecute others for the pleasures of which they have deprived themselves. For my part I don't see or understand anything—except that—by any trivial means—they are attempting to rid themselves of my presence in the Papal States—and were it not for certain *hopes* and *sentiments* (including, *above all*, my love for you) I should very quickly *take myself off*.

[1] The "bigoted relatives" were probably Teresa's grandparents. See Sept. 9, 1820, to Teresa, note 1.

Greet Papa and Pierino.

Elisei has come back and settled in Faenza—here is his letter to me. I don't know the circumstances well enough to give Papa advice. He should know about the character of his relations and of what the government is or is not capable. Of my love you have proofs and shall have more.

I am and shall be

[*November? 1820*] *Nov. 22, 1820 post mark*

D[ea]r Hobhouse—Over the enclosed I leave you a discretionary power—to alter or lop off what may appear "too full of pastime and prodigality"——You may omit the whole—if you think good.— Another letter goes by this post to Whitton.——

yrs. [Scrawl]

P.S.—*I* re-opened the enclosed to Murray for you to pronounce upon in yr. way.

[TO JOHN MURRAY]   *Ravenna. 9bre. 4.o 1820*

I have received from Mr. Galignani the enclosed letters—duplicates —and receipts—which will explain themselves.[1]——As the poems are your property by purchase, right, & justice, *all matters of publication &c. &c. are for you to decide upon.*—I know not how far my compliance with Mr. G[alignani]'s request might be legal, and I doubt that it would not be honest.——In case you choose to arrange with him—I enclose the permits to *you*—& in so doing I wash my hands of the business altogether.—I sign them merely to enable you to exert the power you justly possess more properly.—I will have nothing to do with it further; except in my answer to Mr. Galignani—to state that the letters &c. &c. are sent to you & the causes thereof.——If you can check those foreign Pirates—do;—if not—put the permissive papers in the fire;—*I* can have no view nor object whatever but to secure to you your property—

yrs.

BYRON

---

[1] Byron had received from the Paris publisher Galignani a request for exclusive right to publish his work in France, to prevent piracy.

P.S.—There will be—shortly—*"the Devil to pay" here*—and as there is no saying that I may not form an *Item in his bill*—I shall not now write at greater length;—*you* have *not answered* my late letters;—and you have acted foolishly—as you will find out some day.———

P.S.—I have read part of the Quarterly just arrived.—Mr. Bowles shall be answered[2]—he is not *quite* correct in his statement about E[nglish] B[ards] & S[cotch] R[eviewers].———They Support Pope I see in the Quarterly[3]—Let them Continue to do so—it is a Sin & a Shame and a *damnation*—to think that Pope!! should require it—but he does.———Those miserable mountebanks of the day—the poets—disgrace themselves—and deny God—in running down Pope—the most *faultless* of Poets, and almost of men.———The Edinburgh praises Jack Keats or Ketch or whatever his names are;—why his is the *Onanism* of Poetry—something like the pleasure an Italian fiddler extracted out of being suspended daily by a Street Walker in Drury Lane—this went on for some weeks—at last the Girl went to get a pint of Gin—met another, chatted too long—and Cornelli was *hanged outright* before she returned. Such like is the trash they praise—and such will be the end of the *outstretched* poesy of this miserable Self-polluter of the human Mind.———W. Scott's Monastery just arrived—many thanks for that Grand Desideratum of the last Six Months.———

P.S.—You have cut up old Edgeworth[4] it seems amongst you.—You are right—he is a bore.—I met the whole batch—Mr. Mrs. & Miss at a blue breakfast of Lady Davy's in Blue Square—and he proved but bad—in taste and tact & decent breeding.———He began by saying that Parr (Dr. Parr) had attacked—& that he (the father of Miss E) had cut him up in his answer.—Now Parr would have annihilated him—& if he had not—why tell *us* (a long story) *who* wanted to breakfast?—I saw them different times in different parties—& I thought him a very tiresome coarse old Irish half and half Gentleman and her a pleasant reserved old woman—with a *pencil* under her petticoat—however—undisturbed in it's operation by the vicinity of that anatomical part of female humanity—which would have rendered

---

[2] Isaac D'Israeli's article in the *Quarterly Review*, (July, 1820, pp. 400–434) on Spence's *Anecdotes of Books and Men* quoted (p. 425) a passage from Bowles's *Invariable Principles of Poetry*, in which Bowles corrects a mistake of Byron in *English Bards and Scotch Reviewers* (line 360): "When first Madeira trembled to a kiss."
[3] *Quarterly Review*, Vol. XXIII, p. 407.
[4] *Quarterly Review* for July, 1820, pp. 510–549.

the taking notes neutral or partial in any other she animal above a Cow.—That sort of woman seem to think themselves perfect because they can't get covered; & those who are seem no better for it—the *spayed bitches.*———

[Scrawl]

Ravenna, November 5th, 1820

Thanks for your letter, which hath come somewhat costively,— but better late than never. Of it anon. Mr. Galignani, of the Press, hath, it seems, been supplanted and sub-pirated by another Parisian publisher, who has audaciously printed an edition of L. B.'s works, at the ultra-liberal price of ten francs and (as Galignani piteously observes) eight francs only for booksellers! "horresco referens." Think of a man's *whole* works producing so little!

Galignani sends me, post haste, a permission *for him, from me,* to publish &c. &c., which *permit* I have signed and sent to Mr. Murray, of Albemarle-street. Will you explain to G. *that I* have no right to dispose of Murray's works without his leave? and therefore I must refer him to M. to get the permit out of his claws—no easy matter, I suspect. I have written to G. to say as much; but a word of mouth from a "great brother author" would convince him that I could not honestly have complied with his wish, though I might legally. What I could do I have done, viz. signed the warrant and sent it to Murray. Let the dogs divide the carcass, if it is killed to their liking.

I am glad of your epigram. It is odd that we should both let our wits run away with our sentiments; for I am sure that we are both Queen's men at bottom. But there is no resisting a clinch—it is so clever! Apropos of that—we have a "diphthong" also in this part of the world —not a *Greek,* but a *Spanish* one—do you understand me?—which is about to blow up the whole alphabet. It was first pronounced at Naples, and is spreading;—but we are nearer the Barbarians; who are in great force on the Po, and will pass it, with the first legitimate pretext.

There will be the devil to pay, and there is no saying who will or who will not be set down in his bill. If "honour should come unlooked for"[1] to any of your acquaintance, make a Melody of it, that his ghost, like poor Yorick's, may have the satisfaction of being plaintively pitied—or still more nobly commemorated, like "Oh breathe not his

---

[1] *Henry IV*, Part I, Act V, scene 3.

name."[2] In case you should not think him worth it, here is a Chant for you instead—

> When a man hath no freedom to fight for at home,
>> Let him combat for that of his neighbours;
> Let him think of the glories of Greece and of Rome,
>> And get knock'd on the head for his labours.

> To do good to mankind is the chivalrous plan,
>> And is always as nobly requited;
> Then battle for freedom wherever you can,
>> And, if not shot or hang'd, you'll get knighted.

So you have gotten the letter of "Epigrams"—I am glad of it. You will not be so, for I shall send you more. Here is one I wrote for the endorsement of "the Deed of Separation" in 1816; but the lawyers objected to it, as superfluous. It was written as we were getting up the signing and sealing. * * has the original.

Endorsement to the Deed of Separation, in the April of 1816.

> A year ago you swore, fond she!
> "To love, to honour," and so forth:
> Such was the vow you pledged to me,
> And here's exactly what 'tis worth.

For the anniversary of January 2, 1821, I have a small grateful anticipation, which, in case of accident, I add—

> *To Penelope, January 2, 1821.*

> This day, of all our days, has done
>> The worst for me and you:—
> 'Tis just *six* years since we were *one*,
>> And *five* since we were *two*.

Pray excuse all this nonsense; for I must talk nonsense just now, for fear of wandering to more serious topics, which, in the present state of things, is not safe by a foreign post.

I told you in my last, that I had been going on with the "Memoirs," and have got as far as twelve more sheets. But I suspect they will be interrupted. In that case I will send them on by post, though I feel remorse at making a friend pay so much for postage, for we can't frank here beyond the frontier.

[2] Moore's song (No. 1 in the *Irish Melodies*).

I shall be glad to hear of the event of the Queen's concern. As to the ultimate effect, the most inevitable one to you and me (if they and we live so long) will be that the Miss Moores and Miss Byrons will present us with a great variety of grandchildren by different fathers.

Pray, where did you get hold of Goethe's Florentine husband-killing story?[3] Upon such matters, in general, I may say, with Beau Clincher, in reply to Errand's wife—

"Oh the villain, he hath murdered my poor Timothy!
"*Clincher.* Damn your Timothy!—I tell you, woman, your husband has *murdered me*—he has carried away my fine jubilee clothes."[4]

So Bowles has been telling a story, too ('tis in the *Quarterly*), about the woods of "Madeira," and so forth. I shall be at Bowles again, if he is not quiet. He misstates, or mistakes, in a point or two. The paper is finished, and so is the letter.

Yours, &c.

[TO DOUGLAS KINNAIRD]   *Ravenna. 9bre. 5.0 1820*

Dear Douglas—The enclosed letters contain a representation from the town of Rochdale (of 30000 inhabitant radical Souls) to their liege lord of the Manor—to permit a new market place—owing no doubt to the exuberance of provisions which the times have left in Lancashire.——There seem to be two parties—*for* and *against* the proposed Piazza. To which should I incline?—You are a man of affairs & should know. I am full of philanthropy—but must maintain my Manorial rights.—Read—perpend—pronounce—or ask Spooney. By your papers—I see that her Majesty the *Queen* is likely to triumph over her Tory opponents.——It is a good thing in more ways than one—and the reading of the Evidence will greatly multiply our stock of Grandchildren.—

yrs. ever & truly
BYRON

P.S.—I wrote twice lately to yr. Eminence.—

P.S.—I have written to you—to Spooney—and to the Mathematician—to urge selling out immediately—but I suppose—the friend-

---

[3] The story was told by Goethe in his review of *Manfred* in *Kunst und Alterthum*. See *LJ*, V. 503 ff.

[4] Farquhar's *Constant Couple, or a Trip to the Jubilee*, Act IV, scene 1.

ship of the one—the law of the other—and the Gospel of the third—will be found of the usual practical utility for the absent.—However I have done what I could—and you may all do as you please.——Here there is a political row brewing daily and hourly—it will come upon you like a Water Spout some day, & knock down yr. funds with a foreign war.——

[TO COUNTESS TERESA GUICCIOLI]   *Ravenna. 9bre. 8.o 1820*

Amor Mio +—Non ti scrissi—perche non fu nulla di nuovo a dirti. —"Da *Nulla* Nulla può venire" dice la Matematica—ciò che non è vero pero, poiche ho veduto delle volte da *Nulla* sortire una lettera di sei pagine.—Ma io non ho l'eloguenza di Santa Ch[ia]ra nemmeno della *Fanni*. Tu sai il mio gran'*talento* per il *Silenzio* e dovresti perdonarmi quando non scrivo per ogni piccola occasione.—Il tempo non mi pare molto favorevole per il tuo progetto- -ma ne penserò.——Salutami Papa e Pierino; ed amami—

tutto [Scrawl]

P.S.—Scrivi se ti commoda—altramente credo che non vivresti più —dunque *Scrivi*—gran Santa C[hiar]a +!

[TRANSLATION]   *Ravenna. November 8th. 1820*

My Love +—I did not write to you—because there was nothing to say. "Out of *Nothing* Nothing can arise", the Lady Mathematician said—which, however, is not true, for I have often seen a letter of six pages come out of *Nothing*. You know my great *talent* for *Silence*— and should forgive me when I do not write on every slightest occasion. The weather does not seem to be very favourable for your plan—but I will think about it.

Greet Papa and Pierino—and love me entirely +

P.S.—*Write* if it suits you—otherwise I believe you could not live— so *write*, great Santa C[hiar]a +!

[TO JOHN CAM HOBHOUSE]   *R[avenn]a. 9bre. 9.o 1820*

My dear H.— I admit the force of yr. facetiousness—which it will go hard but I pay off some day or other, as Scrope used to say "I have things in store."—⟨Lazy⟩ Indolent I am to be sure—and yet I can

221

back a horse and fire a carbine, like major Sturgeon "without winking or blinking"[1]—and I can go without my dinner without scolding—or eat it without finding fault with the cooking or quality, and I could slumber as in Turkey when some of my friends were loudly execrating their bed & it's tenantry.——Yours is now a more active life, I admit —you write pamphlets against Canning—and make speeches—and "greatly *daring dine*" at the Crown and Anchor.—And this *is* being active and useful, & justifies yr. reproach of my slumbers.——We will divide the parts between us of "player and poet"—as you have taken up the former one with great success.——Now "I have the best of that" I think—as I used to say to you in the wilderness. And then *you* counsel me to keep out of a *scrape—You!*—why have your prudence and activity kept you out of one?—I think not—you will find some day that your radicals will embarrass you sufficiently.——But in the mean time you are certainly making a figure in point of *talent*—that is a fact —and so you would in any other line—because you *happen to have great talent*—more *I* think than you yourself or others have yet given you credit for—and you are besides sure to train on—because you have strong powers of application—but the *line* itself is not the true one—and was not your own choice—but the result of circumstances united to a little natural impatience for having waited for an opening,—Egad—I talk like an Angel.——Oh—you must know that I sent H[oppner]'s letter without asking him—so say nothing about that—I thought it might serve the *Queen* in her cause—and you in her behalf & sent it—trusting to your discretion—pray—do not compromise him—nor any body else.—"*Young Man*" quotha! he is six & thirty—that is two years older than you—and three years & three months more than me—I see the papers call "*you* young" I am glad of it—but though I am your Junior—I have thought myself *eldern* this many a day.——I hope that you will turn out those Tory Scoundrels.— I do not quarrel with my "*old Cronies*"—nor my "old cronies" with me I hope——and as for the ballad—*you* have *balladed* me fifty times— and are welcome to fifty more—recollect at *Brighton*—at Newstead— & just *before* leaving England—and *since*——

yrs. ever & truly
BYRON

P.S.—Foscolo protests the tragedy—I shall take yr. opinion in good part whatever it is. Will you let Murray have "the Hints" that I may adapt them.——

[1] In Samuel Foote's *Mayor of Garratt*, Act I, scene 1.

Dear Moray—The talent you approve of is an amiable one and as you say might prove "a national Service" but unfortunately I must be angry with a man before I draw his real portrait—and I can't deal in *"generals"* so that I trust never to have provocation enough to make a *Gallery.*—If *"the* person"[1]—had not by many little dirty sneaking traits provoked it—I should have been silent—though I *had observed* him. Here follows an alteration.—Put—

> "Devil, with *such* delights in damning,
> That if at the resurrection
> Unto him the free selection
> Of his future could be given—
> 'Twould be rather Hell than Heaven.—"

That is to say if these new lines do not too much lengthen out & weaken the amiability of the original thought & expression.—You have discretionary power about showing,—I should think that Croker and D'Israeli would not disrelish a sight of these light little humourous things—and may be indulged now & then.———D'Israeli wrote the article on Spence[2]—I know him by the mark in his mouth—I'm glad that the Quarterly has had so much Classical honesty and honour as to insert it—it is good & true.——

Hobhouse writes me a facetious letter about my *indolence*—and love of Slumber.—It becomes him—he is in active life—he writes pamphlets against Canning to which he does not put his name—he gets into Newgate—and into Parliament—both honourable places of refuge—and he "greatly daring dines" at all the taverns—(why didn't he set up a *tap* room at once?) and then writes to quiz my laziness. ——Why I do like one or two vices to be sure—but I can back a horse and fire a pistol without "winking or blinking" like Major Sturgeon—I have fed at times for two months together on *sheer* biscuit & water (without metaphor) I can get over seventy or eighty miles a day *riding* post and *swim five* at a Stretch taking a *piece* before & after as at Venice in 1818 or at least I *could do* & have done [it] *once* & I never was ten minutes in my life over a *solitary* dinner.—Now my friend Hobhouse—when we were wayfaring men used to complain grievously of hard beds and sharp insects—while I slept like a top—and to awaken me with his swearing at them—he used to damn his dinners daily

---

1 Samuel Rogers.
2 See Nov. 4, 1820, to Murray, note 2.

both quality & cookery and quantity—& reproach me for a sort of "brutal" indifference as he called it to these particulars—& now he writes me facetious sneerings because I *do not* get up early in a morning—when there is no occasion—if there were—*he* knows that I was always *out* of bed before him—though it is true that my ablutions detained me longer in dressing—than his noble contempt for that "oriental scrupulosity"[3] permitted.—Then he is still sore about "*the ballad*"—he!! why he lampooned me at Brighton in 1808—about Jackson the boxer and bold Webster &c.—in 1809—he turned the death of my friend Ed. *Long* into ridicule & rhyme because his name was susceptible of a *pun*—and although he saw that I was distressed at it—before I left England in 1816—he wrote rhymes upon *D. Kinnaird* —*you*—and *myself*—and at Venice he parodied the lines "Though the day of my destiny's over"[4] in a comfortable quizzing way—and now he harps on my ballad about his election!—Pray tell him all this—for I will have no underhand work with my "old Cronies".—If he can deny the facts let him.—I maintain that he is more *carnivorously* & *carnally sensual* than I am—though I am bad enough too for that matter—but not in eating & haranging at the Crown and Anchor—where I never was but twice—and those were at "Whore's Hops" when I was a younker in my teens; and Egad—I think them the most respectable meetings of the two.——

But he is a little wroth that I would not come over to the *Queen's* trial—*lazy*—*quotha*!—it is so true that he should be ashamed of asserting it.——He counsels me not to "get into a scrape" but as Beau Clincher says—"How melancholy are Newgate reflections!"[5]——To be sure his advice is worth following—for experience teacheth—he has been in a dozen within these last two years.—*I pronounce me the more temperate of the two*. Have you gotten "the Hints" yet?——

I know Henry Matthews—he is the image to the very voice of his brother Charles only darker—his *laugh* his in particular—the first time I ever met him was in Scrope Davies's rooms after his brother's death—and I nearly dropped—thinking that it was his Ghost.—I have also dined with him in his rooms at King's College.——Hobhouse once proposed a similar memoir—but I am afraid that the letters of Charles's correspondence with me (which are at Whitton with my other papers) would hardly do for the public—for our lives were not

[3] Johnson, *Lives of the English Poets*: "He (Swift) washed himself with oriental scrupulosity."
[4] Byron, "Stanzas to Augusta".
[5] Farquhar, *The Constant Couple*, Act V, scene 2.

over strict—& our letters somewhat lax upon most subjects.——His Superiority over all his contemporaries was quite indisputable and acknowledged—none of us ever thought of being *at all near* Matthews —and yet there were some high men of his standing—Bankes—Bob Milnes[6]—Hobhouse—Bailey—and many others—without numbering the *mere Academical* men—of whom we hear little out of the University —& whom he beat *hollow* on *their own* Ground.—His gaining the Downing Fellowship[7]—was the completest thing of the kind ever known. He carried off both declamation prizes—in short he did whatever he chose.—He was three or four years my Senior but I lived a good deal with him latterly & with his friends.—He wrote to me the very day of his death (I believe) or at least a day before—if not the very day.——He meant to have stood for the University Membership.——He was a very odd & humerous fellow besides—and spared nobody—for instance walking out in Newstead Garden he stopped at Boatswain's monument inscribed "Here lies Boatswain a Dog" &c.— and then observing a blank marble tablet on the other side—"so (says he) there is room for another friend—and I propose that the inscription be "Here lies H—bh—se a Pig" &c—you may as well not let *this* transpire to the worthy member—lest he regard neither his dead friend nor his living one with his wonted Suavity.——

Rose's *lines* must be at his own option—*I* can have no objection to their publication.—Pray salute him from me.——Mr. Keats whose poetry you enquire after—appears to me what I have already said;— such writing is a sort of mental masturbation—he is always f—gg—g his *Imagination*.—I don't mean that he is *indecent* but viciously soliciting his own ideas into a state which is neither poetry nor any thing else but a Bedlam vision produced by raw pork and opium.——Barry Cornwall would write well if he would let himself.——Croly is superior to many—but seems to think himself inferior to Nobody.— Last week I sent you a correspondence with Galignani and some documents on your property.—You have now I think an opportunity of *checking*—or at least *limiting* those *French re-publications*.——You may let all your authors publish what they please *against me* or *mine*— a publisher is not & cannot be responsible for the works that issue from his printer's.——The "White Lady of Avenel"[8] is not quite so good as a *real well authenticated* ("Donna bianca") *White* Lady of

---

[6] Robert Milnes was at Trinity College just before Byron, leaving in 1804. He became M.P. for Pontefract in 1806, but made no great impression in Parliament. In later years he lived in Milan and Rome.

[7] Matthews became Fellow of Downing in 1808.

[8] In Scott's *The Monastery*.

Collalto[9]—a spectre in the Marca Trivigiana—who has been repeatedly seen—there is a man (a huntsman) now alive who saw her also—Hoppner could tell you all about her—& so can Rose perhaps.—I myself have *no doubt* of the fact—historical & spectral. She always appeared on particular occasions—before the deaths of the family &c. &c. I heard Me. Benzone say that she knew a Gentleman who had seen her cross his room at Colalto Castle.—Hoppner saw & spoke with the Huntsman who met her at the Chase—and never *hunted* afterwards.—She was a Girl attendant—who one day dressing the hair of a Countess Colalto—was seen by her mistress to smile upon her husband in the Glass.—The Countess had her shut up in the wall of the Castle like Constance de Beverley.[10]—Ever after she haunted them & all the Colaltos.—She is described as very beautiful—& fair.—It is well authenticated.

[Scrawl]

[TO COUNTESS TERESA GUICCIOLI]   *R[avenn]a. 9bre. 10.o 1820*

Ti ringrazio 1000 volte per il regolo amor mio + gran CANTATA in quel'biglietto tuo!!—Con questo tempo mi pare che i tuoi progetti di andare a cavallo non riuscirebbero troppo bene nei contorni di Filetto. —Non sono venuto ma ritengo la speranza di vederti presto.—Saluta Pierino e Papa—conservati bene ed amami sempre.—Ti bacio + + + +

[Scrawl]

P.S.—Si parla qui di una rivoluzione nata in Inghilterra—ma non credo nulla—poiche jeri ho ricevuta delle lettere di data fresca ed altrettante Gazette da Parigi.—Queste non parlano di nessun' tumulto.—Il processo della Regina va avante colla solita indecenza,— dovrebbe essere ormai deciso.— —

[TRANSLATION]   *Ravenna. November 10th. 1820*

Thank you a thousand times for your present, my love—a fine cantata in your note.

With this weather it seems to me that your riding plans won't be very successful in the country round Filetto. I have not come to you, but I keep the hope of seeing you soon.

[9] Her story is told in Rogers's *Italy*.
[10] In Scott's *Marmion*.

Greet Pierino and Papa—keep well and always love me. I kiss you
+ + + +

P.S.—They are speaking here of a revolution started in England
but I do not believe it, for yesterday I had some recent letters and some
Gazettes from Paris. These did not speak of any riot. The Queen's trial
is going ahead with its usual indecency—it should have been decided
by now.

[TO AUGUSTA LEIGH]   *Ravenna. 9bre. 18.0 1820*

My dearest Augusta—You will I hope have received a discreetly
long letter from me—not long ago.—Murray has just written that
Waite is dead—poor fellow—he and Blake[1]—both deceased—what *is*
to become of our hair & teeth.—The hair is less to be minded—any
body can cut hair—though not so well—but the mouth is a still more
serious concern.——Has he no Successor?—pray tell me the next
best—for what am I to do for brushes & powder?——And then the
Children—only *think*—what will become of their jaws? Such Men ought
to be immortal—& not your stupid heroes—orators & poets.—I am
really so sorry—that I can't think of anything else just now.—Besides
I liked him with all his Coxcombry.——Let me know what we are all
to do.—& to whom we can have recourse without damage for our
cleaning—scaling—& powder.—How do you get on with your affairs?
—and how does every body get on.——How is all your rabbit-warren
of a family? I gave you an account of mine by last letter. The Child
Allegra is well—but the Monkey has got a cough—and the tame Crow
has lately suffered from the head ache.——Fletcher has been bled for a
Stitch—& looks flourishing again.—Pray write—excuse this short
scrawl—

yrs. ever

[Scrawl]

P.S.—Recollect about Waite's Successor—why he was only
married the other day—& now I don't wonder so much that the poor
man died of it.——

[TO COUNTESS TERESA GUICCIOLI]   *9bre. 18.0 1820*

Amor Mio +—Ti prego perdonarmi che non posso in questo
momento andare a Filetto—Tutto ciò che abbiamo a dire si può ben

[1] See Sept. 10, 1819, to Augusta Leigh, notes 1 and 2 (Vol. 6, pp. 222 and 223).

dire a Ravenna,—dunque non è una cosa di tanta importanza.——Nella lusinga di vederti così presto sono sempre il tuo +

[Scrawl]

November 18th. 1820

My Love +—Pray forgive me if I don't come to Filetto at this moment. All that we have to say—can well be said at Ravenna—so it isn't so very important.

Hoping to see you soon—I am always yours +

[TO JOHN MURRAY] *Ravenna. 9bre. 18.o 1820*

Dear Moray—The death of Waite is a shock to the—teeth as well as to the feelings of all who knew him.—Good God!—he and *Blake*—both gone!—I left them both in the most robust health—and little thought of the national loss in so short a time as five years.—They were both so much superior to Wellington in rational greatness as he who preserves the hair—& the teeth—is preferable to "the bloody blustering booby" who gains a name by breaking heads & knocking out grinders.——Who succeeds *him?* where is tooth powder? *mild* & yet efficacious—where is *tincture?* where are cleansing *roots* and *brushes* now to be obtained?—Pray obtain what information you can upon these "*Tus*culum questions"—my Jaws ache to think on't.—Poor fellows! I anticipated seeing both—& yet they are gone to that place where both teeth and hair last longer than they do in this life—I have seen a thousand graves opened—and always perceived that whatever was gone—the *teeth and hair* remained of those who had died with them.——Is not this odd?—they go the very first things in youth—& yet last the longest in the dust—if people will but *die* to preserve them?—It is a queer life—and a queer death—that of mortals. I hear that Waite had married—but little thought that the other decease was so soon to overtake him.——Then he was such a delight—such a Coxcomb—such a Jewel of a Man—there is a taylor at Bologna so like him—and also at the top of his profession.——Do not neglect this commission—*who* or *what* can replace him?—what says the public?——

I remand you the preface—*don't forget* that the Italian extract from the Chronicle must *be translated.* With regard to what you say of re-

228

touching the Juans—and the Hints—it is all very well—but I can't *furbish.*—I am like the tyger (in poesy) if I miss my first Spring—I go growling back to my Jungle.—There is no second.—I can't correct—I can't—& I won't.—Nobody ever succeeds in it great or small.—Tasso remade the whole of his Jerusalem but who ever reads that version?— all the world goes to the first.—Pope *added* to the "Rape of the Lock" —but did not reduce it.———You must take my things as they happen to be—if they are not likely to suit—reduce their *estimate* then accordingly—I would rather give them away than hack & hew them.—I don't say that you are not right—I merely assert that I can not better them.—I must either "make a spoon or spoil a horn".—And there's an end.———The parcel of the *second* of June—with the late *Edgeworth*— & so forth—has *never* arrived—parcels of a later date have—of which I have given you my opinions in a late letter.———I remit you what I think a Catholic curiosity—the Pope's brief—authenticating the body of Saint Francis of Assisi,—a town on the road to Rome.——

yrs. ever
[Scrawl]

P.S.—Of the praises of that little dirty blackguard KEATES in the Edinburgh—I shall observe as Johnson did when Sheridan the actor got a *pension.* "What has *he* got a pension? then it is time that I should give up *mine.*"[1]—Nobody could be prouder of the praises of the Edinburgh than I was—or more alive to their censure—as I showed in E[nglish] B[ards] and S[cotch] R[eviewe]rs—at present *all the men* they have ever praised are degraded by that insane article.—Why don't they review & praise "Solomon's Guide to Health"[2] it is better sense —and as much poetry as Johnny Keates. Bowles must be *bowled* down—'tis a sad match at Cricket—if that fellow can get any Notches at Pope's expence.———If he once gets into *"Lord's* Ground" (to continue the pun because it is foolish) I think I could beat him in one Innings.———You had not known perhaps—that I was once—(*not metaphorically* but *really*) a good Cricketer—particularly in *batting*— and I played in the Harrow match against the Etonians in 1805, gaining more notches (as one of our chosen Eleven) than any except Ld. Ipswich & Brookman on our side.[3]——

[1] Boswell, *Life of Johnson*, ed. G. B. Hill, Vol. I, pp. 385–386.
[2] Samuel Solomon's *Guide to Health* (1795) went into more than sixty editions. He concocted a "Cordial Balm of Gilead".
[3] See August 4, 1805, to Charles D. Gordon (Vol. I, pp. 70–71).

Ravenna, 9bre 19, 1820

Dear Murray,—What you said of the late Charles Skinner Matthews has set me to my recollections; but I have not been able to turn up anything which would do for the purposed Memoir of his brother,— even if he had previously done enough during his life to sanction the introduction of anecdotes so merely personal. He was, however, a very extraordinary man, and would have been a great one. No one ever succeeded in a more surpassing degree than he did as far as he went. He was indolent, too; but whenever he stripped, he overthrew all antagonists. His conquests will be found registered at Cambridge, particularly his *Downing* one, which was hotly and highly contested, and yet easily *won*. Hobhouse was his most intimate friend, and can tell you more of him than any man. William Bankes also a great deal. I myself recollect more of his oddities than of his academical qualities, for we lived most together at a very idle period of *my* life. When I went up to Trinity, in 1805, at the age of seventeen and a half, I was miserable and untoward to a degree. I was wretched at leaving Harrow, to which I had become attached during the two last years of my stay there; wretched at going to Cambridge instead of Oxford (there were no rooms vacant at Christchurch); wretched from some private domestic circumstances of different kinds, and consequently about as unsocial as a wolf taken from the troop. So that, although I knew Matthews, and met him often *then* at Bankes's (who was my collegiate pastor, and master, and patron,) and at Rhode's, Milnes's, Price's, Dick's, Macnamara's, Farrell's, Gally Knight's, and others of that *set* of contemporaries, yet I was neither intimate with him nor with any one else, except my old schoolfellow Edward Long (with whom I used to pass the day in riding and swimming), and William Bankes, who was good-naturedly tolerant of my ferocities.

It was not till 1807, after I had been upwards of a year away from Cambridge, to which I had returned again to *reside* for my degree, that I became one of Matthew's familiars, by means of Hobhouse, who, after hating me for two years, because I wore a *white hat*, and a *grey* coat, and rode a *grey* horse (as he says himself), took me into his good graces because I had written some poetry. I had always lived a good deal, and got drunk occasionally, in their company—but now we became really friends in a morning. Matthews, however, was not at this period resident in College. I met *him* chiefly in London, and at uncertain periods at Cambridge. Hobhouse, in the mean time, did great things: he founded the Cambridge "Whig Club" (which he seems to have forgotten), and the "Amicable Society," which was dissolved in consequence of the members constantly quarrelling, and made himself very popular with "us youth," and no less formidable to all tutors, professors, and heads of Colleges. William Bankes was gone; while he stayed, he ruled the roast—or rather the *roasting*— and was father of all mischiefs.

Matthews and I, meeting in London, and elsewhere, became great cronies. He was not good tempered—nor am I—but with a little tact his temper was manageable, and I thought him so superior a man, that I was willing to sacrifice something to his humours, which were often, at the same time, amusing and provoking. What became of his *papers* (and he certainly had many), at the time of his death, was never known. I mention this by the way, fearing to skip it over, and *as* he *wrote* remarkably well, both in Latin and English. We went down to Newstead together,[1] where I had got a famous cellar, and *Monks'* dresses from a masquerade warehouse. We were a company of some seven or eight, with an occasional neighbour or so for visiters, and used to sit up late in our friars' dresses, drinking burgundy, claret, champagne, and what not, out of the *skull-cup*, and all sorts of glasses, and buffooning all around the house, in our conventual garments.[2] Matthews always denominated me "the Abbot," and never called me by any other name in his good humours, to the day of his death. The harmony of these our symposia was somewhat interrupted, a few days after our assembling, by Matthews's threatening to throw Hobhouse out of a *window*, in consequence of I know not what commerce of jokes ending in this epigram. Hobhouse came to me and said, that "his respect and regard for me as host would not permit him to call out any of my guests, and that he should go to town next morning." He did. It was in vain that I represented to him that the window was not high, and that the turf under it was particularly soft. Away he went.

Matthews and myself had travelled down from London together, talking all the way incessantly upon one single topic. When we got to Loughborough, I know not what chasm had made us diverge for a moment to some other subject, at which he was indignant. "Come," said he, "don't let us break through—let us go on as we began to our journey's end;" and so he continued, and was as entertaining as ever

[1] For Matthews's account of the Newstead visit, see his letter of May 22, 1809, to his sister. (*LJ*, I, 153.)

[2] According to Hobhouse, Matthews hid in a stone coffin in the long gallery at Newstead at night, and rose up from it to blow out Hobhouse's candle. (Broughton, III, 29.)

to the very end. He had previously occupied, during my year's absence from Cambridge, my rooms in Trinity, with the furniture; and Jones, the tutor, in his odd way, had said, on putting him in, "Mr Matthews, I recommend to your attention not to damage any of the moveables, for Lord Byron, Sir, is a young man of *tumultuous passions.*" Matthews was delighted with this; and whenever anybody came to visit him, begged them to handle the very door with caution; and used to repeat Jones's admonition in his tone and manner. There was a large mirror in the room, on which he remarked, "that he thought his friends were grown uncommonly assiduous in coming to *see him*, but he soon discovered that they only came to *see themselves.*" Jones's phrase of "*tumultuous passions*," and the whole scene, had put him into such good humour, that I verily believe that I owed to it a portion of his good graces.

When at Newstead, somebody by accident rubbed against one of his white silk stockings, one day before dinner; of course the gentleman apologised. "Sir," answered Matthews, "it may be all very well for you, who have a great many silk stockings, to dirty other people's; but to me, who have only this *one pair*, which I have put on in honour of the Abbot here, no apology can compensate for such carelessness; besides, the expense of washing." He had the same sort of droll sardonic way about every thing. A wild Irishman, named Farrell, one evening began to say something at a large supper at Cambridge, Matthews roared out "Silence!" and then, pointing to Farrell, cried out, in the words of the oracle, "*Orson is endowed with reason.*" You may easily suppose that Orson lost what reason he had acquired, on hearing this compliment. When Hobhouse published his volume of poems, the *Miscellany* (which Matthews *would* call the "*Miss-sell-any*"), all that could be drawn from him was, that the preface was "extremely like *Walsh.*" Hobhouse thought this at first a compliment; but we never could make out what it was, for all we know of *Walsh* is his Ode to King William, and Pope's epithet of "*knowing Walsh.*"[3] When the Newstead party broke up for London, Hobhouse and Matthews, who were the greatest friends possible, agreed, for a whim, to *walk together* to town. They quarrelled by the way, and actually walked the latter half of the journey, occasionally passing and repassing, without speaking. When Matthews had got to Highgate, he had spent all his money but three-pence half-penny, and determined to spend that also in a pint of beer, which I believe he was drinking before a public-

---

[3] "Granville the polite, and *knowing Walsh*, would tell me I could write." *Arbuthnot*, lines 135–136.

house, as Hobhouse passed him (still without speaking) for the last time on their route. They were reconciled in London again.

One of Matthew's passions was "the fancy;"[4] and he sparred uncommonly well. But he always got beaten in rows, or combats with the bare fist. In swimming, too, he swam well; but with *effort* and *labour*, and *too high* out of the water; so that Scrope Davies and myself, of whom he was therein somewhat emulous, always told him that he would be drowned if ever he came to a difficult pass in the water. He was so; but surely Scrope and myself would have been most heartily glad that

> "the Dean had lived,
> And our prediction proved a lie."

His head was uncommonly handsome, very like what *Pope's* was in his youth.

His voice, and laugh, and features, are strongly resembled by his brother Henry's, if Henry be *he* of *King's College*. His passion for boxing was so great, that he actually wanted me to match him with Dogherty (whom I had backed and made the match for against Tom Belcher)[5], and I saw them spar together at my own lodgings with the gloves on. As he was bent upon it, I would have backed Dogherty to please him, but the match went off. It was of course to have been a private fight, in a private room.

On one occasion, being too late to go home and dress, he was equipped by a friend (Mr. Baillie, I believe,) in a magnificently fashionable and somewhat exaggerated shirt and neckcloth. He proceeded to the Opera, and took his station in Fop's Alley. During the interval between the opera and the ballet, an acquaintance took his station by him and saluted him: "Come round," said Matthews, "come round."—"Why should I come round?" said the other; "you have only to turn your head—I am close by you."—"That is exactly what I cannot do," said Matthews; "don't you see the state I am in?" pointing to his buckram shirt collar and inflexible cravat,—and there he stood with his head always in the same perpendicular position during the whole spectacle.

One evening, after dining together, as we were going to the Opera, I happened to have a spare Opera ticket (as subscriber to a box), and presented it to Matthews. "Now, sir," said he to Hobhouse afterwards, "this I call *courteous* in the Abbot—another man would

[4] The common term then used to refer to for those intensely interested in the art of pugilism.

[5] See March 27, 1808, to John Jackson, notes 1 and 2 (Vol. I, p. 162).

never have thought that I might do better with half a guinea than throw it to a door-keeper;—but here is a man not only asks me to dinner, but gives me a ticket for the theatre." These were only his oddities, for no man was more liberal, or more honourable in all his doings and dealings, than Matthews. He gave Hobhouse and me, before we set out for Constantinople, a most splendid entertainment, to which we did ample justice. One of his fancies was dining at all sorts of out-of-the-way places. Somebody popped upon him in I know not what coffee-house in the Strand—and what do you think was the attraction? Why, that he paid a shilling (I think) to *dine with his hat on*. This he called his "*hat* house," and used to boast of the comfort of being covered at meal times.

When Sir Henry Smith[6] was expelled from Cambridge for a row with a tradesman named "Hiron," Matthews solaced himself with shouting under Hiron's windows every evening

> "Ah me! what perils do environ
> The man who meddles with *hot Hiron*."[7]

He was also of that band of profane scoffers who, under the auspices of * * * *, used to rouse Lort Mansel (late Bishop of Bristol) from his slumbers in the lodge of Trinity; and when he appeared at the window foaming with wrath, and crying out, "I know you, gentlemen, I know you!" were wont to reply, "We beseeche thee to hear us, good *Lort!*"—"Good *Lort* deliver us!" (Lort was his Christian name.) As he was very free in his speculations upon all kinds of subjects, although by no means either dissolute or intemperate in his conduct, and as I was no less independent, our conversation and correspondence used to alarm our friend Hobhouse to a considerable degree.

You must be almost tired of my packets, which will have cost a mint of postage.

Salute Gifford and all my friends.

Yours,

B

[to countess teresa guiccioli]   *9bre. 22.o 1820*

A. M.+—Ma cosa dunque si può fare?—non hai sentito Papa e Pierino? che sono i tuoi prossimi parenti;—e spero anche amici *miei*

---

[6] Sir Henry Smyth was expelled in 1805 for "inciting to a disturbance" at the shop of Mrs. Thrower on Market Hill.
[7] Butler, *Hudibras*, Part 1, chapter 3 (last two words "cold iron").

poiche mi sono condotto con buona fede verso loro.——Quei *altri*,—i buffoni—o del'governo—o (perdonami) di tua famiglia vogliono sacrificarti; si vuole adesso del giudizio e della pazienza.—Se non ti amava—se voleva *disfarmi di te senza biasimo*—ed anche coi ripieghi più bei in favor mio—il modo più certo sarebbe di *venire da te*—e di fare altre simili imprudenze in faccia del' mondo e dei preti—che formano il *mondo qui*—sarò sempre il tuo

[Scrawl]

[TRANSLATION]   *November 22nd. 1820*

My Love +—But what then can be done? Haven't you heard what Papa and Pierino say? who are your nearest relatives and I hope also *friends of mine*, as I have behaved in good faith towards them. These others, *the buffoons*—either in the government or (forgive me) in your family, want to sacrifice you; what is now needed is common sense and patience. If I did not love you—if I *wished to get rid of you without blame*—and also with the best excuse for myself—the most certain way would be to *visit you*[1]—and to commit such imprudences in the face of the world and of the priests—who make up the *world here.*— I shall always be your

[TO DOUGLAS KINNAIRD]   *Ravenna. 9bre. 22.o 1820*

My dear Douglas—You ask me—to *make* Hanson *make Claughton* pay *me*,—I would willingly know how I am to make Hanson do that or any thing else at this distance of time and place?—If you intimate to him that what is taken out of Claughton's pocket will go into his own—in diminution of his "bill of pains & penalties"—he may perhaps condescend to do his duty.—It is useless for me to say more—I have written—& written—and *you* have spoken[.] I suppose he will end by having his own way—and a pretty way it is.——

The affairs of this part of Italy are simplifying—the liberals have delayed till it [is] too late for them to do anything to [the] purpose—If the Scoundrels of Troppau[1] decide on a Massacre (as is probable) the

---

[1] Byron had a hard time convincing Teresa that it was imprudent for him to visit her at Filetto because the Pope's decree stipulated that she should live with her family, and Guiccioli was waiting for an excuse to stop her allowance.
[1] The Congress at Troppau, composed of the great European powers, agreed on a secret protocol affirming the right of the collective "Europe" to suppress internal revolutions.

Barbarians will march in by one frontier and the Neapolitans by the other.——They have *both asked* permission of his Holiness—so to do—which is equivalent to asking a man's permission to give him a kick on the a—se—if he grants it, it is a sign that he can't return it.—The worst of all is that this devoted country will become for the six thousandth time since God made man in his own image—the seat of war.—I recollect Spain in 1809—and the Morea & parts of Greece in 1810–1811—when Veli Pacha was on his way to combat the Russians—(the Turkish armies make their *own country* like an enemy's on a march) and a small [sketch?] also of my own County of Nottingham under the Luddites when we were burning the Frames—and sometimes the Manufactories—so that I have a tolerable idea of what may ensue. Here all is suspicion and terrorism—bullying—arming—and dis-arming—the Priests scared—the people gloomy—and the *Merchants buying* up corn to *supply the armies.*——I am so pleased with the last piece of Italic patriotism—that I have underlined it for your remark—it is just as if our Hampshire farmers should prepare magazines for any two Continental Scoundrels who could land and fight it out in New forest.——

I came in for my share of the *vigourous* system of the day.—they have taken it into their heads that I am popular (which no one ever was in Italy but an Opera Singer—or ever will be till the resurrection of Romulus) and are trying by all kinds of petty vexations to disgust & make me retire.——This I should hardly believe—it seems so absurd —if some of their priests did not avow it.—They try to fix squabbles upon my servants—to involve me in Scrapes (no difficult matter) and lastly they (the Governing party) menace to shut Madame Guiccioli up in a *Convent*.——The last piece of policy springs from two motives—the one because her *family* are suspected of liberal principles—and the second because mine—(although I do not preach them) are known—& were known when it was far less reputable to be a friend of liberty than it is now.—If I am proud of some of the poetry— I am much prouder of some of my predictions—they are as good as Fitzgerald's the Literary fund Seer and Murray's post poet.——

If they should succeed in putting this poor Girl into a convent for doing that with me—which all the other Countesses of Italy have done with every body for these 1000 years—of course—I would accede to a retreat on my part—rather than a prison on hers—for the *former* only is what they *really* want.——She is—as women are apt to be by opposi-tion—sufficiently heroic and obstinate—but as both these qualities may only tend the more to put her in Monastic durance—I am at a loss what to do.—I have seen the correspondence of half a dozen bigots on the subject—and perceive that they have set about it—merely as an indirect way of attacking part of her relations—and myself. You may imagine that I am as usual in warm water with this affair in prospect.— As for public affairs they look no better [word torn out with seal] parties have dawdled till [it is] too late—I question if they could get together twelve thousand men of their own, *now*—and some months ago it was different.——Pray write—remember me to Hobhouse & believe me ever

yrs. most truly [Scrawl]

P.S.—The police at present is under the Germans or rather Austrians who do not merit the name of Germans who open all letters it is supposed—I have no objection so that they see how I hate and utterly despise and detest those *Hun brutes* & all they can do in their temporary wickedness—for Time and Opinion & the vengeance of the roused up people will at length manure Italy with their carcases—it may not be for one year—or two—or ten—but it *will* be—and *so* that it *could be* sooner—I know not what a man ought *not* to do.—But their antagonists are no great shakes—the Spaniards are the boys after all.——

[TO COUNT GIUSEPPE ALBORGHETTI]   *Ravenna* [*9bre?*] *23d 1820*

Dear Sir—You could not have sent me better news[1]—better for England for it will prevent a revolution—though it may *hasten* a *reform*,—or better for Italy for if (as is probable) the Ministry is changed—we shall have a pacific administration, who may perhaps interfere to prevent the "bel paese" from becoming the prey alike of factious citizens or of foreign armies. . . . The news are also personally agreeable to me—for I have obligations to the Queen for the kindness to me when she kept her residence at Kensington Palace. My friends in England have reproached me severely for not being present to do my duty on her Majesty's trial, but it is a satisfaction to me to see by the result that my humble vote and voice were not necessary.

I beg my respects and thanks to his Eminence for his communication and I request your acceptance of my acknowledgments; you write English so well that I need hardly tell you that you were right in *both* your terms—for if London had not been "illuminated" it is prob-

---

[1] The news that Queen Caroline had been acquitted.

able that the people would have "fired" it—and then it would have been "illuminated" with a vengeance.

I have the honour to be your obliged very obedt. servt.

BYRON

[TO JOHN MURRAY]   *Ravenna. 9bre. 23.o 1820*

Dear Moray—There have arrived—the preface—the translation—the first sixteen pages—also from page *sixty* five to ninety six—but *no intermediate sheets*—from ye. *sixteenth* to *sixty fifth* pages.—I apprize you of this—in case any such shall have been sent.—I hope that the printer will perfectly understand *where* to insert some three or four additional lines—which Mr. Gifford has had the goodness to copy out in his own hand.——The translation is extremely well done and I beg to present my thanks & respects to Mr. Cohen for his time and trouble.[1]—The old Chronicle Style is far better done—than I could have done it—some of the old words are past the understanding even of the present Italians.—Perhaps if Foscolo was to cast a glance over it—he could rectify such—or confirm them.—Your *two volume won't* do;—the first is very well—but the second must be *anonymous*—& the *first with* the *name*—which would make a confusion—or an *identity*—both of which ought to be avoided.——You had better put—the Doge—Dante—&c. into *one* volume,—and bring out the other *soon* afterwards—but not on the same day.——The "Hints"—Hobhouse says will require a good deal of slashing—to suit the times—which—will be a work of time—for I don't feel at all laborious just now.—Whatever effect they are to have would perhaps be greater in a separate form, and *they* all must have my name to them.—Now if you publish them in the same volume with "Don Juan"—they identify Don Juan as mine—which I don't think worth a Chancery Suit about my daughter's guardianship;—as in your present code a facetious poem—is sufficient to take away a man's rights over his family.——

I regret to hear that the Queen has been so treated on the second reading of the bill.——Of the state of things here—it would be difficult & not very prudent to speak at large—the Huns opening all letters—I wonder if they can read them when they have opened them? —if so they may see in my most legible hand—that I think them damned Scoundrels and Barbarians—their Emperor a fool—& them-

---

[1] Francis Cohen (afterwards Sir Francis Palgrave) had, at Byron's request through Murray, translated the account of the Doge Marino Faliero in Marino Sanuto's *Chronicle*, which Byron added as an appendix to *Marino Faliero*.

selves more fools than he—all which they may send to Vienna—for anything I care.——They have got themselves masters of the Papal police and are bullying away,—but some day or other they will pay for all.—It may not be very soon—because these unhappy Italians have no union, nor consistency among themselves, but I suppose that Providence will get tired of them at last—& that God is not an Austrian.——

yrs. ever truly

[Scrawl]

P.S.—I enclosed a letter to you for Lady B[yron] on business some time ago[;] did you receive and forward it?—*Adopt Mr. Gifford's alterations* in the proofs.

[TO AUGUSTA LEIGH]   *Ravenna. 9bre. 30.o 1820*

Dearest Augusta—People of sense judge for themselves & not with the opinions of a flock of fools for their standard.——The book I speak of was always open on Lady *Jersey's* table—who I presume is a tolerably reputable authority.—I request therefore you will give a look *only* at the *Stanzas in question*—which *Murray* will *point* out to you—(for fear yr. delicate feelings should be shocked by stumbling again on a Shipwrecke) and tell me if you think there could or could not have been any intention of depicting that woman.[1]——You may do thus much for me—I have done more for you in my time.—Is it true or no that Lady N[oel] is ill, or *was* ill?——Murray said so & quoted *you* as his authority. Believe me ever & very truly

yrs. [Scrawl]

[TO DOUGLAS KINNAIRD]   *Ravenna. 9bre. 30.o 1820*

My dear Douglas/—The enclosed letters of the Hansons with Counsel's opinion will put you in daylight of all their doings.—It is my intention to *appeal* of course.——I have written to you twice or thrice lately. Pray spur the Spooneys on all points—that's the great point.— As to Claughton he must pay.—Murray must come down [hand] somely.——I have another Canto of D[on] J[uan] finished—192

[1] Byron always insisted that the satire on Donna Inez in the first canto of *Don Juan* was not intended for Lady Byron, but none of his English readers could be convinced that it was not a portrait of his wife. Augusta was particularly upset because of her delicate relations with Annabella.

Stanzas—and only wants copying out.——My remembrances to
Hobhouse & so forth—In another month there is half a year's *fee,*
an't there?—

yrs. ever & truly

B

[TO JOHN HANSON]   *Ravenna. 9bre. 30.o 1820*

Dear Sir—I have received yr. letter with Counsel's opinion upon
the Appeal.—You had better then enter the Appeal immediately not
to lose further time.—Mr. Kinnaird acted by my direction about Col.
Leigh's bond.—Let me hope that the Blessington Mortgage will proceed without further delays.——You have my full directions to proceed in making Mr. Claughton fulfil his payments.——I do not know
whether it will be best to send a Courier to Ravenna with the deeds—
or to send them by the post—*Consult weight* & security—and adopt
the mode which will be most speedy.—The *Scotch deeds* directions I
do not understand notwithstanding all the pencil marks—but I will
try to sign them correctly.——My "rough rebukes" as you call them
have been excited by the not very smooth delays which have inter-
vened—what can a man say at such a distance to you gentlemen of the
law?—you best know how far they are deserved.——I shall be very
glad to hear any good news—and with respects & remembrances to
Charles & all your family I am

yours very truly & faithly.

BYRON

[TO COUNTESS TERESA GUICCIOLI (*a*)]   [*Nov.–Dec., 1820?*]

Perdonatemi il non essere venuto questa sera—ma veramente sto
poco bene—cagione forse del tempo—e del non esser stato a Cavallo—
forse delle Gentilezza vostre di jeri sera—e di quest' oggi.——Colla
speranza di rivederci dimane sono e sarò sempre

[Scrawl]

[TRANSLATION (*a*)]   [*Nov.–Dec., 1820?*]

Forgive me for not having come this evening[1]—but in truth I am
not very well—due perhaps to the weather—and to not having been

---

[1] Teresa had returned from Filetto to Ravenna and was living with her father,
Count Gamba.

on horseback—perhaps due to your courtesies of last evening—and of today.—With the hope of seeing you tomorrow I am and will always be

[TO COUNTESS TERESA GUICCIOLI (*b*)]   [*Nov.–Dec., 1820?*]

Io credeva che il tuo venire qui—ti piaceva più per causa della maggiore confidenza—in tanto vengo da voi—per me è eguale.

[TRANSLATION (*b*)]   [*Nov.–Dec., 1820?*]

I thought that your coming here would be more to your liking—because of the greater intimacy—then I shall come to you—to me it is the same.

[TO COUNTESS TERESA GUICCIOLI (*c*)]   [*Nov.–Dec., 1820?*]

A. M.+—Scusi—che ho da scrivere *5 lettere* tutte sopra affari questa sera.—Ecco la causa di così corta & poco cortese risposta—Credimi sempre & tutto il tuo

         B

P.S.—Anche Temo di scrivere *più* chiaramente in circonstanze tue—ti bacio 10000 volte—Ti ringrazio per la bellissima rosa—

[TRANSLATION (*c*)]   [*Nov.–Dec., 1820?*]

My Love +—Excuse me—I have *5 letters* to write this evening, all on matters of business. This is the reason for so short and so little courteous a reply—Believe me always and all yours

         B

P.S.—Also I am afraid to write *more* clearly given your circumstances—I kiss you 10000 times—I thank you for the very beautiful rose—

[TO COUNTESS TERESA GUICCIOLI (*d*)]   [*Nov.–Dec., 1820?*]

A. M. in E.—Come faranno i altri? o come faremo per sapere?—Non sarà gran' gusto andare alla Sala del' Commune per non trovare senoche della canaglia.—Io farò ciò che tu vuoi—decidi.—

         [Scrawl]

My Love to Eternity—What will the others do? or how shall we know?—It will not be much pleasure to go to the Assembly Hall to find only rabble.—I will do what you want—you decide.

[TO COUNTESS TERESA GUICCIOLI (*e*)]   [*Nov.–Dec., 1820?*]

A. M. +—Si può appena leggere qualche parola—l'aqua ha resa il resto poco intelligibile. Domane parleremo più in detaglio—io non son venuto in palco *prima* perche non voleva ricevere delle 'Sgarberie dal' Sr. A. e poi—perche sono venute delle persone—le quali per convenienza come padrone del palco non potrei lasciare—sempre & tutto tuo—

[TRANSLATION (*e*)]   [*Nov.–Dec., 1820?*]

My Love +—One can barely read a few words—water has left the rest scarcely intelligible. Tomorrow we will talk in greater detail— I did not come to the box *first* because I did not wish to receive Insults from Signor A. and then—because some people came—whom I could not leave for propriety's sake as owner of the box—always and all yours—

[TO COUNTESS TERESA GUICCIOLI (*f*)]   [*Nov.–Dec., 1820?*]

Tita non m'ha inteso.—Io lo diceva pregarvi dispensarmi da venire questa sera—per sentire Legniani.—In questo momento capita il vostro biglietto—verrò dunque—perche voi lo desiderate—basta che Luigi m'indica quando viene Legniani.

[TRANSLATION (*f*)]   [*Nov.–Dec., 1820?*]

Tita did not understand me.—I told him to ask you to excuse me from coming this evening—to hear Legniani.[1]—Now your note arrives —then I shall come—because you wish it—so long as Luigi indicates to me when Legniani is coming.

---

[1] Luigi Legnani was a famous tenor.

A. M.+—Ho letto—ma intendo poco—Chi è "Alessandro" di cui parla—è il tuo Marito? Per il resto ci intendiamo qualche cosa dalle procedure antecedente—spiegami cosa è *Sn. Domenico* e "i rescritti" e cosa può o *non* può fare il Cardinale—Mi spiace che Papa non è qui.— Non sono venuto per le ragione già dette—e perche tu stavi male jersera—

+ [Scrawl]

[TRANSLATION (g)]   [Nov.–Dec., 1820?]

My Love+—I have read—but understood little—Who is the "Alessandro" of whom it speaks—is it your Husband? As to the rest we know something about preceding practices—explain to me what is San Domenico and the "rescripts" and what the Cardinal can or cannot do—I am sorry that Papa is not here.—I did not come for the reasons already given—and because you were feeling ill last evening—+[1]

[TO AUGUSTA LEIGH]   [Dec., 1820?]

[Fragment]

...Hobhouse cares about as much for the Queen—as he does for St. Paul's.—One ought to be glad however of anything which makes either of them go to Church.——I am also delighted to see *you* grown so *moral*.——It is edifying.[1]——Pray write and believe me ever dearest A.

yrs.
[Scrawl]

[TO COUNT GUISEPPE ALBORGHETTI]   *Decr. 3d. 1820*

Dear Sir/—I answer you without hesitation.—The Bill is *thrown out entirely* and *completely*—the expression "read again this day six

---

[1] These notes to Teresa ([Nov.–Dec., 1820?], (*a*) to (*g*)) are translated by Professor Nancy Dersofi.

[1] The Queen had gone in state to St. Paul's to offer thanks for her acquittal. Augusta's moralizing comment on that shocking procedure, together with the news that Hobhouse had attended the service, caused Byron to explode about the double hypocrisy of it, since neither he nor Hobhouse really believed in the Queen's "innocence", yet believed that she should have been acquitted. This fragment is from a half-burned sheet.

months" is nothing more than a *form* used on the rejections of *all Parliamentary bills* whatsoever, & which cannot be dispensed with;—it is like saying "the King *never dies*" which is another form of the B[ritish] Constitution.——The great Struggle *now* will be to throw out the *ministers*—How this may end, we cannot yet know.——England at present will *not go to war.*—France and Prussia are against it;—and if the Ministers are *beaten*—there will perhaps be no *foreign* war at all; but this is problematical.—Whether the Ministers in their agony will try some censure or other in a *different shape* against the Queen—is not certain—but if they do they will be beaten probably.—I send you the proceedings.—

yrs. truly
BYRON

[TO THOMAS MOORE (*a*)]   *Ravenna, Dec. 9th, 1820*

Besides this letter, you will receive *three* packets, containing, in all, 18 more sheets of Memoranda, which, I fear, will cost you more in postage than they will ever produce by being printed in the next century. Instead of waiting so long, if you could make any thing of them *now* in the way of *reversion*, (that is, after *my* death,) I should be very glad,—as, with all due regard to your progeny, I prefer you to your grand-children. Would not Longman or Murray advance you a certain sum *now*, pledging themselves *not* to have them published till after *my* decease, think you?[1]—and what say you?

Over these latter sheets I would leave you a discretionary power; because they contain, perhaps, a thing or two which is too sincere for the public. If I consent to your disposing of their reversion *now*, where would be the harm? Tastes may change. I would, in your case, make my essay to dispose of them, *not* publish, now; and if *you* (as is most likely) survive me, add what you please from your own knowledge; and, *above all, contradict* any thing, if I have *mis*-stated; for my first object is the truth, even at my own expense.

I have some knowledge of your countryman Muley Moloch,[2] the

[1] With this authority Moore sold the manuscript of Byron's Memoirs to Murray for posthumous publication for two thousand guineas. But the manuscript was burned after Byron's death, and Moore returned the money. See Doris Langley Moore, *The Late Lord Byron*, Chapter I, "The Burning of the Memoirs".

[2] Thomas Mulock was lecturing on English literature in Paris. Moore attended several of his lectures and pronounced them "mere verbiage". But Mulock curiously found Byron the only person who had a proper notion of religion, and was not even appalled by *Cain.*

lecturer. He wrote to me several letters upon Christianity, to convert me; and, if I had not been a Christian already, I should probably have been now, in consequence. I thought there was something of wild talent in him, mixed with a due leaven of absurdity,—as there must be in all talent, let loose upon the world, without a martingale.

The ministers seem still to persecute the Queen * * *; but they *won't* go out, the sons of b—es. Damn Reform—I want a place— what say you? You must applaud the honesty of the declaration, whatever you may think of the intention.

I have quantities of paper in England, original and translated— tragedy, &c. &c., and am now copying out a Fifth Canto of Don Juan, 149 stanzas. So that there will be near *three thin* Albemarle, or *two thick* volumes of all sorts of my Muses. I mean to plunge thick, too, into the contest upon Pope, and to lay about me like a dragon till I make manure of [Bowles] for the top of Parnassus.

These rogues are right—*we* do laugh at *t'others*—eh?—don't we?[3] You shall see—you shall see what things I'll say, an' it pleases Providence to leave us leisure. But in these parts they are all going to war; and there is to be liberty, and a row, and a constitution—when they can get them. But I won't talk politics—it is low. Let us talk of the Queen, and her bath, and her bottle—that's the only *motley* nowadays.

If there are any acquaintances of mine, salute them. The priests here are trying to persecute me,—but no matter.

Yours, &c.

[TO THOMAS MOORE (*b*)]   *Ravenna, Dec. 9th, 1820*

I open my letter to tell you a fact, which will show the state of this country better than I can. The commandant of the troops is *now* lying *dead* in my house. He was shot at a little past eight o'clock, about two hundred paces from my door. I was putting on my great-coat to visit Madame la Contessa G. when I heard the shot. On coming into the hall, I found all my servants on the balcony, exclaiming that a man was murdered. I immediately ran down, calling on Tita (the bravest of them) to follow me. The rest wanted to hinder us from going, as it is

---

[3] The reference is to a humorous article in *Blackwood's Magazine* called "Shuffle-botham's Dream" (October, 1820, pp. 3–7) which pictures the fraternity of contemporary writers, with "Lord Byron and little Moore laughing behind, as if they would split" at the rest of them.

the custom for every body here, it seems, to run away from "the stricken deer".[1]

However, down we ran, and found him lying on his back, almost, if not quite, dead, with five wounds, one in the heart, two in the stomach, one in the finger, and the other in the arm. Some soldiers cocked their guns, and wanted to hinder me from passing. However, we passed, and I found Diego, the adjutant, crying over him like a child—a surgeon, who said nothing of his profession—a priest, sobbing a frightened prayer—and the commandant, all this time, on his back, on the hard, cold pavement, without light or assistance, or any thing around him but confusion and dismay.

As nobody could, or would, do any thing but howl and pray, and as no one would stir a finger to move him, for fear of consequences, I lost my patience—made my servant and a couple of the mob take up the body—sent off two soldiers to the guard—despatched Diego to the Cardinal with the news, and had the commandant carried upstairs into my own quarter. But it was too late, he was gone—not at all disfigured—bled inwardly—not above an ounce or two came out.

I had him partly stripped—made the surgeon examine him, and examined him myself. He had been shot by cut balls or slugs. I felt one of the slugs, which had gone through him, all but the skin. Everybody conjectures why he was killed, but no one knows how. The gun was found close by him—an old gun, half filed down.

He only said, "O Dio!" and "Gesu!" two or three times, and appeared to have suffered little. Poor fellow! he was a brave officer, but had made himself much disliked by the people. I knew him personally, and had met with him often at conversazioni and elsewhere. My house is full of soldiers, dragoons, doctors, priests, and all kinds of persons,—though I have now cleared it, and clapt sentinels at the doors. To-morrow the body is to be moved. The town is in the greatest confusion, as you may suppose.

You are to know that, if I had not had the body moved, they would have left him there till morning in the street for fear of consequences. I would not choose to let even a dog die in such a manner, without succour:—and, as for consequences, I care for none in a duty.

Yours, &c.

P.S.—The lieutenant on duty by the body is smoking his pipe with great composure.—A queer people this.

---

[1] Cowper, "The Garden" and Thomas Moore, "Come rest in this bosom".

Dear Murray—I intended to have written to you at some length by this post,—but as the Military Commandant is now lying dead in my house—on Fletcher's bed—I have other things to think of.—— He was shot at 8 o Clock this evening about two hundred paces from our door.—I was putting on my great Coat to pay a visit to the Countess G[uiccioli]—when I heard a shot—and on going into the hall—found all my servants on the balcony—exclaiming that "a Man was murdered".——As it is the custom here to let people fight it through— they wanted to hinder me from going out—but I ran down into the Street—Tita the bravest of them followed me—and we made our way to the Commandant who was lying on his back with five wounds—of which three in the body—one in the heart.——There were about him— Diego his Adjutant—crying like a Child—a priest howling—a Surgeon who dared not touch him—two or three confused & frightened Soldiers—one or two of the boldest of the mob—and the Street dark as pitch—with the people flying in all directions.—As Diego could only cry and wring his hands—and the Priest could only pray—and nobody seemed able or willing to do anything except exclaim shake and stare —I made my Servant & one of the mob take up the body—sent off Diego crying to the Cardinal—the Soldiers for the Guard—& had the Commandant carried up Stairs to my own quarters.—But he was quite gone.—I made the Surgeon examine him & examined him myself.— He had bled inwardly, & very little external blood was apparent.— One of the Slugs had gone quite through—all but the Skin, I felt it myself.—Two more shots in the body—one in a finger—and another in the arm.—His face not at all disfigured—he seems asleep—but is growing livid.—The Assassin has not been taken—but the gun was found—a gun filed down to half the barrel.——

He said nothing—but "O Dio!" and "O Gesu" two or three times. The house was filled at last with Soldiers—officers—police—and military—but they are clearing away—all but the Sentinels—and the [body] is to be removed tomorrow.—It seems [that] if I had not had him taken into my house he might have lain in the Street till morning— for here nobody meddles with such things—for fear of the consequences —either of public suspicion, or private revenge on the part of the Slayers.—They may do as they please—I shall never be deterred from a duty of humanity by all the assassins of Italy—and that is a wide word.——He was a brave officer—but an unpopular man.— The whole town is in confusion.—You may judge better of things here by this detail than by anything which I could add on the Subject—communicate this letter to Hobhouse & Douglas K[innair]d—and believe me

yrs. truly
B

P.S.—The poor Man's wife is not yet aware of his death—they are to break it to her in the morning.—The Lieutenant who is watching the body is smoking with the greatest Sangfroid—a strange people.—

[TO LADY BYRON] *Ravenna. Decr. 10th. 1820*

About six weeks ago—more or less—I wrote to you requesting your assent & that of the trustees to the transfer of property in a loan to Lord Blessington.—Since that letter was written—I have had an intimation from Mr. Kinnaird—that the deeds had been examined by Counsel and approved;—and I now once more request that you will take advantage of the present state of the funds to *sell* out—there will be few such opportunities.—Pray attend to this—there is the devil brewing work for mankind all over Europe.———Of the state of things here—I will mention one fact which will confirm what I prognosticated in my former letter.———On the evening before yestereven (Friday) I was putting on my great coat at 8 in the evening (*French* hours not Italian) to pay a visit a few Streets off.—I heard a shot but thought little of it—as it is not uncommon—but on going into the Hall—I found all my Servants staring from the balcony; they begged me not to go out as there was a man just murdered scarcely a hundred paces from the door.—I ran down directly followed by Tita (a stout lad enough) armed of course and found the military Commandant of the troops here,—lying on the pavement *mortally wounded*, but still warm. —He was surrounded by a few Soldiers distracted with rage and alarm —his Adjutant (Diego by name) crying and wringing his hands— with two or three more gathered in haste about the body.— The rest were making off in all directions.——

My first idea was of course to see if he was alive—for nobody else dared to touch him—far less move him—for fear of they knew not what—for they seemed out of their senses.—I had him carried up stairs into my house—sent off the Adjutant to the Cardinal—and the Soldiers for the Guard—made Urbini the Surgeon examine him— and examined him myself—but he was gone—shot in *five* places—

three mortal with Slugs.——The implement was found near him, an old Gun sawed half off.——He never spoke but two or three times —"Gesu"—"Gesu"—and had suffered little pain—& no disfigurement.—He seemed asleep.—He bled very little.——He was placed on Fletcher's bed—and there remained the whole night;—after at least an hour good—they sent the soldiery with their officers and the police—with the Cardinal's thanks to me—for having picked him up—and if it had not been for my happening to be near—it seems they would have allowed him to lie in the Street—Heaven knows how long—& even afterwards—they would not move him till *morning*—allowing the corpse to remain 16 hours in the house of a foreigner who had by accident been near at the time of his assassination.—And this Man was the Commandant of all the troops of the place.——This altogether may show you what a state the country is in—the Commandant murdered in the public Streets—the assassin not taken—nor even pursued at the proper time—nor known even now—for they were like a set of Children—those about him.—I never saw anything like them.——

It is supposed but no one knows that he was killed on account of his having been severe against the Carbonari—(the Liberty boys of the country) but he was a brave Soldier—and it was a pity—for he left a wife and Children quite destitute.——Yesterday things were calmed but nobody seemed surprized, after the night was over—some from one motive—some from another.—The Learned Fletcher is of course horrified—less from the fact—than from the custom—and well he may—for it is common enough.——I even heard a very pretty young woman of very high rank—defend it last night in a considerable company—on the plea of necessity;—which however shocking—and shocking it is—& was to hear her—reminded me of Lord Bacon's observation "that Assassination is a *wild* Justice".—It is the consequence of a negligent administration of the laws, or of a despotic government.——In this state of things—and such things all about—for it is little better any where,—there will be war—and if there is war —there will be despondency—and the funds will fall of course—and then you will regret that you did not have the settled property transferred.—The English Terrier will meddle of course in anything that will keep down freedom—or prop up their own villainy.—Therefore—let the trustees *sell out*—& it will be the better for me—while I last—and the better for you happen what may—you will be the richer widow.—If you think this a strange language—you would not— if you were where we are—with the material [e]vidences there are on all sides.—No man's life is worth much purchase anywhere—but here it is at a discount, & will be more so—if there is a war as is most likely.

yrs. ever [Scrawl]

[TO JOHN MURRAY]   *R[avenn]a. 10bre. 10.0 1820*

D[ea]r M.—I wrote to you by last post.—Acknowledge that and this letter—which you are requested to forward immediately.——

yrs. truly
[Scrawl]

I have finished [a] fifth Canto of D[on] J[uan][1] 143 Stanzas—So prepare.——

[TO JOHN MURRAY]   *Ravenna. 10bre. 14th. 1820*

Dear Moray—As it is a month since I have had any packets of proofs—I suppose some must have miscarried.—Today I had a letter from *Rogers*.——The fifth Canto of D[on] J[uan] is now under copy—it consists of 151 Stanzas.[1]—I want to know what the devil you mean to do?——By last post I wrote to you detailing the murder of the Commandant here.——I picked him up shot in the Street at 8 in the evening; & perceiving that his adjutant and the Soldiers about him had lost their heads completely—with rage and alarm; I carried him to my house where he lay a corpse till next day—when they removed him.—Did you receive this my letter?—They thought a row was coming—& indeed it was likely—in which the the Soldiers would have been massacred.——As I am well with the Liberals of the Country—it was another reason for me to succour them; for I thought that in case of a tumult—I could by my personal influence with some of the popular Chiefs—protect these surrounded soldiers—who are but five or six hundred against five and twenty thousand—& you see few as they are that they keep picking them off daily.—It is as dangerous for that—as ever it was in the middle ages.——They are a fierce people—and at present roused and the end no one can tell.——As you don't deserve a longer letter nor any letter at all—I conclude.

yrs.
[Scrawl]

[1] Murray published Cantos III, IV, and V anonymously at the end of 1821.
[1] As usual Byron kept adding to the canto which grew ultimately to 159 stanzas.

P.S.—The Officers came in a body to *thank* me &c. &c.—but they might as well have let it alone—for in the first place it was but for a common act of decency—& in the next—their coming may put me in odium with the liberals—& in that case—it would do them no good— nor me either.—The other night (since the assassination) Fletcher was stopped *three* times in the Street—but on perceiving who he was they apologized & bade him pass on—the querists were probably on the look out for Somebody, they are very indefatigable in such researches.——Send me proofs of "the Hints" that I may correct them or alter. You are losing (like a Goose) the best time for publishing the Dante and the Tragedy—*now* is the moment for Italian subjects.——

[TO AUGUSTA LEIGH] *Ravenna. 10bre. 21.o 1820*

Dearest Augusta/—Inform Lady B[yron] that I am obliged by her readiness to have Ada taught Music and Italian, according to my wish (when she arrives at the proper period) and that in return I will give her as little trouble as can be avoided upon the subject of her education—tutelage—and guardianship.—A Girl is in all cases better with the mother, unless there is some unusual objection, and I shall not allow my own private feelings to interfere with what is for the advantage of the Child;—She may bring her up in her own way;—I am so sensible that a *man* ought to have nothing to do with such matters— that I shall in another year—either put Allegra (my natural daughter) into a Convent, or send or bring her to England, & put her in some good way of instruction.——Tell Lady B—that I have written to her *two* letters within these *three* or *four months*, I do not say this—because I desire an answer—for I have no such expectation, but simply—that She may know that they have been sent—as the Italian post in these times is always treacherous & sometimes tyrannical enough to suppress letters.——Will you for the same reason inform Murray that for six weeks I have had no letters—although for fifty reasons he ought to have written.—Either the Post plays false, or he is a shabby fellow.——

The State of things here is what cannot be described.——Not ten days ago—the Commandant of the troops—was assassinated at my door—and died as he was being carried into my apartments; he lay on Fletcher's bed a corpse for eighteen hours—before the Government ventured to remove him. He was shot in walking home to his

251

barrack at 8 in the Evening.—All this is little to what will be—if there is a Neapolitan war.——The Italians are right however—they want liberty—and if it is not given—they must take it.—What you say of the Queen is of no consequence, it is the state of things which is shewn which imports.—I have written and written to Lady B—to get us *out* of the *funds*—will she wait till they *go?*—I know more of *those* things—than you or she do—both at home and abroad;—and those who live will see strange things. [End of letter torn off]

[TO FRANCIS HODGSON] *Ravenna, 10bre 22d., 1820*[1]

My Dear Hodgson,—My Sister tells me that you desire to hear from me. I have not written to you since I left England, nearly five years ago. I have no excuse for this silence except laziness, which is none. Where I am my date will tell you; what I have been doing would but little interest you, as it regards another country and another people, & would be almost speaking another language, for my own is not quite so familiar to me as it used to be.

We have here the Sepulchre of Dante and the forest of Dryden and Boccaccio, all in very poetical preservation. I ride and write, and have here some Italian friends and connexions of both sexes, horses and dogs, and the usual means and appliances of life, which passes chequered as usual (& with all) with good and evil; few English pass by this place, and none remain, which renders it a much more eligible residence for a man who would rather see them in England than out of it; they are best at home; for out of it they but raise the prices of the necessaries and vices of other countries, and carry little back to their own, except such things as you have lately seen and heard of in the Queen's trial.

Your friend Denman is making a figure.[2] I am glad of it; he had all the auguries of a superior man about him before I left the country. Hobhouse is a radical, and is doing great things in that somewhat violent line of politics. His intellect will bear him out; but, though I do not disapprove of his cause, I by no means envy his company. Our

1 This letter has been corrected from notations in an annotated copy of Hodgson's *Memoir* in the Birmingham University Library, obviously by someone who had seen the original manuscript. These corrections were supplied me by Mrs. E. E. Duncan Jones, Senior Lecturer at Birmingham University.

2 Thomas Denman defended the Queen as her solicitor-general, though in his peroration he made an unfortunate allusion to the story of the woman taken in adultery. He was later Lord Chief Justice (1832) and was created Lord Denman (1834).

friend Scrope is dished, diddled, and done up; *what* he is our mutual friends have written to me—somewhat more coldly than I think our former connexions with him warrant: but *where* he is I know not, for neither they nor he have informed me. Remember me to Harry Drury. He wrote to me a year ago to subscribe to the Harrow New School erection; but my name has not now value enough to be placed among my old School-fellows, and as to the trifle which can come from a solitary subscriber, that is not worth mentioning. Some zealous politicians wrote to me to come over to the Queen's trial; it was a business with which I should have been sorry to have had anything to do; in which they who voted her guilty cut but a dirty figure and those who call her innocent a not very clean one. Such a Coroner's inquest upon a criminal conversation has nothing very alluring in it, and I was obliged to her for personal civilities (when in England), and would therefore rather avoid sitting in Judgement upon her, either for Guilt or Innocence, as it is an ungracious office.

Murray sent me your "friends," which I thought very good and classical. The Scoundrels of Scribblers are trying to run down *Pope*, but I hope in vain. It is my intention to take up the Cudgels in that controversy, and to do my best to keep the Swan of Thames in his true place. This comes of Southey and Turdsworth and such renegado rascals with their systems. I hope you will not be silent; it is the common concern of all men of common sense, imagination, and a musical ear. I have already written somewhat thereto and shall do more, and will not strike soft blows in a battle. You will have seen that the "Quarterly" has had the sense and spirit to support Pope in an article upon Bowles; it is a good beginning. I do not know the author of that article, but I suspect *Israeli*, an indefatigable and an able writer. What are you about—poetry? I direct to Bakewell, but I do not know for certain. To save you a double letter, I close this with the present sheet.

Yours ever,
[Scrawl]

[TO THOMAS MOORE]   *Ravenna, Dec. 25th, 1820*

You will or ought to have received the packet and letters which I remitted to your address a fortnight ago (or it may be more days), and I shall be glad of an answer, as, in these times and places, packets per post are in some risk of not reaching their destination.

I have been thinking of a project for you and me, in case we both get to London again, which (if a Neapolitan war don't suscitate) may be calculated as possible for one of us about the spring of 1821. I presume that you, too, will be back by that time, or never; but on that you will give me some index. The project, then, is for you and me to set up jointly a *newspaper*—nothing more nor less—weekly, or so, with some improvement or modifications upon the plan of the present scoundrels, who degrade that department,—but a *newspaper*, which we will edite in due form, and, nevertheless, with some attention.

There must always be in it a piece of poesy from one or other of us *two*, leaving room, however, for such dilettanti rhymers as may be deemed worthy of appearing in the same column: but *this* must be a *sine qua non*; and also as much prose as we can compass. We will take an *office*—our names *not* announced, but suspected—and, by the blessing of Providence, give the age some new lights upon policy, poesy, biography, criticism, morality, theology, and all other *ism*, *ality*, and *ology* whatsoever.

Why, man, if we were to take to this in good earnest, your debts would be paid off in a twelvemonth, and, by dint of a little diligence and practice, I doubt not that we could distance the common-place blackguards who have so long disgraced common sense and the common reader. They have no merit but practice and impudence, both of which we may acquire, and, as for talent and culture, the devil's in't if such proofs as we have given of both can't furnish out something better than the "funeral baked meats"[1] which have coldly set forth the breakfast table of all Great Britain for so many years. Now, what think you? Let me know; and recollect that, if we take to such an enterprise, we must do so in good earnest. Here is a hint,—do you make it a plan. We will modify it into as literary and classical a concern as you please, only let us put out our powers upon it, and it will most likely succeed. But you must *live* in London, and I also, to bring it to bear, and *we must keep it a secret*.

As for living in London, I would make that not difficult to you (if you would allow me), until we could see whether one means or other (the success of the plan, for instance) would not make it quite easy for you, as well as your family; and, in any case, we should have some fun, composing, correcting, supposing, inspecting, and supping together over our lucubrations. If you think this worth a thought, let me know, and I will begin to lay in a small literary capital of composition for the occasion.

Yours ever affectionately,
B

[1] *Hamlet*, Act I, scene 2.

P.S.—If you thought of a middle plan between a *Spectator* and a newspaper, why not?—only not on a *Sunday*. Not that Sunday is not an excellent day, but it is engaged already. We will call it the "Tenda Rossa,"[1] the name Tassoni gave an answer of his in a controversy, in allusion to the delicate hint of Timour the Lame, to his enemies, by a "Tenda" of that colour, before he gave battle. Or we will call it "Gli" or "I Carbonari", if it so please you—or any other name full of "pastime and prodigality," which you may prefer. * * * Let me have an answer. I conclude poetically, with the bellman, "A merry Christmas to you!"

[TO DOUGLAS KINNAIRD]   R[*avenn*]*a. 1Obre. 28.o 1820*

Dear Douglas—Having for two months (since the second reading of the Queen's bill) had no news from Murray—who is either shuffling (a publisher can hardly help it—it is their nature) or has been intercepted & suppressed by the suspicious post, of this country (which will be in war in a few weeks) I enclose to you by this post—& with this letter—two packets containing the fifth Canto of Don Juan—155 Stanzas octave—and notes.—Acknowledge the receipt.—War is almost certain—notwithstanding their negociations & talking.——Of the State of this part—judge—on the 7th [9th] they murdered the Commandant of the troops before my door—at 8 in the evening—and he died in my house;—he was at some risk to me and at my own peril taken by myself and servants out of the streets—where he was expiring.—I request an answer.—Tell Murray he is not behaving well.——Above all get my capitals [sic] out of the *funds which are now high*—write to the woman and *trustees*—write—*write*—write—

yrs. ever & truly
[Scrawl]

P.S.—Tell Mr. M⟨urray⟩ that he must settle something yes or no—if no—go to another.—Let me have the half year's Credentials—as soon as convenient.—Consider *war* as certain—The Scoundrels have refused Gallo[1] his passport to accompany the king to Congress.——

[1] Alessandro Tassoni (1565–1635) published in 1622 a mock-heroic poem, *La Secchia Rapita* (The ravished pail), a forerunner of Pope's *Rape of the Lock*. The *Tenda Rossa* (a symbol that he would fight to the death those who took up arms against him) was the title of one of Tassoni's literary polemics.
[1] Marzio Mastrilli duce di Gallo (1758–1833) became Ministro degli Esterl In the Revolution of 1820 in Naples, but was forced out of office with the restoration.

[TO JOHN MURRAY]   R[avenn]a. 10bre. 28.o 1820

D[ea]r. M—I have had no communication from you of any kind
since the second reading of the Queen's bill.—I write merely to apprize
you that by this Post—I have transmitted to Mr. Douglas Kinnaird
the fifth Canto—of Don Juan—& you will apply (if so disposed) to
him for it.—It consists of 155 octave Stanzas with a few notes.———I
wrote to you several times—and told you of the various events—
assassinations &c.—which have occurred here. War is certain.—If
you write—write soon.—

                                                            yrs. [Scrawl]

P.S.—Did you receive two letters &c. from Galignani to me—
which I enclosed to you long ago?—I suppose your answer must have
been intercepted as they were of importance to you & you would
naturally have acknowledged their arrival.—

[TO LADY BYRON]   Ravenna. 10bre. 28.o 1820

I acknowledge your Note which is on the whole satisfactory—the
style a little harsh—but that was to be expected—it would have been
too great a peace-offering after nearly five years—to have been
gracious in the manner, as well as the matter.—Yet you might have
been so, for communications between us—are like "Dialogues of the
dead"[1]—or "letters between this world and the next."——You have
alluded to the "past" and I to the future.—As to Augusta—she knows
as little of my request, as of your answer.——Whatever She is or
may have been—you have never had reason to complain of her—on
the contrary—you are not aware of the obligations under which you
have been to her.——Her life and mine—& yours & mine were two
things perfectly distinct from each other—when one ceased the other
began—and now both are closed.——You must be aware of the reasons
of my request in fa[vou]r of Augusta & her Child[re]n—which are the
restrictions I am under by the Settlement, which death would make
yours, at least the available portion. I wrote to you on the 8th. or
ninth inst. I think.—

Things here are fast coming to a Crisis.——War may be considered
as nearly inevitable—though the King of N[aples] is gone to Congress
—that will scarcely hinder it—the people are so excited, you must
not mind what the English fools say of Italy—they know nothing—

1 *Dialogues of the Dead*, by George Lyttelton, 1st Lord, 1760.

256

the[y] go gaping from Rome to Florence and so on—which is like seeing England in Saint James's Street.— —I live with the people— and amongst them—& know them—and you may rely upon my not deceiving you, though I may myself[.] If you mean ever to extricate the Settlement from the funds now is the time to make the trustees act—while Stocks are yet up—and peace not actually broken. Pray attend to this.—

yrs.
BYRON

P.S.—Excuse haste—I have scribbled in great quickness—and do not attribute it to ill-humour—but to matters which are on hand & which must be attended to—I am really obliged by your attention to my request.— —You could not have sent me any thing half so accept- able—but I have *burnt* your note that you may be under no restraint but your internal feeling.—It is a Comfort to me *now*—beyond all comforts; that A[ugusta] & her children will be thought of—after I am nothing; but five years ago—it would have been something more? Why did you *then keep silence?*—I told you that I was going *long*— and going *far*—(not so *far* as I intended—for I meant to have gone to Turkey and am not sure that I shall not finish with it—but *longer* than I meant to have made of existence—at least at the time.) and two words about her or hers would have been to me—like vengeance or freedom to an Italian—i.e. the "Ne plus ultra" of gratifications.— — She & two others were the only things I ever really loved.—I may say it now—for we are young no longer.— —

[TO AUGUSTA LEIGH]   *R[avenn]a. 10bre. 29.0 1820*

D[ea]rest A.—Forward the enclosed to Ly. B[yron]. Ask Murray if he is mad? or drunk? or stupid? that he has not answered a letter of mine since the 2d. reading of the Queen's bill?—either his letters have been intercepted—[or] he is no better than he should be.— [Pray]—desire Mr. D. Kin[nair]d to press upon the trustees the selling out of the funds—*now* while they are tolerably high.—

[Scrawl]

[TO JOHN MURRAY]   *R[avenn]a. 10bre. 30.0 1820*

D[ea]r M.—In the M. S. sent to Mr. D[ougla]s K[innair]d the other day—being the 5th. C[ant]o of D[on] J[uan]—you will find the following stanza—the ⟨poet⟩ writer has been speaking of Babylon.—

"'Twas famous too for Thisbe and for Pyramus
And the calumniated Queen—Semiramis.—

This Injured Queen by Chroniclers so coarse
   Has been accused (I doubt not by Conspiracy)
Of an improper friendship for her *Horse* * See Pliny &c.
   (Love like Religion sometimes runs to heresy)
This monstrous tale had probably it's source
   (For such exaggerations here and there I see)
In an *Erratum* of her *horse* for *Courier*;
   I wish the Case could come before a Jury here."

Alter the *last two lines* to—

   printing
   ̄̄
   or
   ̄̄

"In writing '*Courser*' by mistake for '*Courier*';
I wish the Case could come before a Jury here.—"[1]

I have written to you often lately and had no answer—I wish you a
New year

                                                   yrs. [Scrawl]

                              _
                              or
                              ̄
Pity! the Case can't come before a Jury cer.—

---

but the other last line ending with "*Jury here*" is better perhaps—&
I think it is—however take which you like, and let me know yr.
sublime intentions & opinions.

[1] This stanza (61 of the fifth canto) was suppressed by Byron at the request of
Hobhouse because of the slur on the Queen.

LIST OF LETTERS AND SOURCES

Date	Recipient	Source of Text	Page
		1820 (continued)	
Jan. 29	Teresa Guiccioli	MS. Biblioteca Classense, Ravenna	26
Jan. 31	R. B. Hoppner	MS. Henry E. Huntington Library	27
[Jan. 31]	Teresa Guiccioli (a)	MS. Biblioteca Classense, Ravenna	29
7 ore [Jan. 31]	Teresa Guiccioli (b)	MS. Biblioteca Classense, Ravenna	30
[Feb.?]	Teresa Guiccioli	MS. Biblioteca Classense, Ravenna	31
Feb. 1	Teresa Guiccioli	MS. Biblioteca Classense, Ravenna	32
6 ore [Feb. 2?]	Teresa Guiccioli	MS. Biblioteca Classense, Ravenna	33
Feb. 7	John Murray	MS. Murray	34
Feb. 7	Teresa Guiccioli	MS. Biblioteca Classense, Ravenna	35
[After Feb. 7?]	Teresa Guiccioli (a)	MS. Biblioteca Classense, Ravenna	36
[After Feb. 7?]	Teresa Guiccioli (b)	MS. Biblioteca Classense, Ravenna	37
[After Feb. 7?]	Teresa Guiccioli (c)	MS. Biblioteca Classense, Ravenna	37
[After Feb. 7?]	Teresa Guiccioli (d)	MS. Biblioteca Classense, Ravenna	38
Feb. 19	William Bankes	Text: Moore, II, 300–301	39
Feb. 20	Lady Byron	MS. The Earl of Lytton	40
Feb. 21	John Murray	MS. Murray	41
Feb. 26	William Bankes	Text: Moore, II, 304–305	45
Feb. 28	John Murray	MS. Murray	45
[March?]	Lega Zambelli	MS. British Museum (Add. 56878)	46
March 1	John Murray	MS. Murray	47
March 3	John Cam Hobhouse	MS. British Museum (Ashley 4744)	49
March 3	Teresa Guiccioli	MS. Biblioteca Classense, Ravenna	52
March 4	Teresa Guiccioli	MS. Biblioteca Classense, Ravenna	53

Date	Recipient	Source of Text	Page
		1820 (continued)	
March 5	John Murray	MS. Murray	54
March 5	Teresa Guiccioli	MS. Biblioteca Classense, Ravenna	54
[After March 5?]	Teresa Guiccioli (a)	MS. Biblioteca Classense, Ravenna	55
[After March 5?]	Teresa Guiccioli (b)	MS. Biblioteca Classense, Ravenna	56
[After March 5?]	Teresa Guiccioli (c)	MS. Biblioteca Classense, Ravenna	56
March 14	John Murray	MS. Murray	57
March 20	John Murray	MS. Houghton Library, Harvard University.	58
March 23	John Murray (a)	MS. Walpole Library, King's School, Canterbury	58
March 23	John Murray (b)	MS. Murray	59
March 28	John Murray	MS. Murray	60
March 29	John Murray	MS. National Historical Museum, Athens	60
March 29	John Cam Hobhouse	MS. Murray	62
March 30	Harriette Wilson	Text: Harriette Wilson's *Memoirs*, pp. 611–612	64
March 31	R. B. Hoppner	MS. Henry E. Huntington Library	65
[April?]	Teresa Guiccioli (a)	MS. Biblioteca Classense, Ravenna	66
[April?]	Teresa Guiccioli (b)	MS. Biblioteca Classense, Ravenna	67
April 3	Lady Byron	MS. The Earl of Lytton	68
April 6	Lady Byron	MS. The Earl of Lytton	68
April 6	John Hanson	MS. Murray	69
April 6	John Cam Hobhouse	MS. Murray	70
April 6	Douglas Kinnaird	MS. Murray	71
April 8	Douglas Kinnaird	MS. Carl H. Pforzheimer Library	72
April 9	John Murray	MS. Murray	73

Date	Recipient	Source of Text	Page
		1820 (continued)	
May 15	Harriette Wilson	Text: Harriette Wilson's Memoirs, p. 614	100
May 20	Douglas Kinnaird, and John and Charles Hanson	MS. Murray	101
May 20	John Hanson	MS. Murray	101
May 20	John Murray (a)	MS. Murray	101
May 20	John Murray (b)	MS. Murray	102
May 20	R. B. Hoppner	MS. Murray	103
May 24	Thomas Moore	Text: Moore, II, 325–327	104
May 25	R. B. Hoppner	MS. Clark Library, University of California, Los Angeles	106
[June?]	Teresa Guiccioli (a)	MS. Biblioteca Classense, Ravenna	107
[June?]	Teresa Guiccioli (b)	MS. Biblioteca Classense, Ravenna	108
[June?]	Teresa Guiccioli (c)	MS. Biblioteca Classense, Ravenna	109
[June?]	Teresa Guiccioli (d)	MS. Biblioteca Classense, Ravenna	109
[June?]	Teresa Guiccioli (e)	MS. Biblioteca Classense, Ravenna	110
June 1	Douglas Kinnaird	MS. Murray	110
June 1	Thomas Moore	Text: Moore, II, 328–329	111
June 7	John Murray	MS. Murray	113
June 8	John Murray	MS. Murray	114
June 8	John Cam Hobhouse	MS. Murray	114
June 8	Douglas Kinnaird	MS. Murray	116
June 8	Douglas Kinnaird and John and Charles Hanson	MS. Murray	116
June 9	Thomas Moore	Text: Moore, II, 333–334	117
June 12	R. B. Hoppner	Text: LJ, V, 43–44	118
June 15	Charles Hanson	MS. Murray	119
June 19	Douglas Kinnaird	MS. Murray	120
June 22	John Cam Hobhouse	MS. Murray	121
July 6	John Cam Hobhouse	MS. Murray	122
July 6	John Murray	MS. Murray	124

Date	Recipient	Source of Text	Page
		1820 (continued)	
Aug. 8	Teresa Guiccioli	MS. Biblioteca Classense, Ravenna	154
Aug. 10	Augusta Leigh	MS. Murray	155
Aug. 11	Teresa Guiccioli	MS. Biblioteca Classense, Ravenna	156
Aug. 12	Teresa Guiccioli (*a*)	MS. Biblioteca Classense, Ravenna	156
Aug. 12	Teresa Guiccioli (*b*)	MS. Biblioteca Classense, Ravenna	157
Aug. 12	John Murray	MS. Murray	158
Aug. 17	John Murray	MS. Murray	158
Aug. 19	Augusta Leigh	MS. The Earl of Lytton	159
Aug. 21	Count Guiccioli	MS. Stark Library, University of Texas	159
Aug. 22	John Murray	MS. Murray	161
Aug. 24	Teresa Guiccioli	MS. Biblioteca Classense, Ravenna	161
Aug. 24	John Murray	MS. Murray	162
[Aug. 25?]	John Murray	MS. Carl H. Pforzheimer Library	162
Aug. 25	Percy Bysshe Shelley	MS. Bodleian Library	162
Aug. 26	Teresa Guiccioli	MS. Biblioteca Classense, Ravenna	162
Aug. 27	Teresa Guiccioli	MS. Biblioteca Classense, Ravenna	164
Aug. 28	John Murray	MS. Carl H. Pforzheimer Library	164
Aug. 29	John Murray	MS. Murray	165
[Aug. 30?]	John Murray	MS. Carl H. Pforzheimer Library	165
Aug. 30	Augusta Leigh	MS. Murray	166
Aug. 30	Teresa Guiccioli	MS. Biblioteca Classense, Ravenna	166
Aug. 31	R. B. Hoppner	Text: Parke-Bernet Cat. 524, Feb. 1, 1944	167
Aug. 31	Douglas Kinnaird	MS. Private Collection	167
Aug. 31	John Hanson	MS. Murray	168
Aug. 31	John Murray (*a*)	MS. Murray	168

Date	Recipient	Source of Text	Page
		1820 (continued)	
Aug. 31	John Murray (*b*)	MS. Carl H. Pforzheimer Library	169
Aug. 31	Thomas Moore	Text: Moore, II, 341–342	170
Sept. 4	Teresa Guiccioli	MS. Biblioteca Classense, Ravenna	171
Sept. 7	John Murray	MS. Murray	172
Sept. 8	John Murray	MS. Murray	173
Sept. 9	Teresa Guiccioli	MS. Biblioteca Classense, Ravenna	173
Sept. 10	R. B. Hoppner	MS. Murray	174
Sept. 11	John Murray	MS. Murray	175
Sept. 14	Teresa Guiccioli	MS. Biblioteca Classense, Ravenna	175
Sept. 14	John Murray	MS. Murray	176
Sept. 21	John Murray	MS. Murray	176
Sept. 21	John Cam Hobhouse	MS. Murray	177
Sept. 23	John Murray	MS. Murray	179
Sept. 25	John Cam Hobhouse	MS. Murray	180
Sept. 28	John Murray (*a*)	MS. Murray	181
Sept. 28	John Murray (*b*)	MS. Murray	182
Sept. 28	Teresa Guiccioli	MS. Biblioteca Classense, Ravenna	185
Sept. 29	Teresa Guiccioli	MS. Biblioteca Classense, Ravenna	186
[Oct.?]	The Neapolitan Insurgents	MS. Carl H. Pforzheimer Library	187
[Oct.?]	John Murray	Text: *Poetry*, VI, 70	188
Oct. 1	Teresa Guiccioli	MS. Biblioteca Classense, Ravenna	189
Oct. 1	Douglas Kinnaird	MS. Murray	190
Oct. 1	R. B. Hoppner	MS. Murray	191
Oct. 6	John Murray	MS. Murray	191
Oct. 7	Teresa Guiccioli	MS. Biblioteca Classense, Ravenna	193
Oct. 8	John Murray	MS. Murray	194
Oct. 11	Teresa Guiccioli	MS. Biblioteca Classense, Ravenna	196
Oct. 12	Douglas Kinnaird	MS. Murray	198

Date	Recipient	Source of Text	Page
		1820 (continued)	
Oct. 12	Teresa Guiccioli	MS. Biblioteca Classense, Ravenna	198
Oct. 12	John Murray	MS. British Museum (Ashley 4745)	199
Oct. 12	John Hanson	MS. Murray	202
Oct. 13	R. B. Hoppner	MS. Facsimile, *The Archivist* April, 1889, p. 12	203
Oct. 16	John Murray (*a*)	MS. Clark Library, University of California, Los Angeles	203
Oct. 16	John Murray (*b*)	Text: Moore, II, 355	204
Oct. 17	John Cam Hobhouse	MS. Murray	204
Oct. 17	John Murray	MS. Murray	206
Oct. 17	Thomas Moore	Text: Moore, II, 358–359	206
Oct. 18	Augusta Leigh	MS. The Earl of Lytton	207
Oct. 25	Teresa Guiccioli	MS. Biblioteca Classense, Ravenna	209
Oct. 25	Lady Byron	MS. The Earl of Lytton	210
Oct. 25	John Murray	MS. Murray	212
Oct. 26	Douglas Kinnaird	MS. Murray	213
Oct. 28	R. B. Hoppner	MS. Carl H. Pforzheimer Library	214
Oct. 30	Teresa Guiccioli	MS. Biblioteca Classense, Ravenna	214
[Nov.?]	John Cam Hobhouse	MS. Murray	216
Nov. 4	John Murray	MS. British Museum (Ashley 5160)	216
Nov. 5	Thomas Moore	Text: Moore, II, 376–378	218
Nov. 5	Douglas Kinnaird	MS. Murray	220
Nov. 8	Teresa Guiccioli	MS. Biblioteca Classense, Ravenna	221
Nov. 9	John Cam Hobhouse	MS. Murray	221
Nov. 9	John Murray	MS. British Museum (Ashley 5161)	223
Nov. 10	Teresa Guiccioli	MS. Biblioteca Classense, Ravenna	226
Nov. 18	Augusta Leigh	MS. The Earl of Lytton	227

FORGERIES OF BYRON'S LETTERS

Feb. 28, 1820: To W. J. Bankes. Schultess-Young, XXXII, 208–9.

March 2, 1820: To Thomas Moore. P. F. Madigan, Vol. 1, No. 4, March–April, 1912.

April 2, 1820: To Douglas Kinnaird. Bixby.

April 4, [1820?]: To Douglas Kinnaird. MS. Gordon N. Ray.

April 9, 1820: To R. B. Hoppner. MS. Lady Anne Hill.

April 9, [1820?]: To [?] MS. Berg Collection, New York Public Library.

April 11, 1820: To Douglas Kinnaird. Schultess-Young, XIV, pp. 176–8.

April 19, 1820: To Sir Godfrey Webster. MS. Murray Collection.

April 24, 1820: To R. B. Hoppner. Schultess-Young, XXVIII, 200–2.

April 25, 1820: To Douglas Kinnaird. MS. Berg Collection, New York Public Library.

April 25, 1820: To Sir Godfrey Webster. Schultess-Young, XXXV, 214–15.

May 27, 1820: To R. B. Hoppner. Schultess-Young, XXIX, 202–3.

August, 1820: To Douglas Kinnaird. Schultess-Young, XV, 178–9.

Sept. 3, 1820: To Douglas Kinnaird. Text: City Book Auction, Oct. 21, 1950.

Sept. 17, 1820: To Douglas Kinnaird. MS. Yale University Library.

Nov. 7, 1820: To [Douglas Kinnaird]. Sotheby, Cat., June 10, 1909, p. 45.

Appendix III

BIBLIOGRAPHY FOR VOLUME 7

(*Principal short title or abbreviated references*)

Astarte—Lovelace, Ralph Milbanke, Earl of: *Astarte; A Fragment of Truth, Concerning George Gordon Byron, Sixth Lord Byron.* Recorded by his grandson. New Edition by Mary Countess of Lovelace, London, 1921.

Blessington—*Lady Blessington's Conversations of Lord Byron*, ed. Ernest J. Lovell, Jr., Princeton, N.J. 1969.

Broughton, Lord [John Cam Hobhouse]: *Recollections of a Long Life.* Ed. by his daughter, Lady Dorchester. 6 vols. London, 1909–11.

Dictionary of National Biography.

LBC—*Lord Byron's Correspondence*, ed. John Murray, 2 vols., London, 1922.

LJ—*The Works of Lord Byron. A New, Revised and Enlarged Edition. Letters and Journals*, ed. Rowland E. Prothero, 6 vols., London, 1898–1901.

Marchand, Leslie A.: *Byron: A Biography*, 3 vols., New York, 1957; London, 1958.

Moore, Doris Langley: *Lord Byron: Accounts Rendered*, London, 1974.

Moore, Thomas: *Letters and Journals of Lord Byron: with Notices of his Life*, 2 vols., London, 1830.

Origo, Iris: *The Last Attachment*, London, 1949.

Poetry—*The Works of Lord Byron. A New and Enlarged Edition. Poetry*, ed. Ernest Hartley Coleridge, 7 vols., London, 1898–1904.

Smiles, Samuel: *A Publisher and his Friends: Memoir and Correspondence of the Late John Murray*, 2 vols., London, 1891.

Wilson, Harriette: *Harriette Wilson's Memoirs of Herself and Others*, New York, 1929.

BIOGRAPHICAL SKETCHES

OF PRINCIPAL CORRESPONDENTS AND PERSONS FREQUENTLY MENTIONED

(See also Sketches in earlier volumes)

COUNT RUGGERO GAMBA GHISELLI

Count Gamba was a respected member of an old aristocratic family in Ravenna. He had allied himself with the aristocratic revolutionary parties from the time of the French occupation. Perhaps Count Guiccioli's temporary alliance with the revolution (he was a wealthy landholder and an opportunist) induced Gamba to give his daughter Teresa, then 18 and just out of Convent School at Faenza, to the 57-year-old Guiccioli in marriage, along with a dowry of 4500 scudi. At first he was alarmed at Teresa's liaison with Byron, but he soon came to like the English lover better than his son-in-law. Byron's genuine interest in Italian freedom contrasted with Count Guiccioli's slippery self-serving politics, and his amiable openness with the suave but scheming ways of Guiccioli.

Teresa had little difficulty in winning her father's confidence in her Cavalier Servente and later in persuading him to seek a separation for her from her husband by appealing to Pope Pius VII. After the separation Byron won Count Gamba's esteem and trust further by siding with him in urging Teresa to observe restraint and prudence in their meetings. "Ask Papa" was his constant admonition. Count Gamba and his son Pietro initiated Byron into the secret revolutionary society of the Carbonari. When the Gambas were exiled, Teresa wanted to stay behind with Byron, but he induced her to follow her father and brother to Florence and later to Plsa where he joined them. From then on Count Gamba accepted Byron as his counsellor as well as his daughter's lover and trusted him completely. After Byron and Pietro left for Greece, Count Gamba returned to the Romagna with Teresa, was jailed in Ferrara for six years for his political activities, and spent his last years on his estate at Filetto, where he died in 1846.

COUNT PIETRO GAMBA GHISELLI

When Byron first visited Teresa Guiccioli in Ravenna in 1819, her brother Pietro was at school in Rome. He had heard gossip about the dangerous and seductive Milord who had shut his wife up in his castle in England, and he wrote to Teresa to warn her. But when he returned to Ravenna the following year, he was, like his father, immediately won over by Byron's charm. After the meeting Byron wrote to Teresa: "I like your little brother very much—he shows character and talent. . . . His head is a little too hot for revolutions—he must not be too rash." It was mainly through Pietro that Byron became involved in the activities and schemes of the Carbonari, and even harboured weapons for them in the Guiccioli Palace at some risk to himself. When the abortive uprising failed in 1821, Pietro and his father were exiled from the Romagna and took refuge in Florence and then in Pisa, where Byron joined them later in the year. From this time on Pietro was his constant companion on their daily rides, and he looked up to Byron for guidance and inspiration.

When the time came to go to Greece, Pietro was full of enthusiasm. Byron wrote to Hobhouse that Teresa was an obstacle to his going, but that "her brother, who is a fine bold young fellow...is even more anxious for him and me to go up to Greece, than anybody else, being a thorough Liberty boy." And Byron let Pietro break the news to Teresa.

In Missolonghi Pietro was Byron's lieutenant and man of all chores. He wrote letters, helped train the wild Souliote corps, ordered supplies, edited the *Telegrafo Greco*, and wrote news of Byron's activities to Teresa, while Byron added a postscript in English. He was the most devoted of all Byron's followers. His naiveté, his sincerity and loyalty, his idealism, and even his impracticality, at which Byron laughed though it sometimes exasperated him, cemented their friendship.

Pietro was desolated by Byron's death. He came to England, attended the funeral, and published his *Narrative of Lord Byron's Last Journey to Greece*. He felt lost without Byron. In the end he returned to fight for Greek freedom as his hero had done, and died of a fever in Methana in 1827.

INDEX OF PROPER NAMES

Page numbers in italics indicate main references and Biographical Sketches in the Appendix. Such main biographical references in earlier volumes are included in this index and are in square brackets.

Cato, 62n
Cavalli, Marchese Clelia, 13, 18, 53, 78
Centlivre, Susanna, 61; *The Busybody*, *The Wonder*, 61n
Cicero, 174
Cicognara, Mme, 25
Clairmont, Claire, [*Vol. 5, 283–4*], her insolent letters to B., 174; and guardianship of Allegra, 174–5; alleged child by Shelley, 191n
Claughton, Thomas, 116, 235, 239, 240
Clodius, Publius, 81 and n
Cobbett, William, 17, 63 and n, 80
Cohen, Francis, *see* Palgrave, Sir Francis
Colburn, Henry, *Biographical Dictionary*, 79 and n
Coleridge, Samuel T., 84
Colman, George, the Younger, *John Bull*, 105 and n; *The Review, or the Wags of Windsor*, 84 and n
Congreve, William, 61
Constant, Benjamin, *Adolphe*, 161 and n, 163 and n
Cornwall, Barry, *see* Procter, Bryan Waller
Cowper, William, 'The Garden', 246 and n; *John Gilpin*, 16 and n; *Retirement*, 101 and n
Crayon, Geoffrey, *see* Irving, Washington
Croker, John Wilson, 223
Croly, Rev. George, 201, 225; *The Modern Orlando, Paris in 1815*, 201n
Cumberland, Richard, *Wheel of Fortune*, 211 and n

Dallas, Robert Charles, [*Vol. 1, 274–5*], accuses B., 47–8
Dante, *Inferno*, 68 and n, 209 and n; *Francesca of Rimini*, B.'s translation, 58 and n, 59, 64, 73, 106
Daru, Pierre Antoine, 132
Davies, Scrope Berdmore, [*Vol. 1, 184n*], 63, 233; an 'irreparable loss to B.', 50 and n; unknown whereabouts, 253
Davy, Sir Humphry, in Ravenna, 78, 95, 105; encounter with a Lady of rank, 98; and Pompeian MSS, 98
de Bathe, Sir James Wynne, Bt, 99
D'Israeli, Isaac, 39n, 223, 253; *Quarterly Review* article, 217 and n

Denman, Thomas (later Lord), defends Queen Caroline, 252 and n
Devonshire, Elizabeth, Duchess of, 95, 188 and n
Dodsley, Robert, *Cleone*, 191n
Dogherty, Dan, bout with Belcher, 233
Dorville, Henry, 27, 118
Drury, Henry, 253
Dryden, John, 83, 252; trns, Juvenal *Satires*, 153 and n
Dyke, Miss, future wife of Moore, 117n

Edgecombe, Clerk, [*Vol. 6, 143n*], 28
Edgeworth, Richard Lovell, f. of Maria, 217
Elisei, Lt. Giovanni Battista, 26, 131, 156, 157 and n, 216; riding accident, 132, 140; offended with B., 147–8
Erskine, Lord, defends the Reformers, 16n

Falcieri, Giovanni Battista (Tita), B.'s servant, *39 and n*; 245, 247
Faliero, Marino, B.'s model, 131 and n, 132, 141–2
Farquhar, George, *Constant Couple*, 220 and n, 224 and n
Faulkner, George, 72
Fawkes (Faux), Guy, 75, 76
Fielding, Henry, *Jonathan Wild*, 49 and n; *Tom Jones*, 132 and n
Fitzgerald, William Thomas, 205, 236
Fletcher, William, B.'s valet, 50, 227, 249, 251; reads Hobhouse's. speeches, 154; illness 179
Foggi, Elise, story of Shelley, 191 and n
Foote, Samuel, *Mayor of Garratt*, 205 and n, 222 and n
Forsyth, Joseph, *Remarks on Antiquities . . . in Italy*, 182 and n, 183
Forteguerri, Niccolò, *Ricciardetto*, 113 and n
Foscolo, Ugo, 205, 238; B. on, 194, 195, 201; *Ricciarda, Tragedia*, 150 and n, 195–6
Frere, John Hookham, 54, 180; 'Whistlecraft', 42, 113 and n
Fyler, Capt., 41

Galiffe, James A., *Italy and Its Inhabitants*, 184 and n

Galignani, John Anthony, Paris publisher, 15, 17, 127; and B.'s French editions, 117 and n, 216 and n, 218, 225

Gallo, Marzio Mastrilli, duce de, 255 and n

Gamba, Attilia, d. of Count Guiccioli, 163 and n

Gamba Ghiselli, Count Pietro, b. of Teresa, 146 and n, 155, 197 and n, 209, 273; *Narrative of Byron's Last Journey to Greece*, 273

Gamba Ghiselli, Count Ruggero, f. of Teresa, 29 and n, 128 and n, 148, 153, 272; and his daughter's liaison with B., 18, 164, 272

Garrick, David, on Johnson and Beauclerk, 16 and n

Gay, John, *Beggar's Opera*, 72 and n, 103 and n

Gay, Mme Sophie, 104 and n, 206

George III, death, 40, 41, 44 and n; insanity, 192

George IV, coronation, 41–2, 50, 65, 86, 120n

Gifford, William, [*Vol. 3, 271*], 168, 172, 179–80; *Baviad, Maeviad*, 175 and n

Ginguené, P. L., *Histoire Littéraire d'Italie*, 54 and n

Giorgione, 'Judgment of Solomon', 45

Giovanni, Don, priest at Filetto, go-between, 185 and n, 186

Gnoatto, Mr, servant to Mme Mocenigo, 65, 79

Goethe, Johann Wolfgang von, review of *Manfred*, 106 and n, 113, 220 and n; dedicatee of *Marino Faliero*, 206 and n; *Faust*, 113

Goldsmith, Oliver, 83; 'Retaliation', 63 and n

Gordon, Lord George, 45 and n

Gordon, Sir John, of Gight (Bogagicht), ancestor of B., 204, 212

Grammont, Philibert, Comte de, *Mémoires*, 202

Grimm, Friedrich Melchior, *Correspondence Littéraire*, 103 and n

Guiccioli, Count Alessandro, [*Vol. 6, 276–7*], 12 and n, 13, 24; and his wife's liaison with B., 17, 67 and nn, 94, 147, 160 and n, 165; B.'s contempt for, 20–1; and Ravenna Theatre Committee, 26n, 52n; borrows money from B., 92, 163

and n; on the eve of divorce, 102–3; papal decree, 125–6, 126n, 136, 165; a Cavaliere di San Stefano, 128 and n, 140; conversation with Alborghetti and Rusconi, 134; a threat to B., 136–7, 143, 155; unpopularity, 149, 165; and Teresa's allowance, 151–2, 152n; relationship with B., 163; alliance with Revolution, 272

Guiccioli, Ferdinando, 29, 30, 172, 174, 176; Lega on his death, 176n

Guiccioli, Countess Teresa, [*Vol. 6, 277–8*], B. and her relations with her husband, 20 and n, 92; B. on their relationship, 22, 88, 105; jealousy, 26n, 151, 185; letter-ending, 26 and n; B. declares his love, 30–1, 33, 34, 92, 140; refuses to see him, 53 and n, 55–6; and his letters, 67 and nn; separation from her husband, 67, 110 and n, 112; on her husband's knowledge of their liaison, 89, 90–1; B.'s wish to marry her, 91 and n, 109; ill with erysipelas, 93 and n; her terms for staying with her husband, 105; papal decree, 125 and n, 126 and n, 127; joins her father at Filetto, 128 and n, 143n; fears for B., 134–5; concerned about gossip, 134n; urges B. to be nearer to her, 143 and n; writes about Elisei, 156, 157; hurt at receiving *Adolphe*, 163 and n; to meet B. again, 174, 176; and Ferdinando's death, 176n; B. calls her Gaspara, 193 and n, 197; date of birth, 193n; B. urges prudence, 235 and n; threat to put her in a convent, 236–7; returns to Ravenna, 240 and n; an obstacle to B.'s Greek venture, 273

Guido di Polenta, 112 and n

Harrowby, Earl of, 62 and n

Heath, Charles, engraver, 165n

Heber, Reginald, bishop of Calcutta, accuses B. of Manicheism, 132 and n

Hemans, Mrs Felicia, 113 and n, 158 and n, 182, 201; *The Sceptic*, 113n

Henley, John, 'Orator', 81

Herbert, the Hon. William, *Edinburgh* reviewer; *Helga, Hedin*, 114 and n

Pope, Alexander, 60–1, 63, 83, 206;
B.'s defence of, 114n, 179, 245,
253; *Epistle to Dr Arbuthnot*, 232
and n; *Rape of the Lock*, 229, 255n
Prideaux, Humphrey, Dean of Norwich,
*True Nature of Imposture . . . in the
Life of Mahomet*, 168 and n
Procter, Bryan Waller (Barry Corn-
wall), 113 and n, 225
Pulci, Luigi, *Morgante Maggiore*, B.'s
translation (1st Canto), 35 and n,
39, 42, 45, 47, 51, 61, 64, 83, 106,
115, 150, 182
Purefoy, Thomas, duellist, 178 and n

Quiroga, General, 155 and n

Raisi, Count Pompeo, 163 and n
Rasi, Dr, 148
Rasponi, Cristino, 24
Rasponi, Count Gabriel, 47 and n
Rasponi, Count Giulio, [*Vol. 6, 247n*],
26, 143
Ravenna, Guiccioli Palace, 13n, 33n;
Albergo Imperiale, 13n, 25
Retz, Cardinal de, *Mémoires*, 180 and n
Reynolds, John Hamilton, *Peter Bell*,
171 and n
Rochdale, possible sale, 69–75 *passim*,
85, 94, 116, 202; prospect of
settlement, 122, 136; failure, 144,
146; to be auctioned, 144, 145;
an Appeal to be entered, 146 and
n, 158, 168, 198, 240
Rogers, Samuel, [*Vol. 2, 286–7*], 181
and n, 223 and n; *Italy*, 225–6
Romilly, Sir Samuel, [*Vol. 3, 255 and
n*], 208
Roper, Major, duellist, 178 and n
Rose, William Stewart, [*Vol. 5, 262n*],
47, 97, 194; *Letters from the North
of Italy*, 202 and n
Rossini, Gioachino, *Barber of Seville*,
87 and n; *La Cenerentola*, 197 and n
Rousseau, Jean Jacques, and Mme
Epinay, 167
Rusconi, Cardinal Antonio, 47 and n,
73, 131, 134, 137, 164
Rusticucci, Jacopo, 68n

San Antonio Abate, 198 and n
Sandri, on Teresa's decree, 130–1
Sandt, Charles, assassin of Kotzebue,
113 and n

Sanuto, Marino, history of Doges of
Venice, 131 and n, 132, 141–2;
Chronicle, 238n
Saunders, Mr., calls *Don Juan* 'all
Grub-Street', 39 and n
Scott, Alexander, [*Vol. 6, 278–9*], 27
and n
Scott, Sir Walter, 45, 48; gazetted
baronet, 83 and n; Works: *The
Abbot*, 204, 207, 212, 214; *The
Bride of Lammermoor*, 48 and n;
Ivanhoe, 48 and n, 83, 113; *A
Legend of Montrose*, 48 and n, 76
and n, 85 and n, 194 and n;
Marmion, 226 and n; *The Monas-
tery*, 48n, 83, 158, 172, 200, 201,
225 and n; *Old Mortality*, 69 and
n; *Rob Roy*, 70 and n, 75 and n, 83
and n; *Tales of My Landlord*, 201
Shakespeare, William, 194; *Antony and
Cleopatra*, 57 and n; *Coriolanus*, 194
and n; *Henry IV, Pt 1*, 50, 170 and
n, 218 and n, *Pt 2*, 179 and n;
Henry V, 82 and n, 118 and n;
Henry VIII, 73 and n; *Hamlet*, 71
and n, 112 and n, 194 and n, 254
and n; *Julius Caesar*, 115 and n;
King John, 102 and n; *Macbeth*, 24
and n, 68 and n, 84 and n;
Merchant of Venice, 79 and nn;
Romeo and Juliet, 118 and n
Shelley, Percy Bysshe, [*Vol. 5, 297–8*],
121; B. nicknames him 'Shiloh',
174 and n, 191; alleged child by
Claire Clairmont, 191n; *The Cenci*,
174 and n
Sheridan, Richard Brinsley, 61, 229;
The Rivals, 154 and n, 211, 212;
Pizarro, 184 and n; *School for
Scandal*, 61
Silvestrini, Fanny, go-between, 143,
161, 209, 210
Sismondi, Jean Charles, 132
Smedley, Rev. Edward, *Churchman's
Epistles*, 201 and n
Smollett, Tobias, *Humphrey Clinker*,
101
Smith (Smyth), Sir Henry, 234 and n
Solomon, Samuel, *Guide to Health*, 229
and n
Sotheby, William, 172, 183
Southcott, Joanna, 174n
Southey, Robert, 89, 102, 253
Spence, Joseph, *Anecdotes of Books and
Men*, 217n, 223